SCOTLAND YARD

A Personal Inquiry

Scotland Yard

A PERSONAL INQUIRY BY

PETER LAURIE

THE BODLEY HEAD
LONDON SYDNEY
TORONTO

For Hilda Harding, to whom
I owe almost everything.

Picture research by Barbara Laurie.
Diagrams by Carola Casson

© Peter Laurie 1970
ISBN 0 370 00451 5
Printed and bound in Great Britain for
The Bodley Head Ltd.
9 Bow Street, London, WC2
by C. Tinling & Co. Ltd, Prescot
Set in Linotype Plantin
First published 1970
Reprinted 1970

CONTENTS

CONTENTS

ILLUSTRATIONS

7

ILLUSTRATIONS
BETWEEN PAGES 168 AND 169 (CONTD.)

INTRODUCTION

This book is the result of eight months spent daily - and often nightly - in the company of various members of the Metropolitan Police as they went about their work. Originally it was intended that it should explain, in general terms, the mechanics of a policeman's life in London, but when I came to write it I discovered what seemed an insuperable difficulty. The problem is that of the 'discretion' which policemen exercise.

There is an enormous difference between what the law allows an English policeman to do, and what, in a given set of circumstances, he actually does. It is common in the daily practice of any government agency to stay within the limits of its powers, but never perhaps as strikingly as in the police. Here the theoretical code bears little relation to the practical code. If the police wanted to - and if there were enough of them - they could find reasons to exercise their powers on everyone every day. They could stop and search people *en masse* in the street, they could search houses, they could arrest and prosecute thousands of drivers for traffic offences and so on.[1]

As a result they would be impossibly overworked and hopelessly unpopular, but in law they could. The difficulty in understanding the police is to understand when and why they do *not* use the ample powers which they possess.

Given moderate intelligence and the will to learn, these powers can be mastered in four months or so. This is the time taken to complete the Metropolitan Police basic training

[1] For an example of what can be done within the framework of peace-time legislation, see the 1940 prosecution described on p. 257

9

course. But this is only a beginning. It takes another three or four years to produce a useful policeman, most of which time is taken in learning how to use his 'discretion'. It is a quality exercised at all levels, from the constable who, as his *Instruction Book* tells him, ignores 'idle and silly remarks' on the street, to the superintendent who decides to prosecute one man but not another for a driving offence, and to the Assistant Commissioner (Crime) who decides that this gang shall be investigated now, whereas that one is to be left until next time.

It would be easy enough to write a book about what the police *can* do. It is all on paper, in *Halsbury's Laws of England*, in text books, judgements and their own *General Orders*. It would be much easier to say what the police *must* do – which is nothing in particular. A Chief Officer of Police has a general duty to enforce the law, but neither the courts nor the government can tell him whom to prosecute, or, without great difficulty, what laws, even in general terms, to enforce.

In strict legal theory, discretion does not exist. Laws are made, the police enforce them, that is an end to it. They are not supposed to choose which will be enforced and which not – that is Parliament's job. But since, in a typically English way, the police cannot be made to enforce any law, no one can in practice prevent them from choosing. Still, they cannot easily admit that a choice is made, or defend the decisions which they reach.

When a Member of Parliament complains, for instance, that he saw a constable in his constituency walk past five untaxed cars in the street and do nothing about them, the police are adrift on this uncharted sea of discretion. They exist to prosecute all crime, so they can hardly excuse themselves with the truth: that if every PC reported every untaxed car he saw, policing in London would come to a stop. They can only admit the fault, trace the PC, and admonish him. Naturally, he had no orders in writing not to report too many untaxed cars. He just knew, as one of the realities of his job, that he and the Force as a whole do not have time to deal with them all.

This was the problem in writing this book. I was trying to explain a peculiar sort of social *savoir faire* which policemen learn almost by instinct. In a few types of case – the admonition of certain traffic or young offenders – the police use it and deliver a caution instead of prosecuting, and the power has become to some extent codified. But otherwise the rules are nowhere written down, no lectures are given on it at the police schools, and perhaps they are not even consciously thought out by the people who exercise them. It would be like trying to give a complete account of contemporary manners.

So it seemed presumptuous to try to *explain* how police worked, because I could never be sure that I had grasped the rules of the game. And in fact, without having had the experience of a seasoned policeman, it was very unlikely that I had grasped them. Wherever I went, I met this latitude, this vacuum within the bounds of prescribed action, which was filled by instinct. It would be extremely difficult to produce a theory of police discretion; impossible without enormous research to substantiate it.

The Author's Relationship with the Metropolitan Police

The idea that a civilian, a journalist, should be allowed to run free among the police and describe things as he saw them was approved by the late Commissioner, Sir Joseph Simpson, in October 1967. From then until the end of June 1968, I spent most of my time with the police. When I had finished my manuscript, several senior officers and officials of the Force were kind enough to read it and let me have the benefit of their painstaking comments. Thanks to their help, most of the grosser errors have, I think, been removed, but whatever mistakes of fact now remain are my fault and not theirs. On matters of opinion several were unsparing in their advice and criticism: again, in many cases

I have gratefully been guided, but where I have not, the perversity is mine.[1] It was agreed when I began that what I described, how I described it and the conclusions I reached were my own responsibility. So this is in no sense an official handbook about the Metropolitan Police.

I am extremely grateful to the Commissioner, Sir John Waldron, K.C.V.O., for allowing me to complete this project after the unfortunate death of Sir Joseph Simpson in 1968. My thanks are also due to Mr G. D. Gregory, the Public Relations Officer, who sponsored me within the Force, and to Mr M. G. Down of his staff, who treated my many small problems with constant helpfulness, and particularly to those policemen of all ranks who put up with my inquiries, took me into their confidence and showed me their work. If nothing else, I owe them all the most interesting year of my life.

The Author's Relationship with Individual Policemen

Before I embark on this account, it is necessary to explain what this relationship meant in practical terms to the policemen who had to put up with my company. I was armed with the Commissioner's approval, expressed in a letter of introduction which I carried on me, so that I could hardly be ignored; yet, on the other hand, I was and still am a journalist by trade. As one detective put it: 'Ever since we first began, we've had it drummed into us: "Journalists are bad. Never speak to journalists." And here you are with *carte blanche* to come and go. Quite frankly, you're a bit of a facer.' With no precedent to guide them, policemen of all ranks found it very difficult to know how to treat me.

The problem was complicated by the archaic regulations of the Metropolitan Police. The counter to every mistake made by a policeman since 1829 is prescribed by one of the 10,000

[1] After the police had finished with the M.S., Lady Wootton was kind enough to read it and suggest some important corrections to the later chapters. I am most grateful to her.

paragraphs of their *General Orders,* a volume now so thick that it takes two hands to pick it up. The draconian code which it prescribes is mitigated by group loyalties and tactful insubordination, but no one could be sure at first that I, as a civilian, would play the game. For instance, if a station officer said to me: 'Come down to the nick at 12.30 – that's when I usually eat – and we'll have lunch in the canteen,' he could conceivably find himself on a disciplinary charge with myself as the principal witness against him, for a General Order then provided (it has since been cancelled) that 'Station Officers' meal times shall be varied from day to day and the time kept confidential.' If the offence were proved, he would have to be reprimanded, and it might be no more than that between him and a contender for vital promotion to Inspector. In this sort of way, I was a continual menace to the officers with me. In fact, any of them who didn't walk smartly out of the room, or, if ordered to take me out with him, didn't contrive to lose me – it sometimes happened – was behaving with some kindness and generosity.

Along with uncertainty about my attitude towards minor problems of police discipline went equal uncertainty about my behaviour vis-à-vis the other side, the criminal. Trust, on such short acquaintance, could only go so far. People were willing enough to take me on small jobs, or to reconnoitre large ones, but when it came to making big arrests, say of robbery teams, it always seemed to have happened the day before. Apart from the constitutional problems of involving a civilian in making arrests, there were other good reasons why I should be left behind. One was safety and efficiency: I would not know what to do, and I could not be relied on to stay safely out of the way. Then, I might get hurt, involving all parties in tedious explanations.

More worrying perhaps was what might happen at the trial. My presence could not be concealed: I would have to be available as a witness. If I was called, the police were in a cleft stick. If I gave good evidence, which agreed with theirs, the defence would allege collusion, the more so because policemen are required to write down the bones of what is later their evidence as soon as possible after the event, and individual officers are allowed to compare notes. When they arrive in the witness-box, they alone read their evidence.[1] But it would be odd, and impolite, if I made full, verbatim notes at the time, and if I had made such notes I could not compare them with the policemen's account, and in the box I would not be able to read my version. In the nature of things, if we were all being honest, my evidence must be less than perfect, damaging the prosecution's case; if it was perfect, there must have been collusion.

So I was not present at the arrest of any prominent criminals. The other definite restriction was on taking me to search premises with a warrant, simply because warrants are addressed to 'each and every constable', but make no mention of journalists. Otherwise I came and went more or less as I pleased and as was convenient to my involuntary hosts.

---

[1] All witnesses are allowed to refresh their memories from notes made at the time or shortly afterwards, but in practice one only sees this done by police or expert witnesses.

CHAPTER ONE

The Physical Presence of The Force

Scotland Yard Itself

Englishmen like to think that everyone in the world, even if he knows nothing else, has at least heard of Scotland Yard. Probably several foreigners have, and many people from far away write there in search of abstract justice: a Canadian factory-worker to complain of chicanery by the management, an Italian mother to denounce neglect of the homeless. Perhaps all police departments get this kind of letter.

Probably, too, the image which these correspondents have of the abstract entity to which they write is something housed in a Grimm's Fairy Tales building, of bastions and steeply turreted towers. That has changed. The Metropolitan Police left the old building next to Parliament in 1967 to make way for the redevelopment of the Parliament Square/Whitehall area with government offices, and also because the headquarters organisation was so squashed that its efficiency was noticeably reduced. Although the old building was cramped, and the Victorian majesty of the downstairs ran out by the third floor, it had a great deal of character and its passing is regretted by some – particularly the more senior officers who lived in the lower parts.

Today the Metropolitan Police Headquarters is an anonymous, two-towered office a few hundred yards away up Victoria Street. It is perhaps better finished than most of its kind, it is kept immaculately clean, and the air-conditioning works almost everywhere, but it has little to recommend it. No one could become devoted to it, there is nothing to replace the marble staircases and enormous mahogany mantel-

15

pieces of the old building. In fact, the new one is so characterless, it is distinctly confusing. The insides of the two towers are identical, each contains an oblong corridor running round a central service core, and one can spend time searching for the right office.

The building was designed as an ordinary office block, and has been little changed. The telephone exchange for the whole Metropolitan Police District is accommodated there. The first floor carries the electronic complexities of the Information Room, Traffic Control Room, and the West London Traffic Computer. One floor, specially strengthened, carries the weight of tons of Criminal Records, and includes a special document-conveyor system. There is a big canteen on the fourth floor of the lower block for the general mob, a mess on the fifth floor for Commanders and above, with waitress service, and for Assistant Commissioners and heads of departments a tasteful dark green and mahogany mess with an ante-room. But the food is the same everywhere.

Office construction and allocation are on conventionally hierarchical civil service lines. Ordinary folk work in open offices, Inspectors and their equivalents have glass booths in the corners, Chief Inspectors share offices in twos and threes, Superintendents graduate to the luxury of a carpet and an arm-chair, Commanders have a conference table, Assistant Commissioners have a corner office with plaster rather than plywood walls – so they can't be overheard – Chippendale-style desk and bookcase, and some have a private bathroom.

The building replaced a four-towered Victorian block full of civil engineers' chambers, part of a mid-nineteenth century development that kept the slums of Pimlico decently out of sight of Buckingham Palace. In 1960 the site was cleared, and taking advantage of the ten per cent increase, allowed to developers on an old building's cubic content, together with the enormous amount of space Victorians wasted on high ceilings and staircases, it was possible to put up a building with a ratio of floor to site area of seven to one, as against the maximum allowed by the then London County

Council's zoning rules of three and a half to one. 'In short,' writes Oliver Marriott, in his book *The Property Boom*, 'the new tenant, Scotland Yard, was able to employ exactly twice as many people on that site as the LCC thought was desirable.' The finished building was worth fifteen million pounds, and Marriott says that the owners, Willetts, make a profit of £570,000 a year to set off against their parent group's losses on the ill-conceived Elephant and Castle shopping-centre development. Although modifications of the building for police use were made at the design stage, the alterations managed to cost £1·85 millions, as against an estimate of £400,000. But apart from these oddities, there is little remarkable about the structure.

From the start it was too small to accommodate even the central administration of the Metropolitan Police. Across the Thames from the Tate Gallery, the police have had another building since 1961, Tintagel House, which accommodates their Planning and Development Branch, a joint computer unit that serves the Home Office and the Metropolitan Police, various training and medical departments and, on occasion, special detective squads. The team that arrested the Kray gang worked there. The Metropolitan Police Laboratory and the Aliens Department are housed in a tall new block in Theobold's Road, behind Holborn. Apart from these, there are 185 police stations spread over the thirty-mile diameter of the Metropolitan Police District which contains a fifth of England's population, a third of its real property and a quarter of its policemen.

These stations vary enormously. Many are tall, boxy Victorian buildings like Paddington (see p. 75 below). Since the war a spattering of new stations have been built. At first, like the one at Kennington, they tended towards the fortalice style, with heavy riot doors and no window less than ten feet from the pavement. After that, the police tried to make their stations light and airy, as attractive as any other public office. This policy was perhaps the child of the unusually calm fifties, and the police may find their up-to-date plate-glass palaces rather difficult to defend in a period of greater public turbulence. The plate-glass front of Brixton police station, built to the new pattern, has a permanent brick hole in it, and the challenge that the future may bring for these buildings is perhaps shown by the urgent use at Bow Street in 1966 of the riot doors which had stood open for half a century.

A police station is a specialised building, and presents some interesting architectural problems. In its simplest form, it falls naturally into an L-shape, with administration down the long arm and the security wing in the short arm. These form two sides of the yard, which has to be sixty foot square, or big enough to turn a prison bus in. The most essential feature is the cell block. A cell should be long and thin, so that the occupant can always be seen from the spy-hole, it should have a lavatory too narrow to drown in, flushed by a lever on the wall from which one can't hang oneself. The teak bench should be held down by half-inch thick bolts, strong enough to resist the most violent madman. The door opens outwards to that the prisoner can't hide behind it, and it used to be built at an angle so that stretchers could negotiate the turn from the cell corridor. But a survey showed that this facility was never used, and it has been abandoned.

The cell corridor opens into the charge room, which has to connect with the rest of the station and with the yard. If it is above the level of the yard, the ascent must be negotiated by a slope rather than steps so that drunks' heels don't flop from one to the other, breaking their ankles as they are dragged in. On the ground floor, the doors are hung so that they swing towards the charge room: this makes it easier to bring in drunk or violent prisoners, and slightly impedes their flight if they break away.

The CID should have a separate entrance, and separate stairs down from their office to the security wing. The canteen should be on the top floor so that cooking smells rise, and should have a separate entrance so that visitors will not meet dustbins on the station stairs. In a station which serves as headquarters for a Division, there is often stabling for the Chief Superintendent's horse, because he will often be mounted when controlling large crowds, and there has to be a shower for him when he comes back.

Headquarters Organisation

Scotland Yard[1] itself is only the headquarters of the organisation. Although 'The Yard' has become the most commonly used collective name for London's police, very few of the 20,000-strong body work there. A thousand detectives, among them the staffs of Central[2], the Flying Squad, C9 and C11[3] have their desks there. There are a few members of the Traffic Department who go out from the Yard, but the rest of the people there, policemen and civilians, are administrators.

The Metropolitan Police is by any standards quite a large firm. It employs getting on for 30,000 people who have to be paid, fed, promoted, chided, provided with white tape, rubbers, cars and dogs, pencils, breakdown lorries, radio sets, ceremonial jackets and several other things. Moreover, the work of police administration is increased by their operations being, in some sense, always a matter of judicial record, so that what in another firm could be dealt with by a telephone call has in the police to be the subject of a report and four attached minutes.

[1] Scotland Yard is the headquarters of London's police only. Although the Metropolitan Police has a quarter of the policemen in England and Wales it is only one of fifty-odd police forces in the Kingdom, each of which is more or less autonomous in its own area. It is often mistakenly thought that Scotland Yard is the headquarters of all Britain's police – this is, of course not so. It does, however, house certain central services, of which the best known is perhaps the Murder Squad, a team of experienced detectives who are available to provincial or colonial forces, for dealing with difficult crimes. Perhaps for this reason 'The Yard' has become synonymous in ordinary speech with the CID generally, although each police force has its own Criminal Investigation Department.
[2] See p. 161 and Glossary.
[3] See pp. 170–178 below.

After a report by a firm of business consultants in 1968, Headquarters was reorganised. As part of this reorganisation the offices of the Commissioner and Receiver, which had been completely separate, were brought together in one organisation. The Receiver is an independent officer who since 1829 has been the financial watchdog, on behalf of the Home Secretary as police authority for the Metropolitan Police and the owner and administrator of Metropolitan Police property. Subject to the approval of the Home Secretary he levies the police rate on the London Boroughs, the proceeds of which provide roughly half the Metropolitan Police expenditure. As part of the merging of the two administrations, he has now, while keeping his independent statutory functions, become the chief administrative officer of the force under the Commissioner, and head of the combined civil staff. He is in charge of 'E', 'F' and 'G' Departments described below, together with the Chief Architect and Chief Engineer's Departments. 'A' Department now deals essentially with the operations of the Uniform (policemen always say 'uniform', not uniformed) Branch; its concern is broadly in keeping order on the streets and in public places. Its various branches deal with complaints against the police, betting, gaming, lotteries, disorderly houses, fortune-telling, importuning, landlord and tenant, licensing of clubs and pubs, living on the earnings of prostitution, music and dancing and public morals. 'A' provides communications, police dogs, mounted police and awards for bravery, staff for courts in the MPD. Its women police look after juveniles in trouble either with the law, their families or their employers. There is a section to encourage harmony between the races, and one to deal with public order, riots, processions, strikes, Royalty, elections, and disasters.

'B' Department is in charge of all machinery moving in the streets. It provides traffic patrols, supervises stopping-places for buses and cab ranks; it inspects traffic signals and road works. It arranges the traffic side of all London's major ceremonials and public events. It licenses cabs and cabbies, bus drivers and conductors, and keeps an index of people convicted of traffic offences. It organises Traffic Wardens and its Central Ticket Office handles the million tickets which they stick on windscreens every year.

Crime is the responsibility of 'C' Department, whose organisation is described in Chapters 6 – 8 in more detail than would be possible here. 'D' provides recruits, training, appointments, welfare, married quarters, cadets. It trains recruits to be policemen, and policemen to be drivers, detectives, pistol shots, radio operators. There is a Catering Branch which provides, at the worst, solid food; a Public Relations Department[1] which provides news, enables articles, books and films to be made about the police, publishes a fortnightly newspaper, *The Job*, and an Inspectorate whose job it is to dissect the running of the force, a department dealing with Management Services, and the Solicitor and his staff.

'E' deals with the administration of civilians working for the Police, but the work of its general section also shows the extraordinary variety of things that the police have to deal with: accommodation addresses, amusements, animals, bravery awards (civil cases), car passes, child adoption and foster-parent inquiries, criminal injuries compensation, deserters, destitute persons, diplomatic immunity and central index of privileged persons, evidence in civil cases, Mental Health Act, miscellaneous and family inquiries, money-lenders, National Police Fund educational grants, parliamentary questions, messengers, pedlars and shoe-blacks, pawnbrokers, radioactive substances index, reference library, street and house-to-house collections. It also licenses lawful owners of firearms and users of explosives. Other sections keep a register of aliens living in London and publish Police Orders.

Finance is provided by 'F' Department in the normal way,

[1] The Press Bureau began in the early thirties as a simple press office liaising with established crime reporters. It had a low position in the hierarchy and was not geared to positive explanation of the police problems and activities. More recently it has become a Department of its own, whose head ranks with Assistant Commissioners.

but with the recent addition of Budgetary Planning and Cost Accounting Branches 'which ... will be working on activity costing, output budgeting and long-term forward estimating with the object of providing financial criteria for the application of management techniques.' 'G' deals with contracts, supplies, runs the stores, printing, accident claims and, curiously, the statistics and map room. Architects and surveyors, under the Chief Architect, are responsible for the Met's buildings, while the Chief Engineer provides and mends cars, ventilation, radios and telephones.

Broadly speaking, everyone down to the Solicitor in this list of functions is a policeman. 'Broadly', because there is now a sensible policy of replacing every policeman doing a job that doesn't absolutely need his physique and training by a civilian. Thus most of the Scenes of Crime officers in C3, the Fingerprint Branch, are civilians; so too some of the people who examine scenes of crime for the Laboratory.

Forces within the Force

Essentially there are four main divisions of policemen. 'A', the uniform Branch, is the largest. With 17,000 men and 470 women it is the foundation for the rest. 'B', the Traffic Department, with 1,300 men, is almost a force of its own. It has its own garages, its own radio, organisation and boundaries. Its job is quite distinct from that of 'A' and there is, in general terms, little organic contact between the two departments. 'C', the Criminal Investigation Department, with 3,100 men and 90 women is 'A's rival. These two departments are inextricably linked. The CID need 'A' to house and transport them, to lock up, feed and charge their prisoners. 'A' needs 'C' to interrogate and prosecute the persons it arrests. Some people in 'C' would perhaps like it to blossom into a national detective force, accountable to no one but the Home Secretary.

It is significant, for instance, that when plans were being discussed to recruit civilian auxiliaries to the CID – for fingerprint and forensic work – it is said that 'C' Department wanted them to have the same powers of arrest as policemen; in effect they were to be policemen, but without having gone through 'A's mill of training and probation, a system that was instituted in the late 1800s to counter a series of disasters with 'direct entry' detectives. This might have been the first step towards independent existence. It must be said that occasional excesses of zeal are probably better restrained by jealous colleagues at the table of power than by any number of enthusiasts for civil liberties outside the police.

The fourth force, the Special Branch, with about 360 men and a dozen women, is technically part of the CID, but functions more as 'A's intelligence arm, keeping it and the government informed of groupings, intentions and leaders among the subversive, and what is likely to happen at the demonstrations or strikes which they organise. The Special Branch is also responsible for the protection of VIPs and inquiries into the backgrounds of aliens living in London who wish to become naturalised British citizens. It keeps itself so much to itself that it seems to play little part in police politics.

Rank Structure[1]

The Metropolitan police is organised in ten ranks as against the eleven of all provincial British police forces. Since I finished the series of visits on which this book is based, the ranks of senior officers have been raised a step to bring them into parity with those enjoyed by officers in provincial forces who discharge comparable responsibilities. For example, some London Divisions, which used to be run by Chief

[1] Unlike the fighting services, police ranks are not properly used as titles. If one is looking for a policeman's office, one asks where *Mr* so and so is to be found, and one would refer in writing to Mr A. B. Xray, Commander, Metropolitan Police.

Superintendents, are as large in policemen, area and population as some provincial forces run by Chief Constables. Chief Superintendents therefore became Commanders in 1969, a rank peculiar to London, but of Chief Officer status and equivalent to a minor Chief Constable or an Assistant Chief Constable in a large County Force.[1] The new ranks are given below, with the old ranks in brackets. Through the *rest* of the book I have left ranks as they were when I met them. In London then, the ranks run thus:

Commissioner, responsible to the Home Secretary for the general running of the Force. The precise relationship between the two parties, or indeed that between any chief of a police force and his Police Authority, has not been precisely settled, and only canvassed for the first time in the courts, as recently as 1968.[2] Then Lord Denning said that the Commissioner is not subject to the orders of the Home Secretary, except that under the Police Act 1964 he can call upon the Commissioner to give a report or to retire in the interests of efficiency. He said it was the duty of the Commissioner, as it is of every Chief Constable, to enforce the law of the land, but in doing so he is not the servant of anyone, save of the law itself: 'No Minister of the Crown can tell him that he must or must not keep observations on these places or those; or that he must or must not prosecute this man or that one. Nor can any Police Authority tell him so. The responsibility for law enforcement lies on him. He is answerable to the law and to the law alone.' Part of his responsibility to the law was made clear in this case. The

[1] There are three different English police rank structures above Chief Superintendent. That of the Metropolitan Police is set out here. The City of London, a sub-Division-sized enclave within the Metropolitan Police District, has, for urgent historical reasons, its own force under a Commissioner and an Assistant Commissioner. All other forces are commanded by a Chief Constable with Assistant Chief Constables and then Chief Superintendents in two grades, followed by two grades of Superintendent.

[2] R. *v.* Commissioner of Police for the Metropolis *ex parte* Blackburn.

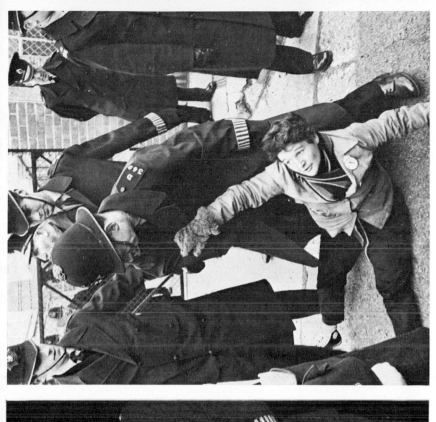

LEFT: The face of the public, as the policeman so often sees him (*Mirrorpic*). RIGHT: Pat Arrowsmith, Field Secretary of the Committee of 100, lies down in the main road outside Ruislip USAF Base in April 1964. She was charged under the Official Secrets Act with 'inciting certain persons to obstruct police officers in the vicinity of a prohibited place' (*Thomson Newspapers*)

ABOVE: Policemen dispersing the crowd at a Fascist demonstration in the East End, October 1936 (*Radio Times Hulton Picture Library*). BELOW: The British Fascist movement in the pre-war years had a profound effect on the attitude of the Metropolitan Police to public demonstrations. Here Sir Oswald Mosley leaves a parade of the National Socialists on the Embankment in 1936. He relies on booted, black-shirted guards for protection, rather than the Metropolitan and City policemen visible behind. (*Daily Sketch*)

ABOVE: The idea that policemen should try not to use physical violence against demonstrators is a comparatively new one. Here bobbies exchange blows with unemployed demonstrators in Trafalgar Square on 'Bloody Sunday', 1887 (*Radio Times Hulton Picture Library*). BELOW: Mounted police in Grosvenor Square, near the American Embassy, at the demonstration, 17th March, 1968. (*Fox Photos Ltd*)

ABOVE: A policewoman takes a photo for a screaming fan at pop-singer Marty Wilde's wedding in 1959 (*Planet News Ltd*). BELOW: Special Branch officers in evening dress, watched by a Yeoman of the Guard, make a routine search of the Royal Box at the Aldwych Theatre in the summer of 1963 (*Bippa*)

Commissioner had decided not to prosecute certain infringements of the Betting, Gaming and Lotteries Act 1963; Raymond Blackburn, an ex-MP, applied to the High Court for a writ of Mandamus to make the Commissioner change his mind, which he did.

Although the Home Secretary has no formal power to order the Commissioner to order policemen to do this or that, the relationship between the two men is so close that it is probably hardly necessary. On the practical level the Home Secretary controls long-term police finance. He advises the Crown on the appointment of the Deputy and Assistant Commissioners. He appoints Deputy Assistant Commissioners on the Commissioner's nomination, and approves the Commissioner's appointments to Commander. On the other hand, the Home Secretary must explain the deeds and misdeeds of the Metropolitan Police to Parliament.

Below the Commissioner come:

The Deputy Commissioner. The Commissioner and Deputy Commissioner, besides administering a large force, have certain other duties: they grant licences – for pub hour extensions, to drive buses and taxis, to possess guns, to hold street collections.

4 Assistant Commissioners (A.C.), at the head of 'A', 'B', 'C' and 'D' Departments. The Commissioner, Deputy and Assistant Commissioners are not policemen. They are not members of the Force and have no more power of arrest than any other citizen. The Commissioner is a Justice of the Peace specially appointed to administer the police force in the Metropolis; the Assistant Commissioners are *ex officio* Justices. This perpetuates the Tudor system of police administration in which Magistrates, appointed by the Crown, directed Constables who have been, since Saxon times, citizens exercising the people's collective responsibility for law enforcement.

17 Deputy Assistant Commissioners (formerly Commanders and Deputy Commanders) who carry the main administrative

burden in the four police departments. They each report directly to an Assistant Commissioner.

39 Commanders (Chief Superintendents), twenty-three of whom command divisions; the rest have jobs of equivalent responsibility at Scotland Yard.

163 Chief Superintendents (Superintendents), seventy-seven of whom are in charge of sub-divisions, the basic unit of policing.

158 Chief Inspectors.[1]

663 Inspectors. This is the highest rank to work shifts. The Duty Inspector is the 'manager' of a busy police station; some small stations are run by an Inspector on his own.

401 Station Sergeants (a rank peculiar to the Metropolitan Police) whose basic job it is to accept charges from arresting officers, satisfying themselves that *prima facie* grounds exist for the arrest and charge.

2,120 Sergeants (PS), each in charge of a section of Constables.

13,318 Police Constables (PC). The Constables are (Uniform Branch) 'A', 'B' and 'D' Departments.

The continuity of rank structure conceals the profound difference of the jobs being done at various levels. Sergeants and Constables are the men who get out on the street and do policing. *They* meet people, they make the decisions that affect the tempers and liberty of the citizen. The job of the Inspectors and Station Sergeants, and to a lesser extent the job of every policeman senior to them, is to check what the Sergeants and Constables have done. As in any big organisation, the higher ranks are necessarily more concerned

[1] Under the regrading of ranks, Chief Inspectors should have become Superintendents. But since this rank does not qualify for overtime payments, its holders would have earned less than they did before promotion. Chief Inspectors have not been promoted *en masse*. So at the time of writing (summer 1969) there are no male Superintendents in London.

with putting the right man in the right job and the general policy of the force than with ordinary policing.

Women Police ranks are (Uniform and CID):

1 Commander
4 Chief Superintendents
3 Superintendents
6 Chief Inspectors
25 Inspectors
55 Sergeants
459 Women Police Constables (WPC's)

In the CID the ranks are:

4 Deputy Assistant Commissioners, in charge of: Administration and Divisions, Operations, Technical Support Services, Special Branch.

18 Commanders. Four are responsible for each of the four districts, supervising their divisional CID staffs: the rest are employed in charge of branches at Scotland Yard.

66 Detective Chief Superintendents, one to each division and the rest at the Yard, ten of whom form the Murder Squad.

109 Detective Chief Inspectors, sixty as Divisional Superintendents' deputies, mostly employed in investigating complaints against policemen.

214 Detective Inspectors (DI), in charge of the Detectives of a sub-division, the basic CID unit.

255 Detective Sergeants, 1st Class, most in charge of sub-divisional CID officers.

757 Detective Sergeants, 2nd Class. This rank carries little administrative responsibility, and means essentially that its holders are fully trained, experienced investigators. Many detectives interested in police work rather than administration do not seek promotion beyond it.

855 Detective Constables (DC), responsible to their DIs for investigating and prosecuting crimes assigned to them.

826 Temporary Detective Constables (TDC or Aid). PCs on two years' probation before acceptance into the CID. Their

main job is to patrol the streets and prove their worth by bringing in an adequate number of arrests.

At the end of 1968 the total strength of the force was 20,521, about the same as it had been at the beginning of the Second World War, although in the interval the working hours of policemen had been reduced and their responsibilities considerably increased. The Metropolitan Police is probably some 5,000 – 6,000 men under strength. 'Probably', because no precise criterion of police manning has ever been discovered. Establishments are arrived at by a process of comparison, instinct and horse-trading.

Relationships between the ranks are in theory as rigid and formal as those in the Army, prescribing hierarchically the 'value' of each individual. But in practice a second, parallel system operates, based on early friendships, experience and usefulness. For instance, one sub-division with many diplomatic establishments had a PC who had made it the work of many years to know personally and informally the staffs of all the embassies and many ambassadors and their families. In a few minutes he could resolve domestic diplomatic problems that would otherwise keep our own and the other country's foreign offices in correspondence for weeks. A man like that is probably as much *use* to a sub-division as a Chief Inspector, and in the informal status system enjoys the same position. This is merely to repeat, in a different way, the observation made above: that the rank structure in the police does not correspond to the difficulty and importance of the jobs being done at different levels. An army is motivated by decisions from the top (and its rank structure reveals the fact): a police force often by decisions made right at the bottom, and its structure conceals it.

Housing and Social Life

Young unmarried policemen live compulsorily in 'Section Houses' of which there are twenty-three spread around

London. The original idea was to provide a police barracks – though that rough term was never used – and a ready supply of manpower for use in emergencies. Until the striking post-war rise in the status of policemen, they were unpleasant homes. A superintendent in his fifties described his first years as a constable: 'You slept in bunks that smelly-footed coppers had slept in since 1832. You were called out twice a night to fight drunken Irishmen, you cooked your own meals – there were no canteens in those days – and I lived on bacon and eggs, until I married to get out of it all.'

The modern Section House is warm and clean, if heavily official in tone, and not very friendly. In the enthusiasm of the force to be above suspicion, it has tended to treat its young constables as irresponsible children: they may not easily live out in their own flats, they may not entertain visitors of the opposite sex except in the common sitting-room under the eye of the Section House Sergeant, and they have to be in by midnight. There was a pathetic story in the police newspaper, *The Job,* about an engaged couple, both members of the police and both inhabitants of Section Houses, who had nowhere private at all to see each other.

The Force has 5,000 married quarters, of which 4,000 have been built since the war. Since married men are apt to be at home in the evenings, they now provide the 'strategic reserve' formerly held by the Section Houses. In the centre of London, married quarters are flats; in the suburbs, houses. A police flat is roughly 12 per cent bigger than one of the equivalent local-authority standard, though some of this goes to provide a bedroom at the back of the building, away from the communal stairs, so that father can sleep in the day when he is on night duty. There is a growing feeling in the police that the literally Victorian design of their older housing is undesirable both on grounds of social policy and personal dignity.

The author of a letter to *The Job* writes: 'A police officer historically comes from the community and is part of the community. We are probably all agreed that large blocks of flats, while apparently necessary at the time, are socially undesirable for police families. They separate them from the community which they serve, promote gossip, fan jealousies and in some cases cause marital disharmony. What are the effects of isolating the (single) man from the community in his stone block of single rooms? How does he feel when he cannot return hospitality or invite someone 'home'? ... what are the psychological effects of section-house residence on personality and behaviour? ... let us ascertain whether there is a correlation between section-house residence and allegations of aggression.'

But the policeman in the community is not altogether enviable. He is never completely trusted by his neighbours. The late Commissioner, giving evidence to the Estimates Committee, was asked, 'Surely there is a prestige element, is there not, which would keep people in the Force?' He replied, 'To the idealist, yes, Sir, but to the realist, no. In fact he will argue the other way, that a policeman is looked down on, that in his neighbourhood he is regarded with suspicion, it is difficult to make friends. In fact he will even argue with some truth that it is inadvisable to make the sort of friends you would make if you were an ordinary member of the public.'[1]

Often his neighbours put him in difficult ethical positions. A uniform sergeant told me how he joined a hockey club whose playing-field lay behind his (police-provided) house. After his first two visits, he lost patience with the other members' defensive needling about his job. 'I went up to the most inquisitive one and said, "Come on, let's hear some stories about your job. When you get in the bank in the morning – what happens? Surprise me." Eventually we arranged a sort of truce; they wouldn't cross-examine me about my job and I wouldn't about theirs. But it *is* a truce. It'll probably take a long time to get on the friendly footing I'd achieve in a month if I weren't a copper.' Another policeman, a constable, told me about his neighbour, whose sitting-room furniture was suddenly re-upholstered in coach-

[1] First Report from the Estimates Committee, Session 1966–7, *Police*, HMSO 1966, para 277.

hide. 'It's ridiculous, it can't have cost less than £500, yet he earns £20 a week. But I'd never nick a neighbour – not unless he did something bad like a robbery with violence – unless he hurt someone.'

In addition to these domestic problems, it is possible that policemen do not make the best of husbands. The average London detective's working day, over a six-day week, is an incredible nineteen hours.[1] Several senior officers also found this hard to believe. This means he spends five hours a day at home and has four days off a month – unless he is needed on a murder inquiry or some such.

But to compensate for these misfortunes, the goodwill and welfare of wives bulk large in the formal and informal management of police life. One of the first things that I learnt about a new group of policemen, and particularly of detectives, was whose wife was ill, whose children were young and needed extra care. A man whose wife was in hospital would be allowed the time that he needed to look after his family, arrangements would be made to find other wives to help him; the community social service that preceded the Welfare State still survives strongly in the police. And policemen are extraordinarily loyal to each other. Their newspaper constantly has stories of generosity and helpfulness: a man's house devastated by a burst water-tank, redecorated by his colleagues in a couple of evenings. Or, on a graver level, this story is typical: a young constable on leave in Sheffield had a car crash and was paralysed from the neck down. Although he had been in the Force only eighteen months, and hardly anyone knew him, the men of his division held a ball, and policemen who had visited him in hospital came from Sheffield, two hundred miles away. Over £1,000 was collected to buy him a motorised bed.[2]

[1] Martin, J.P., and Wilson, Gail, *The Police: A Study in Manpower*, Heinemann, London 1969, p. 147.
[2] *The Job* (24.11.68).

Pay and Budget

Possibly because policemen are not allowed, by law, to call attention to their grievances by striking, the level of their pay in relationship to the cost of living tends to swoop rather erratically. At the end of the First World War, their wages were so far below the cost of living that many constables' families were almost destitute, and forced to apply to the local authority for relief. The unprecedented police strike of 1918 stimulated a swing the other way which in some ranks trebled wages. Since then police pay has tended to fall behind the cost of living, and then to jump ahead after new negotiations. By 1967 the police were ahead; a constable starts at £815 a year, rising to £1,255. He can get up to £130 rent allowance, and, if he is in the CID, £145 a year Detective allowance for twelve hours overtime a week. Chief Inspectors can earn up to £1,865, with £260 detective allowance for those in the CID. Chief Superintendents earn up to £3,090, but detective allowance stops at Chief Inspector. Assistant Commissioners get £5,620 and the Commissioner £8,600.

The Force costs some £70 million a year net, half of which is met from Government Grants, leaving some £4 7s 6d per head for everyone living in the Metropolitan Police District to be met from rates. Of this, £51.5 million goes on wages and allowances of police and civil staff and auxiliary forces. Telephones and teleprinters cost £600,000; wirelesses £530,000. Nearly three-quarters of a million pounds is spent on petrol, and the same amount on new cars. Police dogs cost £32,000, the cost of their food being about £28,000.

Nearly £400,000 goes on travelling expenses, and about a quarter of a million on subsistence and refreshments. Detectives receive £75,000 for expenses allowances; £100,000 is spent on counsels' fees in police prosecutions, and compensation for civil torts, most of which are motor accidents (see p. 256), costs £96,000. The surprisingly small amount of £16,000 is paid out in 'rewards' for information (see p. 187).

CHAPTER TWO

Recruitment and Training

Recruitment

Men can join the Metropolitan Police between the ages of nineteen and thirty from civilian life, or up to forty if they come from the Armed Forces or the Merchant Navy. The candidate has to pass an educational examination, or is exempted if he holds four 'O' levels. The educational standard of recruits in London is higher than in the provinces, but is still not very impressive. Of the ordinary entry, about fifty per cent have no GCE's at all, under a third have four 'O' levels or worse, fifteen per cent have five or more, and six per cent have two or more 'A's. The cadet entry have more 'O's but fewer 'A's.[1] There has recently been considerable effort made to attract university graduates into the service, of which more below.

Physically, recruits must be five foot eight or taller, though several forces require greater height. This is, however, the median height for British men, and gives the policeman a fifty-fifty chance of being taller than any male with whom he deals. The Metropolitan Police get about 9,000 inquiries from potential recruits every year. As part of the weeding-out process, the local police make discreet inquiries of employers and teachers into candidates' reliability, honesty and sobriety. A search is made in Criminal Records, though a minor conviction at an early age would not rule a man out. Vision has to be reasonably good, though people who need glasses are not automatically debarred, as long as they don't squint and are not colour-blind. Physically, too, men must be

[1] *Police Manpower, Equipment and Efficiency*. Report of three working parties, HMSO 1967, p. 17.

C

reasonably wholesome. The principal medical reasons for rejection are bad teeth and diseases of the gums, defects of the feet – flat feet, hammer toes – and diseases of the skin. They must of course be British or Commonwealth citizens.

About a third of those who inquire survive these barriers and are called to the recruitment centre in Borough High Street, Southwark, for examination. Here they sit the educational test, are examined by the Force's doctors and have a quarter of an hour interview with an assistant commissioner, a superintendent and a senior civilian officer. Candidates, nervous and suited, do their best to put on a frank and desirable front; the interviewers do their best to get through the barrier of unfamiliarity.

I sat in on one board which seemed to deal with its customers in a fairly human and perceptive way. Two men from another force, with good reports from their Chief Constables, were accepted almost automatically. One hulking young man, from a rough part of London, confident and apparently well able to care for himself was rejected as unimaginative; another, a mild, stooping ex-Post Office clerk with glasses, whose wife thought he should have an outdoor job and who was desperately eager to overcome the difficulties which the board quizzically proposed to him, was accepted as a good bet. Each year some 1,200 men are selected, or about one in eight of those who apply.

As a means of keeping out qualified, but temperamentally undesirable, candidates, this system is not in itself completely adequate. But the successful go on to an intense three-month basic training course and then spend two years on probation. At the end of that their weaknesses should be apparent.

Once accepted by the board, candidates become policemen on the first day of their basic training course. They recite the following declaration, all at once, in batches of sixty, before an assistant commissioner in his capacity as Magistrate. It has hardly changed since the Middle Ages:

'I . . . of . . . do solemnly and sincerely declare and affirm that I will well and truly serve our Sovereign Lady the Queen in the office of constable without favour or affection, malice or ill will; and that I will to the best of my power cause the peace to be kept and preserved, and prevent all offences against the persons and properties of Her Majesty's subjects; and that while I continue to hold the said office I will to the best of my skill and knowledge discharge all the duties thereof faithfully according to law.'

This makes a subtle but important difference to their legal position. Broadly speaking, anyone may arrest anyone else if he *knows* an offence has been committed and reasonably suspects that the other did it. A constable, on the other hand, is allowed to suppose that the offence has occurred or may occur, and without a warrant he may enter (if needs be by force) and search any place where he reasonably supposes the person to be hiding.[1] This, with numerous but less important statutory additions, is the 'power of arrest' that distinguishes a policeman from other citizens. It is ultimately derived from the State, but unlike anyone else with State powers, except Cabinet Ministers, he exercises it on his own personal responsibility. If he arrests the wrong person, he cannot excuse himself by saying 'My superior officer told me to.' But since constables are hardly worth suing, the aggrieved citizen has, as well as a right of action against him, a right to sue his Chief Officer[2] (in London the Commissioner), or in effect the Force as a whole. So quite apart from anything else, every police force has a vital financial interest in its constables using their powers of arrest correctly.

Basic Training

Each course of students has nineteen to twenty members. One which I saw beginning its training had an average age of twenty-two – the youngest was nineteen, the oldest thirty,

[1] *Criminal Law Act 1967.*
[2] *Police Act 1964*, s. 48.

and three were women. It contained two policemen from other forces, three clerks, a soldier, a shop-assistant, a coppersmith, an animal technician, a trainee manager and, among others, five police cadets. This is an average mixture. The cadets have had up to three years' resident training at the Metropolitan Police's two schools, where they spent half their time on academic subjects, the rest on physical sports, adventure training and the fringes of police work. From the police point of view, they are an excellent source of man-power, dedicated, fit and already half-trained.

Cadets provide about a third of the Force's intake. In the wider perspective they are perhaps rather too young for a job that demands a certain amount of *savoir-faire* and their experience of life is too limited, but as an instructor said, 'They're not grown up enough to be policemen until they're twenty-three, but if we don't grab them at nineteen they're gone for good, so we just have to put up with it.' This view is shared at the top as well, for the head of the Police Department of the Home Office told Parliament's 1966 Committee on the Estimates that 'It has generally been agreed by those concerned with the Service that it would not be satisfactory if one got towards the stage where all, or even a majority of the Police Service, were cadets.'[1]

Once attested, the recruits get their uniforms – high-necked ceremonial frock-coats, day-to-day tunics (but no boots), gloves, capes and a hundred other things, and settle down to learning their trade.

The fundamental aim of the training school is perhaps not so much to produce a finished policeman as one that knows his legal limitations. 'Frankly, these boys are a liability to us in their first years. They can walk out of the nick and make a decision in thirty seconds that might keep the House of Lords arguing for two years and cost more than they'd earn in five lifetimes,' said an instructor.

The course lasts thirteen weeks and is held at Hendon,

[1] First report from the Estimates Committee, 1966–7, *Police*, HMSO 1966, Q 227.

towards the northern suburbs of London. The building stands on the edge of a disused and soon to be built over airfield, was originally a 'twenties clubhouse, then an aircraft factory, and was used before the war for Lord Trenchard's famous Police College. Now it is not in the best of repair and will soon be pulled down and replaced by a purpose-built training centre. The students live in – three to an iron-bedded dormitory. Since National Service ended, few have had experience of barrack life, and some are at first 'rather appalled'.

The bulk of the course consists of law. Policemen have some hundred different powers of arrest, and must know the substance of nearly four hundred other offences. Since the English Law is construed literally by the courts, the policeman has to learn much of it by heart. There is a famous section of the *Children's and Young Persons' Act* which has five 'ands' and 'ors' in it: a mistake in any one could lead to disastrous results.

Here (adapted from Training School material), as an example of only one of the complex procedures which a policeman must keep in his head, is what must be done with a vehicle-driver who seems to have had too much to drink:

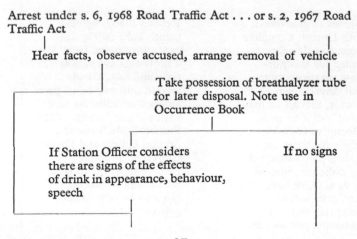

Arrest under s. 6, 1968 Road Traffic Act ... or s. 2, 1967 Road Traffic Act

Hear facts, observe accused, arrange removal of vehicle

Take possession of breathalyzer tube for later disposal. Note use in Occurrence Book

If Station Officer considers there are signs of the effects of drink in appearance, behaviour, speech

If no signs

37

Continued

Inform driver that a doctor will
be called to examine him with his
consent. He can have his own
doctor or a police surgeon. Station
Officer and PC to note, SO to
initial PC's book

Ask for breath test (at least twenty minutes
after arrest)

Negative	Fails to supply	Positive
No evidence of impairment	Evidence of impairment	Ask for blood/urine specimen. Warn that failure may make him liable to imposition of a fine and disqualification: SO and PC to note this warning, which must be repeated whenever a specimen is asked for.
No further action.	ask for specimen of blood/urine. No offence to refuse, but warn driver of s. 2 (1) of 1962 Act.	

CHARGE s. 6 1960 Act before doctor's examination

Agrees to give blood.
Call Doctor. Complete
book 83a. If only
called for this pur-
pose no necessity to
call driver's own
doctor, though he may
have him if he asks.
Doctor to complete
labels for three cups.
Labels to be attached
by police, numbered
1, 2, 3. Offer Nos. 2 or
3 to prisoner. If
accepted, seal in stout
envelope, prisoner and

Refuses blood, agrees
urine. Take two speci-
mens within one hour.
Throw first away, note
time and fact. Divide
second into two equal parts
labelled on adhesive tape
with prisoner's name, date,
Station Code. Prisoner,
Station Officer and Doctor,
if present, to initial over
joint in tape. PC to note
particulars of bottles.
No 1 to be offered the
prisoner

Continued

SO to sign over the flap. Other two cups to be placed in a tin and sealed. Doctor to complete H.O.R.T 5. in triplicate and retain one copy.

Fails urine, refuses blood a second time. If without a reasonable excuse. CHARGE s. 3(3) 1967 Act.

If no breath test taken inside station or outside, CHARGE s. 2(3) of same Act.

If ability to drive is 'markedly impaired' CHARGE s. 6 of 1960 Act. Accused entitled to legal aid.

If SO considers the prisoner shows 'marked impairment' CHARGE s. 6 1960 Act. If he pleads guilty at first hearing, throw specimens away. Otherwise ask for twenty-eight-day remand and send specimens to Laboratory with form 2. Use padded envelope for blood samples. If the prisoner refuses the offer of a sample, repeat the offer at court.
Note fact and reply. If he refuses tell him that the specimen will be thrown away in three days.

If there is no marked impairment, bail the prisoner in his own recognisance to return to station after twenty-eight days if SO is satisfied he will not drive a motor vehicle. If not, detain him until the breath test is negative. Book 12a.

Specimen to Laboratory, using padded envelope. Submit to process department with results of analysis.

When Laboratory report comes

If over 85mg/100 ml serve summons under s. 1 1967 Act, returnable on date of remand hearing. Must be served not less than seven days before hearing Legal Aid

If under 85 mg/100ml refer papers to B.4.

If decided to summons notify him to attend

If no further action,

Continued

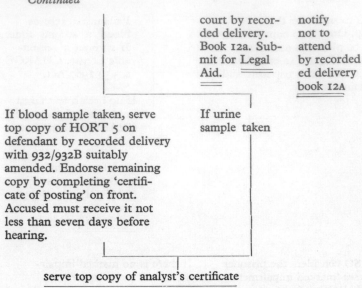

court by recorded delivery. Book 12a. Submit for Legal Aid. ═══ ═══

notify not to attend by recorded delivery book 12A

If blood sample taken, serve top copy of HORT 5 on defendant by recorded delivery with 932/932B suitably amended. Endorse remaining copy by completing 'certificate of posting' on front. Accused must receive it not less than seven days before hearing.

If urine sample taken

serve top copy of analyst's certificate

There is no short cut to learning one's way through the complexities of these laws. But there are mnemonics for procedures. Thus P. MARINERS for a street accident. *P*osition, mark or note; *M*edical aid; *A*bsent from beat – note in pocket-book; *R*emove vehicles; *I*nformation to Local Authority; *N*ames and addresses of people involved and witnesses; *E*xpenses; *R*oad signs needed?; *S*tation Officer informed. And there are litanies to learn:

'How I Put A Prisoner In The Cells:
I get the key
I go down to the cells
I unlock the outer door
I lock it behind me
I unlock the cell
I check the lavatory
I check the blanket
I go back and unlock the outer door
I lock it behind me

I get the prisoner
I unlock the outer door
I take him through and lock it again
I put him in the cell
I lock the cell
I unlock the outer door
I go out and I lock it again.'

In their police lives the students will write hundreds of thousands of words of reports describing every official action they take. Here they learn to say ELBOWS: no Erasures, no Leaves torn out, no Blank spaces, no Overwriting, no Writing between lines, Statements to be in exact words. They have to know that, when the servants on a royal coach wear cockades, there is royalty inside. They have to be able to recognise and deal appropriately with: Fire Brigade Committee Passes, Diabetes cards, Haemophiliac medallions, Steroid treatment cards, Epilepsy lapel badges and cards, Weil's disease cards, Compressed-air worker cards. They must know the flags of Lords Lieutenant, the Imperial Crown Plate, the permanent car pass medal for ambassadors, the ivory pass that the Home Secretary issues to people allowed to drive across the Horse Guards Parade, and many others.

Until recent years, students were required to learn most of the course material by heart; this meant most of their massive Instruction Book, which discouragingly observes 'Instructions cannot be issued to meet *every* case which may arise . . . something must necessarily be left to the intelligence and discretion of the individual.' But few exigencies of urban life are not provided for. Apart from being hard, boring work, which discouraged many potentially useful policemen, the parrot-learning phrases were often of little help when the probationer constable found himself on the street. He had to go through another learning period in which he identified the abstractions he had so laboriously absorbed.

Edwin Brock, one who suffered from the old method, contributed to the symposium *The Police and the Public.*[1] He said that this training had paralysed him. If he had been untrained he would at least have tackled crises in an uninhibited way, but as it was, he needed three or four years' experience before he felt confident of his abilities. One feels there may have been many like him. Now three-quarters of the training is done with visual aids or by acting out little playlets to give the student some idea of the urgencies and irrelevancies of real life situations.

One class is playing at charge rooms. Three instructors, sitting at card tables, are being Station Sergeants, and the students are playing the parts of arresting officers and prisoners. At one table an attractive, freckled girl, one of the WPCs, is being charged with shop-lifting. The student stumbles through his evidence. 'I was on patrol in Oxford Street when' – he looks at his notebook, his finger searching for the right place – 'Mr Peter Stemp came up to me and said . . .'

Instructor: 'Can you tell the Magistrate reported speech?'

'Umm . . . no. As a result of information I received I approached this girl. . . .'

'*Who?*'

'Sorry, this lady.'

'WOMAN.' (Aside to me: 'We drill in this politeness and it confuses them. They say rubbish like, "I'm arresting you, Sir."')

'I approached this woman. Mr Stemp then said in her presence (Instructor: 'That's right'), "Officer, I want you to arrest this woman. She's stolen a pair of nylons."'

Instructor: 'Could any other person have taken them?'

Student: 'Mr Stemp described the box. He said it was green with a pair of brown legs on it. I then searched the prisoner and found this box, here, under her jacket.' He puts the box proudly on the table and stands back. But the Instructor asks: 'Have you proved that this property was stolen?'

[1] Ed. C. H. Rolph, Heinemann, 1962.

'Oh, yes.' He studies his notebook again. 'Mr Stemp then said to me, "I recognise that box. They are my nylons."'

'It's no good you charging her with theft unless you prove something existed to be stolen.' The Instructor charges the prisoner, who says, dutifully, 'I'm sorry, I don't know what came over me.' The student writes this in his notebook, signs the entry, and puts the book away. The Instructor wearily asks: 'Does it look as if I'm waiting for anything?' The student thinks again, then pulls the notebook out and hands it over. The Instructor too signs the entry as a witness of the admission of guilt. Then the student turns her (prop) bag out. Inside the student finds six crumpled 4d stamps, the stub of a Mecca dancing-ticket, a bunch of keys, a dirty handkerchief, a half-smoked cigarette and a metal comb with a sharp handle.

'Should I search under her collar?'

'No, not unless you've changed sex overnight. We'll assume there's a WPC to do that.' The instructor now lists the prisoner's property on the charge-sheet, while the student copies it on the outside of an envelope into which he then puts the things. 'Remember, you take away property that could do harm to herself, or others, anything that is evidence of crime, or shows means to pay a possible fine. Suppose that dance ticket had been a pawn ticket?'

'You'd have listed it, sir, because she might have pawned stolen property.'

'Good again. And I've put the watch in because I've seen someone cut his throat with one. We'll assume she's been put in a cell. Now, you're left with *this*,' says the instructor tapping her baby, a piece of wood wrapped in a grubby shawl, on the table. 'A baby, here in the station, and I expect it's messed itself. What do you propose to do? – 'Right, we'll chase the relatives.' – 'And if there aren't any?' – 'Right again, it goes into care with the council.'

Outside in the yard a group of strikers – a senior class – with planted instructors in plain clothes – is holding a meeting. The speaker is making a good job of subversive speech, and a nervous student in uniform is rocking on the balls of his feet, wondering which of his hazily remembered powers of arrest he is going to have to use.

Suddenly an instructor comes swerving in from behind the student, tears through the crowd, punches one of the planted instructors in the stomach, drops a knuckleduster, hops about shouting at the top of his voice and then gallops away round the corner of the yard. The whole thing is so quick, violent and surprising that the student has hardly taken in what has happened, let alone what laws have been broken and what powers of arrest he has, before it's all over.

The Instructor asks: 'Now, what do you plan to do?'

'Arrest him?'

'Yes, you've got a *power* of arrrest, I'll give you that, but what are you arresting him for? – Public Meeting Act! Try again.' Long pause, while the 'strikers' pick themselves up and crowd round the student, shouting, waving the knuckleduster, each trying to complain louder than the others of his injuries.

'Look, sonny, get on with it. Right now you're in a shocking state. The meeting's broken up; chummy's in the next county by now.'

Indoors again, the canteen has been re-set as the bleakest sort of pub; mugs filled with cold tea stand on the formica tables. Half a dozen instructors are lounging about, arguing, sleeping, staring moodily into space. Those who play these little sketches have become polished actors. They achieve characters who have a real, daunting presence; people with their own lives and worries, to whom the police are an irritating irrelevancy, or something automatically to hate. Part of the point of this training is to teach the students to assert themselves, to dominate older, bigger, angrier men. In real life the people whom they will have to dominate will be strangers, but here they are their own awe-inspiring instructors. It is a sort of psychological battle-course with live ammunition.

The first two students are put outside, and the rest of the class settles down at the back of the room to see the play. A 'Salvation Army Captain' complains to the pair in business that a man inside the pub is drunk and asleep. He says he is wearing a tweed jacket. They go inside and find two men who fit the description. While they talk to the nearer, the other starts throwing chairs about. Whichever one they talked to first, the other would be 'drunk'. Moral: find out *exactly* what it's all about, and then take one each.

The next two students are sent out, and come back to find two men with their heads together, furtively writing out a list. One says to the other: 'Two and six place.' This suddenly makes sense to the students, who dive at the table, snatch the money – coins roll all over the floor – tear the list, because they think that the men are writing out a heinous betting-slip on unlicensed premises. The two instructors get up and swear loudly, angrily, convincingly at the young men. They fiddle with their chinstraps, they don't know what to do next, and when they are told the list was for fish-and-chip orders (two and sixpence-worth of *plaice*) they're like to sink. As they pick the chairs up for the next run, one of the instructors whispers: 'You see why this is such a valuable form of instruction. They'll never drop a bollock like that again. You see them maturing overnight.'

The next two students have to break up a quarrel. The instigator was the biggest and most menacing instructor. They gamely carried him out, kicking and squealing; he fought his way back in again, and then everyone in the 'pub' started to fight. The two students looked like people who had stepped into a warm bath and found that they were swimming for their lives. But they pushed their helmets forward and tried again. When the riot was broken up, their class instructor held a post-mortem.

'Did you assert your authority? No. It isn't enough to carry the man out. You've got to produce calm. Could you hear what the landlord was saying? No. That's because you didn't take charge and shut everybody up. If *you* start fighting

45

it panics people, they'll press on all the harder. Now, you carried him out and he came back, and you carried him out again and that time you kept hold of him. What did you do that for? Why did you arrest him?'

'Quarrelsome, sir.'

'Indeed! Under the Prevention of Breathing Act, I suppose.'

It was the end of class. A new recruit, pale under his freshly cropped hair, reflected, 'I was just thinking. From now on I'll have to be like these boots – round and shiny. This would be an easy job if you didn't have to think about it; but when you have ideals about how much people should influence each other, it gets difficult.'

The Superintendent in charge of the school, an immaculately scrubbed, fresh-faced man, whose head and hands are somehow precisely the proper extremities to his uniform, says, 'We try to get across to them that they are "servants and guardians of the public". After a while you can't beat about the bush any longer. You have to take a calculated risk, push them out on the street and see whether, when someone is *really* rude to them, they really ignore it. Some will definitely get their knuckles rapped in division, but that's part of the learning process. We can only simulate reality so far.'

Wastage

After the recruits leave the school and are posted to their divisions, training still goes on. Until they have been two years in the force, they are on probation, and the subject of two-monthly reports to their Divisional Chief Superintendents. They also spend two days a month at classes, learning remoter points of the law. During this time, more misfits are weeded out.

One such might be the subject of the sort of comments suggested here. To save wounding feelings, I asked a Chief Superintendent to put together an imaginary personal report on a police failure. John Doe's file opens with a portrait. He looks like Tommy Steele, and on the day that he was photographed he had a black eye. The form gives his size in respirators, gumboots and steel helmets. Lower, the Chief Superintendent in charge of the school had written, 'This man really had to struggle hard all the way, and is going to need a great deal of help and guidance if he is to survive his probationary period and make a sound policeman.'

The boy plays cricket and likes athletics. By his eighth month in division, his new Chief Superintendent called for a monthly report. In the first of these his Section Sergeant said that he is 'shy and reserved, but a pleasant-natured man with colleagues and the public. He appreciates encouragement, and has been advised (see Vocabulary) about stops on the street.' His Inspector found him: 'Well turned out, but very reserved.' The Superintendent: 'Satisfactory start, should improve quickly, responds well to guidance.' The Chief Superintendent: 'Think it a little early to assess him.'

The second report repeated the first, except that his Sergeant has discovered an interest in cinematography. The man possessed his own first-class equipment. The District Training Officer said that he was poor on theoretical knowledge and resented being corrected. The third is much as before: the Inspector said that he wasn't a good mixer, the District Training Officer commented on his poor reporting, the result of carelessness, the Chief Superintendent found room for considerable improvement.

With the fourth report the Inspector put the boot in. 'He tells me he has always wanted to be a police officer and that he is happy in the Force, yet his whole attitude leads me to believe that he has little interest in the service. When spoken to he appears resentful (though that might be timidness). If this man does not show rapid improvement, I cannot see how he can be a useful member of the force.' The District Training Officer found a great improvement. His Superintendent wrote, 'In my opinion, this PC is *not up to standard*. He is so completely lacking in self-confidence that he cannot possibly be happy in the service. He must always be apprehensive that he will be called on to exercise his police powers. He lacks strength. He is of no use at present.'

The Chief Superintendent called for the unfortunate, read it all to him, and he resigned. This boy is an example of what is called 'annual voluntary premature wastage' by people in the police-recruiting business. In his case it was probably for the good of both parties, and since a policeman cannot be considered fully trained until he has had three or four years' service, his loss after only a year was not serious. But more disturbing, the AVPW for the Metropolitan Police runs at about 460 a year, or more than a third of annual recruiting. Half of these leave *after* their probationary period and represent a serious loss. Although this rate is comparable with the wastage from the prison and fire services and from the civil service clerical officer grades, and is perhaps a fact of bureaucratic life, the police feel that it is pointless to have to recruit twelve men to get seven useful ones.

A survey, taken in four other forces, by a firm of management consultants, suggested that 'apart from pay and hours of duty . . . unsatisfactory man management seemed to cause considerable unrest; and two aspects of man management in particular were mentioned. These were (a) unnecessarily strict adherence to the letter rather than the spirit of the regulations; and (b) thoughtless application of disciplinary measures.'[1] As a result of this, 'man management' had become a sort of Star of Bethlehem to the Uniform Branch at the time of my visit, and what had been an autocratic service was trying, with some contortions, to democratise itself.

As an example of the way things were going the description of the parade on p. 59 will perhaps stand, but the emphasis on man management seemed at first to impose considerable strain on the lower supervisory ranks, who are expected to apply an almost unworkable accretion of

[1] *Police Manpower, Equipment and Efficiency*. Report of three working parties, HMSO 1967, p. 22.

48

orders and instructions without upsetting their men. A young Inspector said: 'Our ground is a miserable one to work, and if I got all regimental and made the lads fill in the books properly it would be the last straw and they'd all leave. For instance, white gauntlets for directing traffic on point duty. You're supposed to book them in and out, but people just collect them and put them back, and what does it matter if a pair gets lost occasionally? But I can hardly go to the Superintendent and say, "I have to report, sir, that the books are not correctly kept." Making the system work puts people like me in the middle.'

The problem is being tackled at one of its roots by rewriting General Orders, so as to cut out an enormous quantity of petttifogging rules that have accumulated over the decades. But this is only part of the problem. A more fundamental difficulty, perhaps, is that there is no way of measuring how well a policeman is doing. In business the test of success is profitability; in war it is who won the last battle, but the police job is essentially compromise built on compromise. There is no single quantity that one can measure to test the uniform policeman's work.

For instance, if he reports too few people for process, he can't be doing his job because the streets are certainly full of law-breakers. But if he reports too many, he damages the public relations of the force, and shows that another police responsibility, traffic management, has been neglected. The *real* effect of policing lies in its social symbolism rather than in any mechanical effects which it produces by restraining law-breakers, and is therefore almost impossible to measure.

But a disciplined bureaucracy has a built-in hunger for quantifiable facts. It needs to be able to assess people and schemes, it needs something to measure, and if the real objectives are not measurable, then surrogates are drawn inexorably into their place. And for want of any better absolute criteria, they are used to make judgements about people. So one finds, willy-nilly, minute analyses being made of crime and arrest rates, although most of the factors affecting these lie wholly outside the control of the police. At least things have improved since pre-war days, when the ability of a superintendent was judged by the number of discipline charges which he managed to bring against his men.

The CID have a much simpler objective: to arrest every available criminal. A detective's arrest score is closely related to his ability: the existence of something real and measurable seems to simplify management enormously. It is interesting that 'man management' as a problem is not recognised by the CID, and although relationships between the ranks are often brutal, the wastage rate in this department is negligible.

Specialisations

After their two-year probation, recruits become proper policemen and can opt, if they wish, for a specialist job: the CID, Special Branch, Traffic Department, Mounted Branch, River Police or Dogs. Of these the largest, if not the most important in every policeman's opinion, is the CID. Selection for the department is by means of another two-year probation period, during which the candidate, now with the rank of Temporary Detective Constable, but always called 'Aid', patrols the streets and carries out observations. He is expected to bring in roughly an arrest a week for the whole two years. If he manages to fulfil his quota without being the subject of a complaint from a member of the public, he is likely to be accepted into the department as a Detective Constable and sent to the Detective Training School. This brute criterion of suitability is typical of the CID's whole attitude to life.

The CID school deals with some 1,400 students a year, most of whom are Metropolitan officers, but some of whom come from neighbouring forces. There is an advanced course for potential Detective Superintendents, one for promotion to Detective Inspector, and the largest, the basic Detective Constable's course. There are smaller courses for Aids, Fingerprint, Photographic and Scenes of Crime officers. The school also provides instructors to train uniform officers on divisions in their new (in London) role as investigators of minor crime.

The school is at Peel House, near Victoria, the old uniform basic training school. Students on the basic course undergo thirteen weeks of almost solid criminal law, salted with lectures on explosives, pathology, a BBC film on interrogation, a demonstration of a thermic lance, and other diversions. It has its own Black Museum; unlike the famous one at Scotland Yard, the exhibits are chosen for their instructive qualities rather than for their associations with famous cases.

The body of the course is the English Criminal law – complete – and the pass mark in the final examination is a stiff eighty-five per cent. In contrast to the uniform policeman's basic training, the teaching is almost completely academic. Little use is made of playlets, and, in fact, there is little attempt to teach *detection* as such. It is characteristic of the conservative CID that the only book on the practical details of catching criminals – how to search a man, or a house, how to follow people, how to get information about companies was written by a retired *uniform* inspector,[1] and I never heard it mentioned at the school.

The Telecommunications School trains 1,500 officers a year in simple voice and telex procedures. The Dog and Mounted Schools have perhaps been often enough described not to need attention here. The Driving School is also very well known. Based at Hendon, it processes nearly two thousand officers a year through an elaborate scheme of five qualifications in car-driving and two in motorcycling.

Since the British Police are traditionally not armed with guns, the most interesting school is perhaps that which teaches pistol-shooting. The intention is simply to enable policemen to defend themselves when they have to tackle armed

[1] Meek, V. *Private Enquiries*, Duckworth, 1967.

criminals. It is a necessary response to the new criminal fashion of carrying guns, but one that is regretted by many policemen. Until now (summer 1969), British policemen have only fired twice in anger since the siege of Sidney Street in 1911. In both cases crazed gunmen were killed by police rifles: once in Chatham in 1951, again in Glasgow in 1969.

Initially this takes four days, the first of which is spent at an old military camp in Epping Forest. Stout and worried CID officers in baggy denim overalls try to remember their infantry tactics as they cover each other in dashes towards the hidden instructor. They learn how to get out of a car under fire, how to hide behind the wheels and the engine block, and not to forget to take the radio microphone on its stretchy cord with them. In an old, dark bunker they learn how to search buildings for gunmen. Their instructors are hiding with starting-pistols: the bangs echoing in the concrete rooms are extremely unnerving.

The problem in gun-training policemen is to teach them when *not* to shoot (like teaching recruits when not to use their legal powers). In this bunker exercise, a female tailor's dummy, wearing blue overalls and mending a radiator in the dark, nearly always gets shot in embarrassing mistake for the villain. Proficiency is maintained on indoor ranges under three police stations in central London. At one, officers shoot at street photographs projected on a wall: bishops, villains and nannies pushing prams alternate with startling rapidity.

Some 1,000 men, or five per cent of the force, have qualified on this course.[1] Guns for operational use are kept at most stations in the care of the Station Officer; only the Special Branch, who protect important visitors, and, on occasions, PCs outside embassies carry guns as a matter of course. They have 9 mm Walthars, the rest use ·38 Webleys. The Walther is light and comfortable to carry, but it will jam if the trigger is held back too long, or if it is dropped. The Webley is a brute to carry but will stand up to a lot of rough treatment.

[1] Eighty men are qualified as marksmen with the rifle.

Broadly speaking, all these specialist schools teach the use of tools that are often useful to policemen: radio sets, indictments, fingerprint forms, Acts of Parliament, cars; but they do not teach policing itself.

Bramshill and the University Man

There is nothing very controversial about the vocational training. It is a necessary adjunct to the police job and often to promotion, and policemen accept it. But the Home Office's National Police College at Bramshill is rather different. This is intended, as a pamphlet given to visitors explains, to enable its students 'to broaden their outlook, to quicken their mental powers, and to improve their professional skill and knowledge'.

The courses appear to be an amalgam of university and military-style education, modelled perhaps on the Army's Staff College. The aim is possibly to 'civilise' the rough copper, and if the government wanted to spend money on that alone, few policemen would object. Typical of the many comments that I heard from London policemen was this one from an experienced uniform Inspector: 'I don't think it has much bearing on your professional career, but it's a marvellous opportunity to think a bit, to stand back from the chaos, to take stock and do some reading.'

Housed in a beautiful, simple, seventeenth-century brick mansion near Reading, with less successful Ministry of Works modern outbuildings, courses are run at the Police College at four levels. The Senior Command Course is designed to produce men capable of promotion to Chief Constable level from within the ranks of the police. Until the last thirty years, most such people were retired senior officers from the services, who brought with them some breadth of experience. They are selected by a three-day civil service board at Eastbourne, where candidates, in small syndicate groups, debate current affairs, draft proposals to deal with some desperate concatenation of civil problems, and are interviewed.

The course aims to produce some twenty qualified men a year, from whom in time the thirty Chief Officers[1] needed annually by the English and Welsh police can be selected.[2] Their syllabus includes a broad spectrum of civic knowledge: economics, international affairs, state security, public speaking, a parliamentary exercise. On the professional side, students learn about leadership, management, welfare, and assessment for promotion within the police. They do public order and disaster exercises, they learn the techniques of administration. They are initiated into the mysteries of traffic engineering and management.

The Intermediate Command Course is similar, but at a level designed to fit men for Superintendents' jobs. About fifty students pass through it each year; the national requirement is about 300-400. Next there is the Inspectors' course, designed to take ordinary policemen and broaden their outlook. One in three of the 900 annual promotions to Inspector pass through it. A witness before the 1967 Committee on the Estimates said of it, 'We seek to impart what one might, I think, justifiably call citizen knowledge, the kind of knowledge every professional man should have in common with every other professional man. A professional man should be an educated man in the sense that he knows the values of his society very thoroughly, he is at ease and confident, considers himself very much to be a guardian.'[3]

None of these causes trouble and they doubtless do a lot of good. It is the fourth, the Special Course, that poses a problem to the police as a whole. This was begun in 1962 with 'the aim of accelerating the careers of young officers of outstanding promise.'[4] Candidates apply for it at the time that they sit

[1] Chief Constables, Deputy and Assistant Chief Constables in provincial forces; Commanders and above in the Metropolitan Police.
[2] The Scots, with a different system of law, have their own police college.
[3] First report from the Estimates Committee, Session 1966-7, *Police*, HMSO 1967, para 840.
[4] *Ibid.*, para 756.

their Sergeant's examination, after a minimum of two years' service. They spend a year at the College, and if successful, are promoted Inspector a year later at the end of five years' service in contrast to the ordinary process of promotion, which might take nine or ten years. This causes some jealousy, although the Special Course provides only three per cent of the promotions to Sergeant and Inspector.

But the difficulty is not just over accelerated promotion to Inspector. It is that these highflyers affect every policeman's chances of promotion to higher ranks. One of the important things about Napoleon's armies was the baton that every soldier carried in his knapsack. This is in theory true of the police, who now have an active policy of promotion to all ranks from within the service, but the stimulating effect is vitiated if those who are eventually to command are marked from the beginning. The 'stars' might, as many policemen feel, be better brought in at a senior level, as they were before the last war. This would free many more intermediate ranks for the promotion of people who may not rise very far, but would like to enjoy some authority towards the end of their service and a higher pension on retirement.

The apparent necessity of having two 'streams' in the police, one, the 'A' stream, as one might call it, destined for higher things, and the other much larger, destined for routine jobs, presents the police administrator with a very tricky problem. He has to have enough stars to make sure that the needs of the service will be supplied, but if he has too many, he discourages the stars themselves, and, more seriously, he kills off almost all hope of promotion for the rest, who then have little motivation to soldier on in what has become a sterile and hopeless job. This is all the more serious in the police because junior policemen, PCs and Sergeants, are in many ways the most important ranks and by no means the least responsible.

The whole problem is coloured by the memory of Lord Trenchard's Hendon Police College, which ran from 1933 to 1939. In effect it recruited men, who, after a courtesy period as PCs and two years' training at the College, immediately became Inspectors. At the beginning of the scheme, in 1933, the Metropolitan Police was given to understand that no one in future could hope for promotion above Inspector unless he had been through Hendon. Although the late and present Commissioners, six Assistant Commissioners, at least twenty-one Chief Constables, and seven members of the Inspectorate were among the 188 Hendon graduates, the scheme aroused frantic opposition and cast suspicion in advance on any proposal which appeared to create a privileged officer class.

The conundrum is exacerbated by the need to recruit university graduates. The Chief Constable of Lancashire put the administrator's point of view, '... I am very keen to get some university-trained men into the police, not because a university-trained man is *ipso facto* a better policeman, but because a much greater proportion of grammar school boys today are getting into the universities and the police service ought to be getting its fair share of these boys. We have failed completely to do so.'[1]

In the context of the Robbins Report, and its intention that, within the foreseeable future, 80 per cent of young people should have university degrees, it is even more essential that the police should 'get their fair share'. But to get and keep graduates in competition with industry, the police have to guarantee quick and certain promotion to the highest ranks. Their thinking is now that Commanders or Assistant Chief Constables should be appointed at about the age of thirty-five, as against forty-five to fifty in the past.

Graduates arrive in the police in two main ways. Either they are recruited under a special scheme which, if they earn their superiors' approval during basic training and probation, and pass the Sergeants' examination, guarantees them a place on the Special Course, or, as policemen passing out of the Special Course in the ordinary way, they do well

[1] Note 3, p. 54. para 1257.

enough to win a Bramshill Scholarship to a university, where they take a degree without leaving the Police Service.[1]

Altogether nineteen graduates were offered places in the police in 1968, and twenty Bramshill scholarships were awarded. This total of forty is negligible in comparison with the total intake into the police service (700 in London alone), and is only three per cent of the promotions to Sergeant, or four and a half per cent of those to Inspector. But it represents twenty-six per cent[2] of the promotions to Superintendent, and no less than 130 per cent of those to Chief Officer. And this is at a time when there are some fifty police forces in England and Wales. If, as may be possible, the Home Office amalgamates these into some twenty forces with correspondingly fewer Chief Officers, the graduates are that much more certain to swamp the promotion lists.

Eventually a log jam may develop in promotion that may have to be cleared by reserving a proportion of top jobs for 'B' stream people, by early retirement on generous pensions of middle-rank men who are unlikely to progress, and by compensating the essential, long-service PC with increases of pay in proportion to his experience. It is not surprising, then, that 'graduate entry' is a loaded phrase among policemen. It is necessary and inevitable, and perhaps the surprise is that graduates and special-course men are as well accepted as they are.

---

[1] Of the policemen at university in 1968, fourteen were reading for LL.B., nine for B.Sc. Econ., one for a degree in Government studies, two in economics, two in history, one in psychology, five in law, two in history, one in politics and sociology, and two in social studies.

[2] An average figure: 40% in 1967; 10% in 1968.

CHAPTER THREE

Uniform Police

On the Beat

The basic policeman is the man on the beat. Every police-man, whatever he does for the rest of his career, starts with two years on the beat, and a great many continue all their service doing this job on and off. A beat in Central London is an area roughly 400 yards by 200 yards; 4,000 people live on it and the beat man walks round it.[1]

In the old days the Metropolis was divided into seventeen divisions, each division into two or three sub-divisions, each sub-division into two sections, and each section into eight beats. Three men were provided to each beat – one for each of the three reliefs – and set walking. Apart from

[1] While I was researching this book a new system of beat policing was being introduced. Instead of assigning constables to beats for their eight-hour turn of duty, as only one of several jobs they might do, the new system of Unit Beat Policing puts a constable perman-ently in charge of each beat. His job is to get to know the people who live on it, to investigate any minor crime that occurs there, and in general to establish the sort of relationship a village policeman has with the community in which he lives. In this scheme there is also, for every two beats, a 'Panda Car' – a light car driven by an ordinary PC, and controlled by personal radio from the station, which deals with small but urgent problems to which it is not worth getting an Area Car. In order to make the best use of the Unit Beat men's knowledge of their beats, there is also a new appointment of 'Intel-ligence Collator', whose job it is to keep records of crime in the station's area, and to evaluate trends on his own and neighbouring grounds. Since this system was still at a rather tentative stage during my visit, and its effect is to improve the quality of policing rather than to change its nature, I have not described it at length.

a few officers to staff the stations, make reports, receive charges, and manage the men on the beat, this was all that there was to policing. Time has built on this simple idea an enormous organisation. Now, only one uniform policeman in eight is actually walking a beat at any given moment.

The first time that I walked with a beat-man was at night, out of Paddington. This used to be one of the busiest stations in the MPD, and starred in the film 'The Blue Lamp'. But demographic changes have – from the police point of view – sadly altered it. What used to be slum streets, full of prostitutes and criminals, have been pulled down, and a vast and expensive redevelopment carried out. In other parts the better-heeled bourgeoisie have been buying up the rooming houses and rebuilding them as family homes. Nowadays, in police terms, Paddington is quiet.

It is ten o'clock; the PCs going on patrol for the 'night turn' are gathered in the parade room, down in the basement. Round the walls are a few photographs of wanted men: the coloured portrait of the Cannock Chase murderer, distributed by the Daily Express, that then decorated every police station in the land, an Identikit picture of a bushy-haired Irishman who nearly killed a policeman in Liverpool with a crowbar, a few blurry snaps of a twenty-year-old who lives on the sub-division and is thought to be making a promising career in housebreaking.

The sixteen or so men on beat duty are sitting round three sides of the room – bulky in their heavy winter coats and scarves, their boots stretched before them. The Section Sergeant is leaning on a desk in the middle, debating with '216' what to do about some empty houses on his beat where prostitutes are taking their clients. 'Do you think it's worth taking a dog down there?'

'I don't know that we'd need it really . . .'

'I'll tell you what we'll do. We'll get eight blokes in the van after refreshments (about 2 a.m.) and we'll go down there and sort it out.'

'513' puts in: 'You need to, there's a room they use as a lavatory – it's disgusting really.'

The Sergeant went on, 'The Superintendent's very pleased with the stops – keep it up.'

At that, the Night Duty Officer, an Inspector, comes down, and the Sergeant calls out 'APPOINTments!' They all stand up with their truncheons held upright in one hand, their whistles and keys over the back of the other hand, the finger through the ring (when constables in less formal county forces are attached to the Metropolitan Police for some special job, this ceremony always makes them laugh).

The Inspector sits them down again and the debate continues. 'Who has Three beat with the cinema?' '120' says he has. 'Well then, watch out for taking and driving away while the people are inside.'

'All right, but they're showing *Quatermass and the Pit* – it's a crap film, I don't reckon there'll be many there.'

'Mr Anderson, at 105 Northumberland Place, has left a heater on in his front room to dry the wallpaper. His house isn't on fire.'

Another PC: 'You remember that job we had the other night when we turned over the pusher's drum and all he had was a boy-friend who said that drugs weren't his interest? Well, I saw him hanging round Queensway this evening as I was coming on.'

This briefing session provided one of those correspondences between theory and practice that are rare in any walk of life, for a recent report on police manpower and efficiency said: 'The briefing officer and the constables he is briefing should regard themselves as confidential colleagues engaged in a joint enterprise, in which the sharing of information and the planning of tactics are matters for the whole group.'[1]

Two PCs have permission to police a football match at Chelsea. Only local policemen get inside the ground to see the game, but they will earn £5 a head even after tax. At that the meeting breaks up and we proceed on our beats. Until quite recently PCs marched out of the station in single file on the

[1] *Police Manpower, Equipment and Efficiency*. Report of three working parties, HMSO 1967, p. 124.

outside of the pavement – as they had since the force began – but now the whole procedure is simpler and less formal.

I am attached to a solid, intelligent Scot, about thirty years old, who transferred a couple of years ago from Glasgow. Our first call, a few doors away from the station, is on an Irishman in a boarding-house. After some banging and ringing he emerges: a toothless man with a yellowish moustache and a large belly. My companion tells him that his sister died a few hours before in Ireland, he thanks us politely, says he expected it and retires, apparently unmoved. 'I reckon every PC in the Met has to do this three or four times a year. It's one of the worst things you have to do. This bloke was easy, but when it's a mum whose kid has been killed, or her husband ... Like one I had not long ago – he was a steeplejack working up a 300-foot chimney who took a pace back to admire his work. He fell head first onto a lot of reinforcing-rods – that wasn't too nice, but the way his poor wife carried on ... and all you can do is pat their hand and make tea for them.'

We plod on, and I try to get used to letting my legs swing at their own natural speed – this saves energy and gets one along at about half ordinary walking-pace. In court policemen describe this as 'proceeding' and get laughed at for it by intellectuals, but, as I think C. H. Rolph once pointed out, this accurately describes what they do – they are neither coming nor going, nor even walking, in the ordinary sense of the word: 'I was proceeding on my beat.'

We proceed some more and come to an empty house which we mark by tying a piece of black cotton across the area steps and tucking a leaf in the jamb of the door, so that if someone breaks in the beat-man will know and can get the place surrounded. If he's lucky the intruder might still be there. We proceed a lot more, up and down, round and round – the Duty Officer believes in getting his men mobile, so only half a dozen of the beats are being patrolled on foot this evening, and we have to cover three of them. 'In theory,' says my friend, 'I'm here to prevent crime, but how can I? Any villain with an ounce of sense in his head is going to see me coming a mile off and duck out of sight. He knows I'm not likely to come back for an hour or two and he just gets on with it.'

Every fifteen minutes we pass or are passed by a police car – a mini with a couple of aids parked up a dark alley keeping observation – the PC notices them but doesn't tell me until we're past so that I shan't give them away by unnatural curiosity. Then we find the empty area car parked outside an Indian restaurant from which comes a confused shouting noise. The station's general purpose car, a grey Hillman with a give-away black whip aerial on the roof, putters past with a wave, then the area car again going fast with the blue light flashing.

After an hour my companion admits that a beat in a good residential area is the slowest sort of policing that there is. The dark houses slide past, we meet a boy with a little tartan suitcase and a grubby mackintosh – my friend stops him, asks his name and where he's going. The conversation is casual, a bit drawn-out, the policeman is looking for nervousness, signs of wanting to rush away. But this boy is just sleepy. He stand there feeling timeless. He doesn't mind a bit if we open his suitcase and accurately predicts the uneaten cheese sandwiches which we will find inside. He is an apprentice with the electricity board, coming off his evening shift; we apologise for bothering him and wish him good night.

This is a 'stop' under Section 66 of the *Metropolitan Police Act 1839* which gives the Metropolitan Police power to stop and search any person and/or vehicle they reasonably suspect of carrying stolen property. Curiously, only a dozen or so forces have it[1], yet it is a very powerful crime-fighting weapon. A thief can pick the time and place of a crime to reduce his chances of detection, but this power subjects him to an extra hazard coming and going. Section 66 stops produce about 40% of the Metropolitan Police's

---

[1] These are: the City of London, Newcastle-on-Tyne, Macclesfield, Salford, Oldham, St Helens, Burnley, Birmingham, Rochdale, Manchester, Birkenhead, Liverpool, and one county, Herefordshire.

50,000 crime arrests a year, although only one stop in twenty is fruitful. Some of the other nineteen produce trouble for the police, usually because an eminently respectable person has been stopped and doubts that a constable could 'reasonably' suspect him of carrying stolen property.

'What does "reasonably" mean, anyway?' asked my companion. 'Burglars don't go about with masks on and bags marked "SWAG" any more. In a smart district the intelligent breaker goes to work in a bowler, pin-stripe suit and a monocle, but the chap you stop is likely to be a retired colonel. You tell him this is one of the best ways of catching thieves, and it might be his property you get back, but there's some of them won't have it. Often it's just a feeling you get, something about their eyes – I don't know. Some coppers are better at it than others. But you can hardly get up in court and say "I had a feeling in my stomach". After all, who does most of the crime in this country? Young men – anyone between fifteen and twenty-five. If there's more than one, or it's late at night, or they're carrying something, then a stop is indicated.'

Occasionally a 'feeling' pays off in a handsome way. In the spring of 1968 a large emerald was stolen. The owner of the jewel was approached by an intermediary bearing a handsome offer of £15,000. After negotiations, a meeting was arranged in a private sitting-room in a big hotel. Instead of the buyer, a ruffian turned up, hit the seller on the head, took the jewel and left. The bulging briefcase which he left behind was full of magazines, not money. Although the 'buyer' obviously knew why and how this happened, he would not say anything, and there were apparently no leads at all.

Three days later, a PC on the beat near Victoria stopped a car for having no road-fund licence. The young man driving was so rude that the PC took his car keys and made him wait while he checked him with CRO and the car with CVI (see p. 213). The man had previous convictions for car theft and assault on the police. He would not explain where the car came from, so he was arrested on suspicion of having stolen it. When the car arrived at the station it was thoroughly searched and a .45 revolver-round found under the seat. His flat was searched, and there was the pistol used in the robbery and a lot of magazines wadded to make more 'money'.

The reaction of one outraged citizen is recorded by John Chandos McConnell, in *The Police and the Public*[1], who was pulled one night on 'A' Division's ground, taken to Gerald Road Police Station and searched. He made a great fuss about it and began to sue the Commissioner. In the end he got £50, his costs and an apology from the officers concerned. This happens about a dozen times a year: but the number of arrests so outweighs aggrieved respectability that it seems to be the policy of the force to pay up and apologise with good grace. Certainly I met no constables who felt they weren't adequately supported over stops.

We stroll back to the station for a cup of tea poured from an urn balanced on the edge of the counter – the grill is down, the canteen staff gone home – to the strains of Radio Caroline, then illegal and on her last legs. Afterwards I go out with the Duty Officer, an elderly, grizzled inspector, respected by his men as a practical copper. He collects a driver and we get in his staid car – but at least it has a radio and puts us in touch with the rest of life in the MPD. I ask him what he's looking for: 'At night you watch for moving goods vehicles – in London there aren't many honest ones that need to move after midnight – saloon cars with two to three men, expensive-looking cars with very young men – they're often joy riders – men on the pavement carrying goods.' But our first customer is a shadowy figure walking an unsteady figure of eight round the pillars in front of an office. We pull up and watch him.

'He'll come' says the Inspector, but the driver says 'No – he's settled down for the night.' At that the man ups and dashes into the middle of Edgware Road where the traffic is still heavy and fast. The Inspector runs after him and

[1] Ed. C. H. Rolph, Heinemann, 1962.

brings him back. He is put in the back of the car explaining monotonously that he has to get home, his wife will be worried because he only went out at six to get her some medicine. In between repeating this, he digs me in the ribs and asks why I'm not saying anything. At the station he blows the Inspector a kiss and slumps happily on the charge room bench. He says he is called Fred and is charged in that name with being drunk and disorderly. 'Drunk', he says, very shocked. 'I'm very ashamed of you', he adds, waving a waggish finger at the Inspector.

Drunks are a perennial problem. There is no intrinsic reason why the police should deal with mild alcohol poisoning. But for their own safety – like Fred – they can't be let loose. There is no medical treatment for the condition and many are violent, so it's pointless and unfair to the nurses to send them to hospital. But mixed with the heavy-breathing drunks are a few almost indistinguishable people with fractured skulls. Of the 34,000 arrests for drunkenness made every year in London, in spite of the attention of Police Surgeons and the intuition of wary Station Sergeants, perhaps half-a-dozen die in the cells. It is difficult to know what to do about it.

The Inspector gets a radio operator and we go out again. We sew a seam in and out of the little mews, up and down the small streets. At this early stage I haven't much idea what to look for and I completely miss an old Vauxhall crossing a street a hundred yards down on our left. Our driver doesn't. We dart up the next street, left, right and emerge just behind it. We hover menacingly in the hope that the driver – if he has evil intentions or something incriminating on board – will panic, but he doesn't and we pull him.

There are four boys. The driver knows the index number of the car, he can turn the ignition off with the key, he has licence and insurance in the appropriate names, the car's age agrees with its licence plates, the road-fund licence is apparently in order. The radio operator is in rather an aggressive mood. He makes the passengers get out during these formalities, to watch him rummaging the boot, but to no avail. We say good night under the flat yellow sodium lights and continue our monotonous, dream-like cruising, up and down.

The main radio has been quiet for several minutes when the personal radio lying on the back seat comes up with an alarm bell ringing by Hyde Park. We are close by, and when someone winds a window down we can already hear the deep clanging echoing between the buildings. From the street we can't see where the bell is, what flat, if any, has been broken into, so the Inspector calls the nick to check the keyholder's register and see who can let us in. The answer comes that only one flat in this block has an alarm – it belongs to a wealthy owner of a civil engineering firm – so it's deduced that it must be his.

The keyholder is the caretaker of the flats: after a great deal of ringing he comes to the door and lets us in. As we go up in the lift the PC reports this to the station by radio – which rather impressively works though surrounded by sheet steel and brick – and at the top we find that the flat has infrared alarms that are constantly being set off by pigeons or falling leaves. We search the place, listen to the self-important and slightly drunk owner's account of his last burglary but one, and retire irritated. 'Let's get back and do some police work – we're not insurance agents,' growls the Inspector.

On the way back, the operator suddenly calls out, 'Left, and take the second right, then stop.' The driver does, and we wonder what the operator knows that we don't as he walks off into the darkness. We wait three minutes and he comes back. 'What were you after then?' asks the Inspector. 'I'm getting me dinner, aren't I?' he says biting into a pie from the cabbie's coffee-stall.

Past eleven, a PC calls on his personal radio for a little help to clear out a pub. It is just round the corner, so we stroll over and find one of those stupid pub crowds, balancing on the edge of the pavement and hoping that A will hit B. At the same time the area car arrives, the spare car and

a van with four PCs. I am indistinguishable from the rest of the
crowd, and a sergeant, as he walks behind, gives me a shrewd
prod between the shoulder-blades with his elbow – a silent
warning to a largish young male not to mess with the police.

We move on again. Ten minutes later the main radio
produces a call to a disturbance at a club in Queensway.
Almost as the operator finishes logging the message, the
driver pulls over for an area car coming up fast behind us
with its lamp flashing. Queensway isn't on their ground and
no one is quite sure where in the one-way system this club
stands, so to save time finding it we follow. When we come
near it's easy to pick out the right place by the mob outside –
we push our way in and go downstairs. The décor is rustic,
the benches made out of rough pieces of branch. In the
corner by the stairs a small CID man has a much larger man
backed into a corner and he is hissing at him 'Don't ever
speak to me like that again. You've got no sense, you've
got no manners, you've got nothing. Now get out and never,
never threaten me again.'

He – the detective – and his partner were eating their
supper when one large Irishman touched up another one's
girl. Without more ado the second man rose, picked up a
bench and hit the first in the face. The centre of the room
was now cleared of furniture. In the middle there was blood,
surprisingly in clotted heaps. One of the combatants had
been arrested; the other was leaning against the bar. He is
about six foot two, handsome and radiates hardness; his
face is blotchy white and mauve, and beneath the skin his
nose looks like chunks of broken paving.

A small constable comes up to him and grabs his hand
with the confidence of a nurse. He turns it over and spreads
a wound with his two thumbs. 'That looks like a stab –
you sure he didn't have a knife?' While he conducts this inquiry the policeman keeps opening his mouth in an odd
way and rolling his lower jaw about. An hour before, he was
escorting a drunk into the station when the drunk suddenly
turned round and athletically kicked him hard on the chin.

The club empties sooner than one expects, leaving its tired proprietress to pick up the broken china and wash the blood away. Witnesses are rounded up and go off with the assaulted man to Harrow Road Police Station; we go back to Paddington Green for a meal. By this time exhaustion is creeping on, I take a glazed look at a drug addict in the charge room – a patient of the eccentric doctor Petro who was soon afterwards struck off the register for carelessness over heroin. Petro used to hold his surgery in various odd places: one of them was the waiting-room of Paddington Railway Station. The Inspector is shocked: 'If the lad's got to be like this, then let him, but it annoys me to see the doctor making £2 a time out of his necessity. To me drugs say beatniks, lay-abouts, dirt, kids going to ruin. That's all I see of them – I freely admit my attitude is emotional.' After apologies for such a quiet evening, I go home. It is 2.30 a.m. and the 'night-turn's' working-day half done.

Another week, another beat: this time out of Gerald Road on Royal 'A' Division. My companion is a tall, intelligent young man, who spent several successful years as an apprentice instrument-maker, got fed up working at a bench and joined the police. His youthfulness is characteristic of PCs on the Inner London Divisions, where sixty per cent have less than five years' service. As they mature and marry, they move to the outer suburbs, where houses are cheaper. At Bushey, on the north-west extremity, for example, only one constable has spent less than ten years in the force.

He is in a sunny temper, pleased with the world owing to a very neat crime arrest he and his friend achieved a couple of weeks before. 'There's this square behind Knights-bridge Tube Station, packed with expensive cars, and natur-ally there's always one or two being stolen. But about a month ago there's a regular spate of it – a dozen going in a week – it's all extremely aggravating. My mate and I reckon we'll go and have a look after work. We're on days then; so every evening we get down there in my car and cruise round from ten o'clock onwards till about two. We do this for three nights and don't get a sausage – we stop lots of people but they're all relatively straight, and whatever they're up to isn't stealing cars.

'The fourth night we reckon will be the last and on that too nothing happens. It's getting quite late when we see these two lads getting into a Jaguar. We think, oh well, just another pair of playboys, but as soon as we go up to them and say "We are police officers," the one getting in slams the door and roars off, nearly running my mate over. I don't know how he jumped out of the way. The one who's left yells out: "Stan, you bastard," and then we claim him. In his pocket he's only got a little diary full of police call signs and a list of types of cars he's got to steal. He doesn't much want to talk, but there's a couple of addresses in the diary and so we get warrants and go round them inquiring for "Stan". Luckily someone knows him and he gets nicked.

'He doesn't want to help the police in their inquiries either, until it's explained that he can have attempted murder of a police officer for nearly running my mate over. Then he unburdens himself. He and his friend have been stealing cars at £30 a time, making themselves a couple of hundred pounds a week. What they'd do was to get a list of cars from the ringer, go out and get them, move them somewhere quiet, then telephone the number of the car key and where the car is parked. All the ringer has to do is buy a key, come along as innocent as pie, open the door and drive off to wherever he does his ringing.'

An arrest like that is a good start to a CID career. However, this afternoon's stint involves nothing criminal. On the way through the quiet squares of Belgravia, an odd lady with a scarlet parasol, a scarlet hat, an elaborate embroidered cloak and the short scarlet ankle socks that seem to be the uniform of the mentally ill-synchronised, asks my friend the way to Victoria. He explains in detail, bending courteously over her with one thumb tucked in his belt, and when he's finished, she says, 'God is very good to me. I send the Commissioner a Christmas card every year and he rains his blessings on me.'

She potters off ahead of us and evidently asks the next PC she meets the same question, for he too makes 'how to get to Victoria' gestures while she looks earnestly up at him. 'She'll ask every copper on the ground the same thing and then go home after a pleasant afternoon. I don't know what it is, this job seems to draw the nuts.' In Knightsbridge, though, we get a succession of pretty girls asking the way, and in a moment of exhilaration he takes a deep breath of the pale blue January air, looks around happily and says: 'Who could be bored with this marvellous street to walk up and down?'

Ninety-nine hundredths of the time patrolling beats is spent being a walking, visible symbol of law and order. The uniformed constable on the beat represents rather than executes effective policing. Very occasionally a patrolman meets crime in progress. This crime entry is abstracted from the CID night duty book at a station south of the river. The night-duty detective sergeant recounts the crime of the night for the information of his superiors; it is a purely internal document, and also illustrates the difference between the public and private voices of the police:

'The brothers K . . . , being music lovers, were desirous of collecting equipment to enable them to enjoy their hobby. Unfortunately they were without the wherewithal to enable them to do so. An ingenious plan crossed their minds; i.e. to screw a radio shop. With all the cunning of a couple of congenital morons, they climbed to the roof of a lock-up shop at 127 High Road, made their way through the asbestos roof, and commenced shopping. Unfortunately, another music lover, none other than PC 323 'O' Division, was also admiring the display, and got very jealous of the K . . . s who were at that moment removing the best items. So he nicked them.

Many items of property were recovered from the roof and are in the store. The elder K . . . is already on bail for a similar offence. The younger one maintains that he went along to persuade his brother that honesty is the best policy.'

More often the patrolling constable is involved in domestic accidents: fire, floods, suicides, births or, even in the trendy 1960s, runaway horses, as the following citation testifies:

Police Constable William WHYTE (Warrant Number 150135)
Joined the Metropolitan Police
force 15 May 1961.
(No previous decorations)
London Gazette
(No. 436689)
Awarded Queen's Commendation. dated 29.6.65.

'At about 12.55 on 18th January 1965, a scrap-metal dealer left a horse-drawn cart in Camden Road, N.W.1., while he was collecting scrap metal from a shop. He had chained one of the cart wheels and placed a nosebag on the horse before leaving it. For some reason unknown the horse, a six-year old gelding standing twelve hands, took fright and bolted, mounting the pavement and galloping towards "The Nag's Head". The dealer came out of the shop and tried to stop the horse by grabbing an ear and its mane, but after travelling some forty yards was forced to let go to avoid being pushed through a plate-glass window.

The animal, completely out of control, bolted along the north pavement towards the junction of St Pancras Way. The pavements were busy with shoppers and traffic was fairly heavy.

As the horse neared the junction the lights were changed to allow cross-traffic to flow, and Police Constable Whyte, who was seeing children across the road, ran across the junction between the traffic to try to intercept the horse and cart, but before he could do so the cart struck a stationary van. The horse then made a 'U' turn and, mounting the pavement at the corner, passed between two trees and returned to the roadway. It continued running back along

71

Camden Road and the officer, chasing after it, managed to jump on the cart. He then worked his way forward in an attempt to seize the reins, but they had apparently fallen off with the bridle when the horse first took flight. The constable then stepped on to the shafts, jumped on to the animal's back, and endeavoured to reach its muzzle, but as the cart collided with a cab he was thrown to the roadway, and had to roll over several times to avoid being hit by the cart which was skidding sideways because of the chained wheel. Regaining his feet, Police Constable Whyte continued his pursuit and again managed to jump on to the cart and then on to the horse's back.

By this time the horse was heading straight for the back of a stationary vehicle and the Police Constable, tugging violently on the horse's mane, managed to swerve the animal into a lane clear of traffic. Finally, at the junction with Royal College Street, the cart collided with a concrete bollard and finished up on an island. Again Police Constable Whyte was thrown off into the roadway, grazing his chin and injuring his left thigh.

Fortunately, the cart was so jammed that the horse was unable to continue its flight and members of the public assisted in quietening the animal. Police Constable Whyte gave instructions for securing the horse and remained at the scene until the arrival of other officers.

He was then taken by ambulance to University College Hospital, but was discharged after treatment and was placed on the sick list for two days.

Police Constable Whyte, who has been highly commended by the Commissioner, has been awarded £20 from the Bow Street Metropolitan Magistrates Court Reward Fund.'

Personal Equipment

How is a policeman equipped when he sets forth on the streets? He wears, naturally enough, his uniform with as many vests and jumpers under it as he thinks fit, heavy boots, a long heavy coat or mackintosh – though in the summer at the discretion of his Chief Superintendent, he may strip to shirt-sleeves. On his shoulder – sergeants and constables only – he wears his divisional letter and his number[1]. In the police force this is officially his name, and, curiously, policemen resent strange senior officers calling them by name rather than by number. They are numbered so that the aggrieved public can identify them; but experience shows that very few people who make complaints get either the letter or the number right.

He wears the helmet, odd-looking but practical headgear, since it makes its owner easy for his fellows or others to see in a crowd or down a street. He wears the chin-strap under his lower lip (a) by tradition, (b) so that the evilly-intentioned can't pull the helmet off the back of his head and garrotte him. In a special pocket down the right-hand seam of his trouser he carries his stick, a heavy piece of turned mahogany, and is careful, when he wears shirt-sleeves, to tuck the leather strap out of sight. He very seldom draws it and uses it still less often.

He has a whistle on a silver chain, which runs from the second button of his tunic to his left-hand breast pocket. He can, if he likes, buy himself a pair of handcuffs (Messrs. Hiatts of Birmingham, one of many manufacturers, make the Regulation pattern: 27/-, or the Peerless with nickel-plated finish: 84/-). Few policemen do, since the courts give heavy damages against those who use handcuffs unnecessarily; and as one man said: 'If chummy's not desperate to get away you don't need to handcuff him to you; if he is, he's got to kill you. I wouldn't touch the things.'

The policemen who guard palaces, and in times of stress embassies and the homes of Cabinet Ministers, are armed with 9 mm Walthers. One I met guarding the Bolivian Embassy just after the death of Che Guevara was loaded

---

[1] Divisional letters run from 'A' to 'Z', omitting 'I' and 'O'. Policemen attached to Scotland Yard wear 'CO', and members of Traffic Department 'TD'.

with a big radio set, a pistol, and because of the frosty night was wearing thick woollen gloves, so that he could neither run nor shoot. One feels that guns are provided more as a reciprocal gesture than as a serious deterrent to the bomb-thrower.

More to the point, the uniformed policeman is armed with a formidable quantity of paper. In his various capacious pockets he stows: an A-Z map of London – for his own navigation and the benefit of his frequent questioners; if he is young he probably also carries a book of twenty-seven specimen reports which tell him how to record such events as: cab-bilking, escapes of gas, ejection of a rowdy councillor from a council meeting, a fire, a sudden death and a dog-bite.

He has a leather wallet embossed with 'MP', a crown, his divisional letter and number. In this he keeps a yellow Accident Report Book, *Death or Personal Injury,* in which he can quickly record the details of road accidents, another white one for *Damage Only* accidents, a *Process Report* book for summonsable offences – incorrect parking, driving carlessly – a pocket book with the Judges' Rules on the inside cover and four inches of ruler on the back cover in which he writes all his other reports. All these are numbered and logged at the station so that he cannot be suspected of forging reports to fit his case.

He has a book of slips to give people, to remind them to produce their driving-licences within five days at their nearest police station, and a little pad of plain memos. He is issued with a *Pocket Directory and Duty Hints* which tells him *inter alia* about animal clinics; birth, marriages and deaths; choking; Consulates, Foreign; the Holger Nielsen method of Artificial Respiration; Homeless persons; Hydraulic Power Companies; National Assistance Officers; RAF vehicles, removal of, broken down; Refuges for Destitute persons; Silvester Method of Artificial Respiration; Turnocks; and Wards casual. It details his literally one hundred and one powers of arrest without a warrant – and the fervent hope that he won't invent a hundred and second one breathes from the page. He may also provide himself with *Hopker's Summons*

Headings (364 of them), Police Review Publishing Co., 1960 and *Calvert's Powers of Arrest,* Butterworth, London, 1962.

A Police Station

This station is a big, gaunt, brick block, soon to be pulled down, that now stands alone in a wilderness of cleared buildings and a growing motorway. The silhouette is distinguished by its air-raid siren on a wooden pylon and a long whip aerial for the personal radios. In the yard there are the usual parked police cars. Civilian cars that have been stolen or in accidents and are being kept as evidence stand in a pound nearby. At the far end there is usually one car behind a 'DO NOT TOUCH AWAITS FINGERPRINT EXAMIN-ATION' notice. Up the side of the yard runs a block of latter-day stables – they used to be CID offices.

There are two doors in front; the conspicuous one leads to the front office, the counter, and the charge room. The other leads to the main staircase, offices, the canteen. It was built, as were many Metropolitan nicks, in the 1880s. The décor is strictly functional, based on glossy pastel paint and polished brass, the windows are small, the offices inconvenient, yet the buildings of this stamp – often distinguished by grotesquely large chimneys – have a pleasant, brute amiability about them. There is lavish steam central-heating and since few windows will open, it is always warm.

Indoors, in the used parts, there is an air of chipped paint; documents are kept in old wooden cupboards, report books are piled on mantelpieces and counters. To the left, as you enter by the main door, there is a door for the public to get to their side of the counter. If you go straight ahead, through the door marked 'private', you're in the charge room – a bleak apartment furnished with a bench for prisoners to sit on, a wooden table on which to turn out their possessions, a tall school-masterly desk where the Station Officer can rest the crime book while he is taking charges, a number of coats, scarves and hats, and several conical yellow 'No Waiting' notices.

Opening out of the left hand wall there is a passage which leads, via the open air, to the canteen, and the door to the detention-room (see p. 232) on which someone has pasted a cartoon from the *Evening Standard*. It shows two convicts eating a hearty Xmas dinner and is captioned: 'Celebrating with conviction.' On the inside of the door someone else has written 'No exit via this door. Please leave by alternative exit.' The detention-room contains a rickety chair, a tatty mattress and a barred window.

Further along a locked door leads into the cell corridor. Half a dozen cells lead off it. They are constructed on old-fashioned lines. A wooden bench runs along one wall, with a lavatory let into the last three feet, a brass handle by the door for flushing the lavatory, a bell-push, which can be switched off outside. Being winter, the cells are cold. There is also a blanket.

On the far wall of the charge room there is a blackboard divided by white lines so that the gaoler can scribble up the names, cell numbers and crimes of his prisoners. Lastly, there is a door onto the yard so that prisoners can be brought in from vehicles.

Off the passage from the charge room there is a squalid den where Reserve sits and looks after the personal radio transceiver. Here also is the station's teleprinter linking it with CO: as it chatters out its messages, Reserve nimbly tears off the pieces of paper and sticks them in a loose-leaf message book along with written-down telephone calls. A lot, if not all, of human life is there:

'An inquiry to be made *re* relatives of a lady, Mrs Edith Hannah J ... found dead at 15 Northumberland Avenue'. An employer has rung up about a girl who lives on the ground floor. From a telephone conversation he has had with her he thinks that she may have taken an overdose of drugs. 'A 1963 Ford green Cortina, registration unknown, offside damaged, cardboard in offside window, contains three wanted men, DI Jones C9.' A message to D2 surveyors' department: 'Drain in station yard blocked; the spring and hinge on reserve room door broken.' Indeed it is; the door leans open, leering. 'Boy 11, slim build, fair, spotty face, white denim battle dress, trousers, yellow nylon socks, found at QR. Gives no name.' A Relief needed for WPC who took a girl home from the ice-rink in Queensway who had broken her ankle. 'Persons found: James HARVEY, collapsed and in St Mary's, no known relatives or friends.' 'Seventeen-year-old girl, light brown hair, big curved mouth, pierced ears, common London accent, violent temper, wearing red mini-skirt, believed two months pregnant, and her son, one year old, peaked cap, teddy bear, left home after quarrel with mother. Child possibly in need care and attention.'

On Friday nights and Saturday mornings there are dozens of missing girl messages, as they set off for week-ends with their boy-friends without telling Mum.

Pushing past Reserve, who is often propped on one elbow reading a cowboy story, you come to an elderly lady who runs the switchboard, knitting away in a cloud of cigarette smoke. She has a little trapdoor to the Station Office, through which she passes the frequent cups of tea that lubricate all police work. There the Station Officer, a policeman with the appropriate rank of Station Sergeant, is busy briefing a recruit on his responsibilities towards five parking tickets. Each one is numbered, logged out in a book kept for the purpose, and wrapped in a polythene bag. 'Here you are son. Don't go mad with them.' The recruit departs with his mentor for the day, a more experienced PC, and the Station Officer begins painstakingly copying officers' notebooks into the Occurrence Book – the station's official diary – writing with great neatness and care.

The top one relates in 500 words how Mrs Evelyn FORBES (43) struck Mrs Delilah GALASHIELDS (38) on the head with an iron, and what the witness Mr John THOMAS (62) saith of it; all written out by the PC who was called to the disturbance, in pencil, being careful to fill up each line, put all names in capitals, and to cross out and rewrite all mistakes. The copying looks and is anachronistic: it will soon be replaced by photocopying or central dictating-machines and audiotypists, but it at least assures the Station Sergeant that the men for whom he is responsible are making their reports literately, legibly and in the prescribed form. If they do not, he is to blame.[1]

By his side the duty state board shows the complexities of modern policing. Of forty-two PCs on 'early-turn' – the morning shift:

2 are lent to Marylebone Lane, to watch the Chinese Legation.
1 is sick
4 are on leave
3 are drivers
1 is on maintenance
1 is Reserve
3 are writing reports on accidents
2 are attached to the Divisional Vice Squad at Harrow Road
1 is on vehicle moving with Traffic Division
2 are at Court
1 probationer is at refresher classes
1 probationer is learning beats
1 probationer is learning courts

Leaving:
19 on beats, or 1/6th of the station's complement of PCs.

Of 2 Inspectors and 6 Sergeants:
1 Sergeant is 'strapping' on the Lambeth prison-van service
1 Sergeant is on a promotion course
1 Inspector ⎫
1 Sergeant ⎬ are on weekly leave
1 Sergeant is with the Divisional Vice Squad

Leaving:
1 Inspector as Duty Officer
1 Sergeant as Station Officer
1 Section Sergeant.

---

[1] Since this was written, the reporting of minor incidents like this has been revised, and would now only merit a couple of lines in the officer's pocket book.

78

A red-faced boy with a pleasant expression and curly hair is revealed hanging nervously against the door jamb. He leans over the counter and asks for Detective Sergeant Shmiff, who eventually comes down and looks blankly at him across the counter. 'You remember me, guv? – you know, the X Hotel motor car job?' The Detective Sergeant reacts slowly, then says heartily, 'Yes – Henry that's it, isn't it, I nicked you, didn't I, lad?' The boy allows this is so and looks conspiratorially round the room. Then the DS takes him off upstairs where doubtless he has some news that might be worth the price of a drink.

His departure leaves room for a Cockney family complete: a stocky and aggressive father, a large flowery mum with an elaborate coiffure, and their small button-eyed son wearing a peak hat and with his thumb in his mouth. The PC perceives they have a lot on their mind and takes them up to the end of the counter. They stand under the *IN MEM-ORIAM* board with its list of names of dead policemen and 'At the going down of the sun and in the morning we shall remember them.' The three lean on the great heap of crime books and confer. It concerns this neighbour of theirs, the 'old feller', an aspirant taxi-driver like the man here, who failed his 'knowledge' (of London's geography[1]) when our friend got his, so that began the bad blood; now wife can't meet wife on the stairs of the buildings without calling of names, and there's bullying among the children. Husband: 'It's the wife really – but if I go down and see them, I'm bound to end up hurting him.' She puts in, 'She goes for days without saying a thing, then it all seems, you know, to get too much for her and she really screams at me and says the most awful things.' They unburden themselves with urgency and passion to this young constable, who could well be their son. 'I know what it's like, I live in flats myself,' he says.

After a long discussion, he decides that there might well be insulting behaviour or a potential breach of the peace in it, and he'll get a late-turn beat-man to go round and see

[1] See p. 125

79

the woman. The wife: 'He'll have to do something – we live in a show flat. The GLC send visitors from Russia and all over to see it, but we'll have to move. They think we're mad.' And so it goes on.

Area Cars

The man on the beat was designed for a static immobile population without telephones: he put the police force on the ratepayer's doorstep. But during the development of London and the Metropolitan Police it became apparent that he alone wasn't enough, and cars with radios were added as a quick reaction system. The point of the car is to get policemen quickly to where something has just happened. While they're cruising around waiting for action, they also bring under surveillance a great many miles of road – the Metropolitan fleet covers some fifty million miles a year[1], but although they stop suspicious cars and walkers, they are ineffective against the thief hiding in a garden waiting to break in, or the man at work on an office safe who might be seen through a chink by a policeman on foot. On the other hand, car crew work has the advantage of being much more interesting and of not wearing men out so fast by exposing them to the elements (often seen in Old Police Orders: PC SNOGG, retired, *worn out*).

The area cars are big black saloons – usually automatic Rover 2000s, 3 litres or 3.5s, or Jaguar Mark 8s, or Triumph 2000s, with hardly any of the old Wolseleys left that were *the* police car for a generation of post-war filmgoers. The normal crew is two: a driver, who does nothing else but drive police cars, a uniform radio operator and also, if necessary, an observer who wears plain clothes appropriate to the area so that he can be put out to keep an eye on shady characters. The car is fitted with an eight-channel radio set, and

[1] Since there are 8,600 miles of road in London, this implies that a police vehicle passes an average spot 5,800 times a year or 16 times a day.

the crew probably take with them a couple of personal radios which work as well in a car as outside – one to keep them in touch with events on the ground, and the other for the observer to wear under his jacket to keep in touch with them if he gets out of the car.

The crew by itself can operate as a tactical unit. The operator sits in the front nearside seat with the radio, the observer sits in the back nearside so he can hit the pavement quickly – if it's a Jaguar with little leg-room, he lies along the back seat. There are usually one or two truncheons rolling about on the floor, a radio log-book in a plywood holder and the car's diary on the back window-ledge in which the observer keeps some sort of account of their doings. At the back of the log-book there is a record of 'persons apprehended', and each crew vies with the previous one to take more in their thirteen-week tour. The visitor's seat is the offside rear, and there I spent many interesting hours, for the boredom, intimacy and occasional spasms of urgent action of area car work are very conducive to friendship.

The area car's brief is to be first at scenes of crime – in case any arrestable bodies are hanging about – to check ringing burglar-alarms, to deal with fire, flood and minor social unrest. Less urgent jobs are tackled by the appropriate station, and traffic accidents by another organisation. But most of the time we were a quick-reaction public relations force. By the time we arrived the action was all over: the arrival of the big black car with the flashing blue light showed the victim of a housebreaking or the people standing round the beaten up man on the pavement that, somewhere, *someone* cared.

This afternoon, just at the beginning of spring, I am riding with the late-turn crew of Alpha One. The crew is lively and argumentative. All the way from the far end of Kensington High Street to Knightsbridge we have an urgent debate on capital punishment – all four of us displaying different and irreconcilable views. The driver is a bearded liberal – his father is a publisher and his brother a professor somewhere. 'Careerwise I'm the black sheep of the family.' We take a turn through the Park, and already the lovers are settling down in their cars beside Rotten Row. He looks idly at them as we whisper past. Love in cars has a loaded connotation to the Metropolitan Police after a *cause célèbre* a few years ago. 'I'd never touch a sex case,' observes the driver. 'I could come up here or St. James's Park any night of the week and get half-a-dozen, but these are the only courting grounds for miles. It'd be a shame to spoil them – you never know when you might need them yourself.'

Eight hours spent riding an area car is an amusing way to spend a working day. Several things contribute to it. There is the incessant police broadcast. Channel One – which we're on this afternoon – is full of life. Over it one is kept in touch with what's happening, the breakings, the disturbances, and even the occasional prize offer of a stolen high-value load, which means a very nice ten per cent for a non-policeman to spot.

I scribble all these numbers down and keep my nose pressed against the window. There is the occasional chase that clears the air for commentary: over the operator's microphone come the screaming tyres, the clangour of his car's horn off the flying buildings. Since everyone hears what everyone else says, the air too is an informal, real-time seminar on crime. To go out in a police car that has no radio is like going to a party in ear-plugs – missing the help, friendliness and chat one knows is flowing all round; even if it's seldom of any concrete use it's painfully missed.

The controller's voice is hypnotic: he reads out the assignments with a calm rhythmical cadence, taking what seems at first absurdly long over each word and between words, but in fact, as he knows very well, it is better for the operator to get the message down right first time. The controller knows too that if he sets the car going in the right direction, he has at least a couple of minutes to fill in the details, so he puts the essentials first. 'Delta One, Delta One' on a rising and falling cadence. Then a pause, and he starts again as if it were a completely new message. 'At number one hundred and forty three, Oxford Street, West One – a disturbance. The informant: a Mrs . . . . at number wun fower niner, ring the second bell up. Message timed at wun seven fiyiv two.'

A great advantage to cruising round London with nothing to do but look out of the windows is the amazing prevalence of pretty, and often beautiful girls. Their long legs swim past the window like animated statues like the figures of an opium dream – occasionally a particularly fine sct will stop conversation in the car as dead as if it had been switched off. It is noticeable too, how many girls like the police – often a pretty driver gives us a smile, and it's lucky she can't hear the comments that are coming out of the dignified but amiable smiles back. 'The only thing wrong with this force, mate,' confided one driver, 'is that it's randy and it doesn't get enough.'

But more worrying, mixed in among the pretty legs, are the perpetrators of London's annual quarter of a million indictable crimes. Non-policemen see the black cars with the blue lights and the impassive faces cruising shinily about, and we think: 'They *know*'. From inside the car you think: 'Out there on the pavement are three quarters of the villains. *They* know'.

The patrolling policeman's problem is to distinguish the evildoer from the probably honest citizen. Naturally the first does his best to resemble the second, and the policeman, unless he is fortunate enough to catch a villain in the act, has to base his judgement on tiny indications, like a doctor diagnosing a subtle disease. Almost by definition, he identifies a criminal by illegal or anti-social acts, and he hopes that a man who offends in big things does so in small ones. So the policeman in a car looks for the small actions that show disregard for society: driving too fast, braking too hard, cornering too noisily, jumping the amber light, racing pedestrians on a zebra. These may all be the outward and visible signs of an inward and hidden criminal disposition. So too could be a surly manner, rudeness, unhelpfulness.

We swish along quietly, working back towards our proper ground, keeping a weather eye out for trouble. Stopped at traffic lights, we watch a big lorry going the other way through the red light. 'We could go after him and caution him, or stick him on even, but it wouldn't be worth it. Like as not he'd complain against us – say I was rude or something, and it's just not worth it for something minor. It ties you down writing stupid reports when you should be out doing proper police work. I've known motorists done for speed complain that the traffic bloke's fingernails were dirty – *and* get the charge dropped.'

It's Thursday – late shopping in Oxford Street, and the usual weekly 'shout' arises relating a robbery of a shop's take on its way to the bank. The robbers have escaped: the first witness says they drove a beige Austin 1100, ZXT 262 T. We turn on the light and gong and go. We have two and a half minutes left in which to catch them – twenty seconds later the radio comes up with the car's proper description: a *grey* 1100, number XZK 262 T, stolen yesterday in the docks. 'Did they come from the docks? They'd perhaps drive north-west' – useless speculations as the driver hurls us through the one-way systems and we nearly break our necks trying to scan each side-street as we shoot past.

A description comes up: 'One man is twenty-two to twenty-four, short blue mac, five foot eight,' which must suit about 26,000 men in the West End at this moment. Charlie One comes up with an inquiry: 'Re the robbery ...' they don't have to say that, for north of the river everyone is thinking of nothing else, sitting in dark cars, fifty or sixty crews hoping *they* will be the ones to see the 1100. After five minutes and no news we begin to relax; at R plus eight minutes Charlie One comes up again: they've found the car neatly parked in a tiny street opposite a building site.

We go round – there is Charlie Two – a brand new Jaguar with polythene covers still on the seats: the getaway car

84

is properly parked, a steering-wheel glove on the wheel, and the blue mac neatly draped over the front seat. Everyone has their hands in their pockets so they won't touch it and have a run in with the District Fingerprint officer. As we drive away someone says: 'Who says crime isn't worth it? Look at us. We'll take home £15 this week and that team will split £400 for a tenth of the work.'

The radio now starts handing out alarm calls – shops and houses in the West End with burglar alarms ringing. Delta One, Marylebone Lane's car is, they say, nothing more than an automatic alarm car – it gets a hundred or so a week and one of those might be caused by an actual burglar. The rest are wind, falling leaves, pigeons getting in amongst the infra-red beams. We deal with a couple and then get a house-breaking up at the north end of the sub-division.

The victim is a neat little spinster who got home at five-thirty to find the curtains blowing into her room and all her things spread about. Outside the window there's a flat terrace and a gentle range of roofs leading away. She waited until nine before she reported it, 'because they must be watching every move we make.' The landlady, a formidable Pole, confirms this. She has for some days had a funny feeling every time she went out. We look round the room, and the spinster shyly produces her savings – fifty-three pounds in notes in a jam-jar under her bed. 'Honest to God,' says one of the policemen, 'what can you do to help these people? There are banks to put money in and telephones to call us, but they won't use either.'

The relief ends pleasantly with yet another break-in, this time in the flat of five spinsters – all young, two pretty and all pleased because their over-insured costume jewellery has been stolen. We are asked to stay for coffee by the fire: the light and the room after the dark and rather smelly car are delightful. The crew are off duty in ten minutes so there is a suggestion that they get some bottles and come back for a party. Perhaps they did.

But 'Night's the time; it's so simple. Either chummy put

85

his hand through the window or he didn't.' After a while I began to see the police like a huge cat sprawled over London, that dozes during the day, cleaning itself, writing reports, going to court – a process one might compare to digestion – and only at night waking up to go out hunting. Most policemen I met much preferred night duty, even though it separated them from their families, it took a long time to get used to sleeping in the daytime, and if they arrested someone during the night who wouldn't plead guilty, they had to get up at nine to give evidence.

It's five to eleven, a warmish evening, in the station yard at Brixton. Three crews are standing about chatting, drivers stooping to take tyre pressures, observers rummaging in the boots to check the gear they ought to have – a flying spot of light round the dark walls as someone tests his seek-and-search lamp. The radios buzz and mutter out of the open doors of the cars. Our operator is still in the nick getting together his log-book: a cheerful clatter of tea cups comes out of the canteen overhead.

Our first 'shout' comes before our operator. We pile in and roar up Brixton Hill to a pub disturbance: twenty people are standing on the pavement round a lady with teeth like small black pebbles in a richly painted face behind a Niagara of tinted hair. She's leaning on a man's shoulder shouting that she will "break the focking cont's teeth down the focker's focking throat!" We stand about looking massive and implacable until the audience and finally the principals drift off.

'Like a drink, gents?' asks the shirt-sleeved bartender confidentially. The policemen can't say yes, possibly because of me[1], and anyway the breathalyser is a great deterrent to them, so we regretfully refuse. The operator comes over plaintively on the personal radio and we promise to pick him up. Brixton is said to be the busiest ground in the Met, but tonight it is dead quiet. 'We have the highest oil-fire fatality rate of any London Borough,' someone says as we

[1] See Introduction, p. 12

pass a coloured man carrying a can of paraffin – 'nothing you can do about it, but the results are messy.'

We get a shout to a chemist's where a large scruffy man with long yellow hair over his dandruffed collar is debating with a young pharmacist. He wears a short white coat: under the glaring fluorescent light his face is green with exhaustion. He excitedly waves a prescription for amphetamine tablets – purple hearts. He's certain the doctor's signature is forged, but he can't ring him to check. The scruffy man says, 'Sure, he doesn't know a thing about it; he was asked by a feller in a pub to collect the tablets. Yes, he'd be pleased to point him out to the gentlemen.'

On the way to the pub the crew guess who it's going to be, and when we peer through the leaded windows and our new friend points, right enough, it's the man. They push in through the swing doors, caps on the back of their heads, burly and hard; the observer who, north of the river, would wear a white collar, club tie and tweed jacket, here has a knitted cotton shirt under a lumber-jacket. The man we want is a curly-haired Irishman, rather drunk, who insists on finishing his porter before we go. He probably won't get another drink for a long time, so we let him suck it up; chatting the day's Cup Semi-Finals with a tableful of equally large men.

Back at the nick the two are sat in the charge room well apart so they can't pass things to and fro as first one is searched and then the other. Here the charge room is, by an architect's oversight, a vestibule off a corridor, so people keep coming and going. When the Irishman is searched he has 7d and a steel comb, and keeps bursting into song.

The informant is sat down in the interview room among a crowd of coppers. 'Stand up for height' – he gets up and three people make a guess, someone takes an average; they get his name and age and ring CRO. The driver, a cunning, hungry copper comes back three minutes later: 'I asked if you had any tattoos and you said no, you naughty man. Roll up your sleeve. They're fading? Crossed hands and

87

Love Mother?' Shouts of laughter then quietly: 'You are
nicked, my love, well nicked.'

The driver reads from a piece of paper: 'You are identical
John Stuart Mill Gazette 777777 '68, wanted for fraud on
National Assistance at Torquay.' Not a whit perturbed, the old
man goes on: 'Sure, I didn't know the script was forged. 'Twas
just a feller in a pub asked me would I step down the road.'

A thin-faced, cross duty detective is called down to deal
with the charges. We go into a store-room to explain the
offences. 'It's all rubbish really,' says the driver and the DC
couldn't agree more. There are some odd objects lying
against the wall – I ask their use. 'That's the work of some
git at CO with nothing better to do. Riot shields, he says
to himself, are just what the lads need in rowdy Brixton, so
he sends us these. One of the boys was fool enough to take
one to deal with a demented Jamaican with a knife – he
grabbed it and gave him a right clouting.' Indeed the edge
of one of these prehistoric objects has a dark brown stain.

Then we get a shout to go to a motherly person standing
in a phone-box nearby. She was walking home, thought she
saw a man lurking up an alley and retreated. We cram her
in the back, drive her home with a 'Sleep well, love', scout
round with torches through the jungly front gardens, but
find no one. A cruise round again, and we spot a gaggle of
youths sitting on a wall down a side-street – not illegal, but perhaps not innocent nearly at midnight. We go round the block
and park opposite them until they break up and go their ways.

Straight away a shout: 'Woman needs police'. We think
of stranglers and rape and rippings; at this hour there's
nothing about, and with the blue light and gong going we
hit eighty mph down the Brixton back-streets. But the
driver's so good it feels like riding a piston down a cylinder
bore. We're Lima Three – Lima Two comes up to say they're
on their way – and just then we see the flicker of their blue
light going down a parallel street. It becomes a sort of race,
which we win because the others get a one-way street
wrong and have to go round the block. The woman who

needs us is a quaking old dear in an immaculate, cheerless basement flat, whose senile husband has fallen out of bed *again*. If he lies on the floor all night he'll get pneumonia and die and perhaps half her agitation is because it would be such a good thing if he did.

So the seven of us troop down, lift the scrawny old thing up and dump him in the middle of the bed. He lies there in a ring of dark blue with his knee up. We can't tuck him in, so someone says: 'Put them down, Pop, or you'll get a smack-bottom' – not sarcastically or to raise a laugh, but because the old man has gone back to babyhood and his very first practical jokes. He puts them down, turns over and goes off to sleep amongst us. She says: 'It's a good thing I didn't take my sleeping-pills – I usually do Mondays. He'd have been there all night.' 'Well, Mum, if he falls out again, you just call us up. That's what we're here for.'

This is Saturday night: for an hour after the pubs close it's quietish, then the air is alive with the fights and injuries and accidents that don't surface until midnight. This delayed reaction – directly related to the speed at which alcohol seeps from the stomach to the blood-streams and to the brains of the anonymous hundreds of thousands in the dark round us – is manifest in a flood of calls. By 2 a.m. the excitement dies away. For long periods the radio is not just quiet but silent.

Our operator taps it disconsolately, adjures it: 'Speak to me, speak to me, even if it's only rubbish.' They gossip about their colleagues: 'So John tells the skipper, "I'm not spending eight hours in a car with Fred's feet. I'd rather go back to walking," and for John that's really something.' 'Some years ago,' says the driver, pointing out a corner house, 'I got a call to there – "Man needs police" – that's all it said. So I get dropped off and knock on the door. A lovely bird comes out, a real cracker, but she's all sad and in tears and drooping. Then this bloke totters out, haggard, he's got four days growth of beard, his eyes are all red; he's in a shocking state. His hands and knees can't stop trembling. It's now

Monday – he met her Thursday night at the Palais and she won't let him go. He says, "Please, please could you stay around while I get some things on?" ' We don't believe that one either. The traditional spice of area car work used to be the chase, but London is now so crowded with cars that tearing about after villains in the old style is officially discouraged.

The last happening of the evening, after twenty minutes complete silence, is a garishly painted mini-van lurching round a corner in front of us, patently going too fast. We turn everything on, daring him to play, but he doesn't and we pull him. Five thin crew-cut boys crawl out and try to melt away into the night – they have to be herded back like sheep. The driver, barely out of his adolescence, is being difficult. He claims to be twenty-seven years old and to have just come out of prison after doing three years.

Our driver strolls over with his thumb in his belt: 'You were stupid to get caught. I can't say I'm impressed. And you're stupid now. You think you've told us, but you've just forced yourself on my memory. Whenever I see this old banger of yours I'll remember that you're a stroppy little lad, and I shall watch you with care. So you haven't done yourself any good, and if you're over twenty I'm Jack Solomons.'

He's the one who told the silliest jokes; now he becomes studious and makes the boy read the Section on *Road Craft* at the beginning of the AA book: we stand about like children at school waiting for someone to construe. Meanwhile the observer's been put in like a ferret to search the back of the van. The best he can do is a speedometer which one of the boys admits came off a derelict car. It's thrown back: 'We used to do them for larceny from persons unknown, but now the courts reckon a derelict car has no owner so you can't steal from him.'

That was our chase for us. An untypically busy evening: many merge into one soothing dark continuum.

CHAPTER FOUR

Public Order

The Metropolitan Police exists, historically, to control the London mob. It was created because the military had shown itself in several incidents unable to do the job. Crowd control is therefore the oldest police skill, and to the outsider perhaps the most esoteric. There are three kinds of crowds and they present two complementary problems to the police. In the first case the crowd's aims are perfectly lawful, it is expected to behave well, and the police problem is simply to shepherd it, to prevent it – like a delicate animal in a concrete maze – from hurting itself.

Remembrance Sunday presents an annual job of this sort. About two-thirds of the way along Whitehall, the Cenotaph stands in the middle of the road, commemorating the dead of two world wars. On the Sunday in question several ceremonies take place there besides the official 11 a.m. wreath-laying. Afterwards, people who have been held back on the pavement by a cordon of police want to look at the tributes. If the police just let the crowd through, it would converge on the Cenotaph and soon the people in the middle, round the monument, who had seen their fill and wanted to go away, would be trapped by the others pressing in all round them. An impasse would develop.

To prevent this, a second cordon is formed inside the first, making a funnel that opens towards the monument. People are allowed to move along Whitehall until they come to breaks in the first cordon about fifty yards west of the Cenotaph, then they go to the middle of the road and merge in a stream going towards the monument. A barrier erected a few minutes after the ceremony protects the wreaths and, as a finishing-touch, a mounted policeman is posted in front of it: his height warns the crowd that there is an obstacle ahead, so they separate round him.

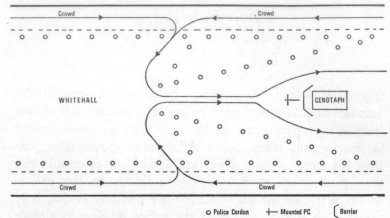

O Police Cordon   +— Mounted PC   [Barrier

Crowd Control at the Cenotaph on Remembrance Sunday

It is also necessary to close side-streets to prevent traffic moving into Whitehall, and also to close off streets to let the military processions get to the Cenotaph and back uninterrupted. After everything is over, streets are opened up again in reverse order to make sure that traffic can get out at the far end before it is let in at the near one. Experience teaches important little precautions: a man has to be posted to prevent people falling down the steep little steps at the end of Richmond Row: probably he has been there on every public occasion since the Metropolitan Police was formed.

In the files and the collective memory of the Metropolitan Police, there are schemes for controlling crowds on every imaginable public occasion. The operation orders and subsequent reports for every Coronation and every Royal Lying In State are preserved, to be built on and modified to fit the new but eternally similar circumstances of the future. Churchill's funeral was ten years' planning, and it probably contained, percolated through a succession of intermediate heroes, elements of Nelson's. The appearances of life change: the slogans and the banners alter: to the police one crowd is very like another.

Flower Power and the Fuzz

The Inspector in charge of Hyde Park has descended from his family residence over the nick – desirable situation, country air, five minutes from Oxford Street, – and is briefing the dozen and a half PCs drafted in for the afternoon to help cope with the second annual Legalise Pot Rally. They stand in a semi-circle in a room behind the canteen. The Inspector, a small man with a pudgy, experienced white face, says: 'The main thing we've got to look out for this afternoon is obscene language. I expect you'll know about this recent case at Brighton? No? well, I'll tell you. There was a hippy gathering on the front, and some fellow got up and read a poem of Allen Ginsberg's which included the line – here he looks over his shoulder at the small and innocent WPC standing behind him – 'Do you object to strong language?' 'If I'm going to hear it this afternoon, I might as well hear it now.' But the Station Sergeant led her away.

'As I was saying, he got up and read this poem which contained the line: "Go fuck yourself with an atom bomb." Naturally he was done by the local police, but the magistrate dismissed the case. The police appealed, but the High Court said that it was a good old-fashioned word, we all used it and knew what it meant, and dismissed the appeal. Well, that doesn't touch us. The Hyde Park Regulations prohibit the use of obscene language in a public speech and that's good enough for us. No one has to be insulted or shocked or offended. You take his name and address and report him for *process*. There *is* a power of arrest, but go easy because the courts have been criticising us for using it too much.'

'Now about hippies. They'll be reading poetry, and in case you haven't heard hippy poetry, it's like this:

The Moss
Me!
The Sky
Sticks sticks ugh ugh ugh!

93

'You'll find the average hippy is a nice enough bloke. He'll give you daffodils to show he loves you – or whatever flower's in season – but don't let that bother you. If they get stroppy, jumping over benches and annoying people, and you have to deal with them, *you have to tell each one individually,* because they don't believe in leaders or organisation. But you're not likely to get bother. In case there's any "fucks" flying about, me or the Station Sergeant will be at the bottom of the platform ready to deal.'

The meeting dissolves, the PCs nip back for a last cup of tea and then we set out across the grass to the meeting. The Inspector: 'We're in a slightly odd position here: we police the park, as you see, for the Ministry of Works – there's an agreed establishment and they pay for the job. But they expect us to pay as much attention to a radio playing as someone getting his head bashed in. They say, "Yes, but couldn't you have gone to the head-bashing *via* the radio and dealt with that as well?" They don't see it from the point of view of my lads – when there's a job of work to be done they don't want to mess about with radios.

'Our forward-looking Minister authorised a pop concert here the other night. It was supposed to come off on the bandstand – which isn't really suitable – so it was moved to the Cockpit[1]. It was an hour late starting, but the audience was as good as gold, and what amazed me was that the performers could actually play their instruments. Tyrannosaurus Rex and the Pink Floyd they were called. When it was over they picked up all the rubbish and left the place immaculate. But you can't get it into the hippies' heads that one concert in one spot once a year doesn't entitle them to play radios all over the place all the time, or musical instruments.'

We arrive at the meeting: a circle of a couple of thousand

[1] The Cockpit is the semi-circular depression, shaped rather like a Greek theatre, on the north side of the Serpentine. The police use names for several places in the Park which date from its occupation in 1666 by refugees from the Great Fire.

people with a step-ladder in the middle and a cloth banner that says 'Legalise Pot'. The Ministry have not permitted amplifiers, so the speaker is quite inaudible and any obscenities that he is giving out are wasted entirely. The usual hippy crowd: beads and shawls and the usual aimless wandering to and fro with sullen uncommunicative faces. The police stand about very tall in their helmets: every few minutes people come up to ask them how many people are there, or to complain about the hippies.

One such is a hawk-faced sunburnt young man, about twenty-six, with a pretty girl on his arm.

'Believe me, sir, we don't like it any more than you do. But it's been ruled that as policemen we can't be shocked or disgusted. We can't do anything about it without complaints. What did you actually hear – any obscenities?'

'Well, no, I just object to the tone of the whole thing. "Legalise Pot" indeed.'

'Very well, sir, I'll take your name and address.'

Another young, cheerful-looking copper stands with his arms crossed on his chest and his helmet pulled down over his nose: many of the helmets are still stained with flour from the Grosvenor Square demonstration. They keep old ones for riots: 'The boredom gets on top of you if you don't keep your eyes open.' A small but delicious hippy lady in big blue glasses smiles sweetly at him as she brushes past. 'See?'

On the ordinary meeting-ground business is as usual, three policemen wander to and fro, two each are stationed at the Communist and the Black Power stalls – at the latter because the speaker keeps three or four henchmen who are apt to deal drastically with hecklers unless restrained. 'When you feel it's time for tea, just get your notebook out and pretend to write down what he's saying. For some reason he don't like that,' the Inspector had told them.

The rest of the meeting-ground is a bedlam of slightly cracked speakers and their hecklers, salted with American tourists. There's a strong smell of the herbal cigarettes which the hippies use, hoping the police will arrest them for mari-

95

juana. But the police know the dodge and pay no attention. The police walk up and down, and boredom begins to settle round their boots. In the hippy circle an inept Balinese dancer is waving his hand about: he has a train made of inflated balloons carried on sticks and weaves through the crowd, dipping and swaying as he treads on people's feet.

Outside the ring, the Station Sergeant can just see this: 'I suppose that's a "Performance or Representation" contrary to the Park Regulations, and I suppose you could make out that the tambourines are "instruments", but if I go in there and ask for his address, he'll give me a wrong one, and I'll have to borrow him and we'll have a scuffle, half a dozen hippies down the nick and everyone aggravated. I don't suppose anyone will complain to the Ministry about it, so I won't bother.'

Rain, the best policeman of all, begins to fall; the organiser comes past and thanks the Station Sergeant for his help – he seems to have made most of the arrangements for the meeting. And it all dissolves away.

Fun on the Terraces

A more routine problem is hooliganism among football spectators: hardly a ground in London is free of it. A survey commissioned by the Ministry of Sport in 1967 found that the sort of person convicted is typically in his early or middle teens and that, interestingly, two in three have previous convictions for other offences. A Chief Superintendent with two large grounds to police says 'They're not football hooligans really, they're not decent villians; they're just hooligans who go to a match and carry on the same way as they always do.'

This was a routine Saturday at a moderately troublesome ground. Forty-nine men were detailed to manage traffic outside the ground: they put up temporary one-way signs, controlled junctions and pedestrian crossings. An Inspector and forty men were assigned to controlling queues in the ground, sixty men were inside, allowing one PC to every

thousand spectators. A Chief Inspector was in charge of them:
I found him a few minutes before the game started, watching
anxiously by the main gates. 'I may have to decide to shut the
gates to prevent the crowd overfilling the ground – it's always
unpopular and the people outside think I've done it to spite
them. But I can't risk a stampede and people getting crushed.'

We run in under the stands to a little office where electric
counters show the rate of flow through the turnstiles. Ten
minutes before kick-off it has fallen from the maximum possible of 800 a minute to 500 a minute: he watches the flying
orange numbers in the vacuum tubes, then decides that
the ground will be about 1,000 spectators short, and that he
won't have to shut the gates, as in fact it turns out. A minute
before the kick-off, the stream through the main gates has
died away to one rather feeble-witted boy who wants directions somewhere quite different. In the directors' car park
next door, the sheepskin-and-tweed-jacket set have got out
of their fawn Jaguars and gone up too.

The Chief Inspector has the gates closed and goes off
to his strategically placed seat in the director's box. The
police have a little brick room with a heater in it and a telephone. On the window-sill there's a crime book for the ground
and a register of people ejected by them on behalf of the
management – a tactic often used because it saves policemen having to go to the station with their charges. Inside
the hut there are four policemen: one, a Sergeant, sitting
warming his hands at the electric fire, and facing him, also
warming his hands, a tall youth with lank blond hair and
a scarf as long as himself wound round his neck.

On a chair between them are spread out some objects
in issue: an Arsenal football-club scarf – he is not an Arsenal
supporter, 'I found it on the ground,' – several odd leaden
disks the size of shillings – either for putting in ticket
machines or for throwing at people, 'I don't know where
they came from,' – and a surgeon's lancet with the blade
ground into a hook which he could use privily to cut
through the clothes and flesh of people standing in front

of him: 'I tell you again, I just found it on the ground. I was going to give it to someone.' 'You didn't make much effort to give it to me,' said the Sergeant without emphasis, 'It's all one to us: you can have larceny-finder, or offensive weapon. When you get up to the station, you let them know what you've decided.'

One of the PCs standing by the door, a dark, cross-looking man of about forty, shrugs himself into his coat again, buttons the scarf inside the collar, sets his helmet forward on his head and sallies out. I attach myself to him. He is one of four experienced men on anti-hooligan patrol. We go under the stand, where there is a large space, roofed by the sloping undersides of the seats. A revolting tea bar is set into one side; elderly and aimless fans wander about trying to find their seats. As we walk across, a tide of young boys pours round us, yelping. The PC braces himself against them like a stream and yells, 'STOP RUNNING!' They take no notice and disappear down one of the concrete tunnels like a pack of hounds.

We run after them, through the tunnel and up, on to the end terrace where the group dissolves into the crowd. But the leader, conspicuous in white trousers and a blue and white striped singlet, is left sitting at the base of a pillar. We say simultaneously, 'I fancy that one'; the policeman because he warned him half-an-hour ago to stop running about, I because he looks dangerous. When the boy stands up he is taller than either of us. The PC scoops him and another boy up with his free hand and we go back to the hut. We wait in the hut for ten minutes, then a van comes from the nick to collect the half-dozen prisoners that have accumulated. The van backs up to a side gate, the boys are led out and get in, and a couple of PCs go with them. In the van one discusses the match with the young policeman nearest him; the rest sit silent, as they do at the station, while the police work away at the charge sheets, writing up their notebooks for court, and telephoning the boys' parents. In the charge room, dark with a wood block floor, the boys sit round the edges with their hands out of their pockets, looking like children.

Eventually it's the stripey one's turn to be dealt with: he is summoned to the desk where the Station Sergeant is sitting, and the PC says in a formal voice: 'For a period of twenty minutes this youth was running up and down knocking people out of his way. He was arrested and told it was for insulting behaviour. He was cautioned and made no reply.' He has nothing to say to this and sits down again to await his father, who will probably not be best pleased to have his Saturday afternoon interrupted.

The Duty Officer, an elderly inspector with an almost bald head and a careworn expression, watches this with his arms folded: 'I can understand modern teachers and parents not caring to be strict – after all, there's not much point being firm if the others aren't. But sooner or later someone has to draw the line or the kids get out of hand. You didn't get this teenage hooliganism ten years ago. It was unheard of to find boys this age at police stations. Increasingly, I'm afraid, it's us that have to draw the line and we aren't loved for it.'

Ho! Ho! Ho Chi Minh!

The series of four anti-Vietnam demonstrations held in London over 1967–68 combined the ideology of the 'Legalise Pot' Rally with the self-expression of the football hooligans, inflated to a massive scale. Each one posed the Metropolitan Police a severe test of its organisation, morale, and public relations sense; taken in series they show a most interesting development in police policy, and in general they illustrate very well the delicate and contradictory role of the police in society.

Of the three sorts of crowd – the totally respectable, the overtly respectable with an unlawful intention, and the riot, the second is the most difficult for the police to deal with, and these four all fell into that category. Before we look at each in turn, it may be interesting to consider, in the abstract, the problems of controlling this type of crowd. The essence of the affair is a public relations contest, in which the demonstrators try to force the police to be seen to be violent.

The police are the State made flesh: in their single blue bodies they focus a thousand resentments against the omnipresent machinery of government. However the demonstrator thinks the State has wronged him, he hopes to make it visible to the world through the action of a policeman. The policeman, on the other hand, is usually subject to several conflicting impulses.

Firstly, he must succeed. In this case he must not let the demonstrators enter the Embassy. Secondly, he is an actor on the international stage. The American Government would protect our Embassy against a similar demonstration, but would doubtless use far more vigorous means. But he uses violence at his personal peril; with telescopic lenses on the roof-tops around, he may find himself a national enemy the next morning. Fourthly, he knows that he is outnumbered, but he can't lose interest and go home as the demonstrator can. Fifthly, he knows nothing of how the day is going elsewhere.

If I had been a policeman at the rougher demonstrations, knowing no more than what I could see across a hundred yards of shouting heads, I feel that I could well have panicked. Although demonstrators may know that it's a public relations exercise and that *they* mean no real harm, the police remember how many officers have been maimed in excursions of this sort. The second man to die on duty in Metropolitan Police – back in 1833 – was stabbed in a mob embroilment. The demonstrator can be reasonably confident that a policeman will not draw out a knife and cut his kidneys: the policeman cannot.

Constitutionally, too, the police are in a difficult position. Under the heading *Duty to Disperse Unlawful Assemblies and Riots,* Wade and Phillips remark, in their *Constitutional Law,*[1] ' . . . a police officer must hit the exact line between excess and failure of duty and is guilty of criminal neglect

[1] Longmans, 1960.

if he fails to judge rightly.' A consoling thought to the honest citizen, safe at home, but one which gives concern to the senior police officer – with pennies singing round his ears and a pension at stake.

In an ordinary street disturbance, a policeman is entitled by law to use as much force as is necessary to prevent a breach of the peace. Naturally, in the proto-typical situation where one man is attacking another, the force is going to be used against the aggressor. Although people behave less rationally than usual, and more aggressively in a crowd, the law takes no notice of this. It disregards the cheerers-on and concentrates only on the policeman and the man who is causing a breach of the peace.

This is admirable and civilised, but it means that the policeman can legally do nothing to discourage the cheerers-on, who may well physically prevent him getting at the person who is throwing rocks or prodding with a pole. He cannot arrest or subdue anyone that he isn't prepared to charge with an offence, and although he doesn't have to arrest anyone to prove his point, it obviously makes for better public relations to be able to produce a body in court the next morning.

But tactically, in the mob situation, arrests are a luxury which the police do their best to avoid, because one constable has to go with every person arrested to give personal and immediate evidence before the Station Officer. Since the police are ordinarily outnumbered by ten to one, this means that each arrest weakens the police ten times more than the crowd. This constitutional one-for-one relationship was exploited by the Committee of a Hundred's tactics in the nuclear disarmament campaign of the early sixties. They hoped, by mass sit-downs, to provoke more arrests than there were Metropolitan policemen, thus paralysing the administration of law and order. Because each arrest not only takes a constable off the street, it creates a minimum of six police man-hours of work.

So, although the Americans might defend the British Embassy with water cannon, tear gas, slippery foam, paralysing gas, and armed militia men, and would expect us to achieve the same effect in defence of their Embassy, the British police are precluded by law and their own practice from using these methods. In England it is quite possible that someone knocked over by a water cannon could sue the police for assault. If there was no evidence that he was committing a breach of the peace the case would be heard in court almost as if the demonstration did not exist, as if he were walking through Grosvenor Square and a policeman wantonly turned a hose on him. There is, and has been for two hundred odd years, a very severe inhibition on the protectors of public order not to take *general* action against a crowd until disorder has become spectacular.

Quite apart from the distaste which people feel for violence done by the police – whether it is justified or not – there is a sound commercial reason for the police not to help to start a riot. Once one has begun they have to pay for all the damage done by the crowd. The existence of a riot is a matter of fact for the court to decide on the events of the day. For example, in 1945, a crowd climbed over houses outside Chelsea Football Ground to see a match against Moscow Dynamos: the High Court held that this had been a riot, so the Metropolitan Police had to mend the damaged roofs.

Although we like to think of public stampedes and trampled bodies as things that only happen abroad, the English are not immune. Twice in recent times crowds have got out of hand, with fatal results. A crowd going to shelter for the night of March 3, 1943, in Bethnal Green Tube Station, was panicked by the firing of a salvo of anti-aircraft rockets a mile away. They surged forward, and a woman carrying a baby tripped on the third step from the bottom of the improvised stairs. A man fell with her; the people at the top, fearing that the platform doors had been closed against them, pushed harder. It was a quarter of an hour before the police could control the situation; when the mass of people at the bottom of the stairs was cleared away, 27 men, 84 women and 62 children were found crushed to death; 62 were injured.

Then, in 1946, 33 people were killed in a rush to enter Bolton Wanderers football ground. Every senior police officer has these nightmares at the back of his mind, and one that allowed such a situation to develop in a crowd under his control would be held very much to blame. So for one reason or another, the police have to renounce general methods against an unruly crowd, and are limited to man-to-man techniques. The operational solution is a difficult matter.

The Chief Superintendent of a division visited by the marches explained some of the police problems thus: 'People always tell you that the difference between the police and the army is that in the army it doesn't matter what you do as long as you do it quickly; in the police it doesn't matter how long you take as long as you're right in the end. This is true of most police work, except crowd control. There you've got to be both quick *and* right, but this is just what the ordinary copper isn't trained for. He isn't good at quick action in squads. All his experience is as a lone operator – his instinct is to set off and settle the bother straight away.

'Suppose there's a crowd of 40,000 people and you've got a couple of thousand coppers, average age twenty-three or so, to control it. If you said "Away you go, lads, sort it out," they'd wade in and get slaughtered. Systematic violence against crowds makes no tactical sense for us, because we're outnumbered at least ten to one. You have to play a crowd along.'

There are tricks to this that only experience can teach: 'One of the things is to catch a crowd off balance. During one of the Grosvenor Square marches, the Anarchists came up Wigmore Street to burn down Dow Chemicals. They arrived outside Dow, and started to surge about and debate what they should do next. I could hear their voices: "Go on: bust a window." "Did you bring the matches?" "No, let's leave it alone – anyway it's raining." "We *said* we would" – and all this sort of thing.

'Just then we could hear fire engine gongs pelting down Baker Street and the crowd started saying, "The dirty sods – we haven't even set light to the place yet." "Sit down, sit down." So they all were getting down when it became apparent the fire engines weren't coming our way at all – there'd been a false alarm in Grosvenor Square. So they started to get up again. With their bottoms half-way between heaven and earth, I thought, "This is my moment," and got the police cordon behind to give them a push – we got the whole mass moving away down the street before they realised what had happened – and by then it was too late.'

Rather like electricity, a crowd always has to have somewhere to go, and as long as it is moving, it presents no real problem. Trouble-makers are swept down-stream, while the defenders stay still and improve their positions. But a crowd that comes to a halt, or gets into a space too small for it, is a danger to itself and its shepherds. So, for example, if the police have to barricade a street, they always put the barrier at the entrance, even though the point to be protected may be right at the other end, because once a procession gets up a dead end, it can easily panic and fight its way out.

The same officer continues: 'It's very important to stand right up close. Our instincts are all for face-to-face crowd control. It's something to do with facial expressions, something basic about the nature of human aggression. It's very difficult indeed to hurt a stranger badly when you're nose-to-nose – much easier at a distance. There's a bit about it in *The Naked Ape* which, I think, explains why our crowd control methods work so well. When people stand twenty yards apart throwing things, then you get injuries. And as soon as you bring impersonal things like tanks or water cannon into the picture – or you make your own men impersonal by using gas and putting them in gas masks – you take away these restraints from people and they get really violent.

'We've studied all these new methods of crowd control – water cannon, for instance, don't work well, they just make people very angry indeed. In New York they've come back to our methods: men and horses close up.' Also, which he didn't say, vigorous personal action on either side in the middle of a jam-packed mass of demonstrators and police is almost impossible to photograph, and so doesn't count in the public relations battle.

The four pro-Vietnam demonstrations formed a developing sequence. The first, in October 1967, seems to have surprised the police by the determination of extremists to break into the American Embassy, and the complete inability of the organisers to control their followers. The assembly in the Square degenerated into a dispersed, large-scale scuffle: the demonstrators used whatever weapons the ground afforded – park benches as battering-rams, metal fencing as pikes. The police, caught off balance, did much the same; horses and dogs were brought up, and buses were driven forcibly into the crowd to split it into more manageable lumps. The next day there was criticism of police violence.

The second demonstration took place on March 17, 1968. I went as a spectator among the crowd. It began with a mass meeting in Trafalgar Square, remarkable for its apathy. A few policemen wandered about among the crowd – and one got thrown in a fountain by Sussex University militants carrying a banner: 'Death to Yankee Imperialists.' Film stars and well-known protesters made routine speeches: Vanessa Redgrave read out messages of encouragement from Godard and other continental film-makers in a voice like the Queen's. She concluded: 'I feel that my presence here to-day speaks for itself.' Some of the idealists wore white ribbons round their heads: the practical felt they were unnecessary invitations to truncheons. The very sensible German delegation appeared in light-weight helmets. There was, in the square, a listless, almost nauseous indolence; a mass feeling of stage fright.

Normally, the police agree route and timing with the organisers of demonstrations, and after that rely on them to carry the programme out. But the previous march had got completely out of hand. Downing Street had nearly been stormed – for the first time in living memory – and on this occasion the police were going to do some shepherding themselves. Even so, in Grosvenor Square itself, the police adopted a rather half-and-half strategy. The Square runs east and west, the Embassy taking up the whole western end. The back and sides of the building were easily defended with cordons across the narrow streets; the theory was that the march should enter the square at the north-west corner and progress *away* from the Embassy around the other three sides, back up the south side, and that the leaders should halt at the south-west corner to deliver a petition. The Embassy was fenced off by cordons diagonally across the intersections at each side, and a cordon joining them along the western edge of the gardens. Reserves and thirty mounted police were held behind the Embassy.

It was no secret that there was to be an attempt to storm the Embassy. For instance, the *Guardian* had reported, rather irresponsibly, that posters advertising the march carried stickers: *Come Armed*. In Ladbroke Grove, Notting Hill, a largely coloured area, someone had written on a conspicuous wall: 'The War Starts March 17.' Police on the outskirts of London, presumably acting on Special Branch information, stopped several coach-loads of students on their way to the demonstration, and removed marbles for throwing under the horses' hooves, pepper (invisible on TV) for throwing in police faces, and sachets full of red paint to simulate blood from police wounds. These armaments emphasise how much the march and the preparations to counter it were, as it were, two elements in the production of a drama for television and newsreels. The police hoped to emerge as firm but gentle; the demonstrators as innocent victims of police brutality – or if the day turned in their favour and they carried the Embassy, the righteous avengers of the Vietnamese innocents.

Very slowly the edge of the square fills up with spectators; the faces of the policemen in the cordon harden from Sunday afternoon amusement to apprehension. By the time all the pavements are full, roaring noises are heard from the North Audley Street entrance and a long while later, as a pathetic anticlimax, the tiny head of the procession arrives outside the Embassy, led by an inspector from Cannon Row.

They pause for a moment, looking self-conscious in the middle of the road, like a Bateman drawing, then they are shooed off into oblivion down South Audley Street.

The roar increases. Big red banners appear up North Audley Street – the roar becomes hard and frightening. It's like going to Lands End in a westerly gale: inland, before you get there, it seems exciting and romantic, then at the promontory, it's apparent that the wind, the rocks and the sea are dangerous. The crowd makes a noise like a huge animal: I remember the barefoot girls with white tape round their heads and the babies on their hips who set out from Trafalgar Square.

The noise lowers again and then becomes several times louder. Suddenly the crowd spills over the hedge into the gardens. Police horses tittup round the south end of the Embassy and are put in. The trees are full of people, like fruit: an elderly mounted policeman with a red face and almost white hair clings to his horse's neck, sheltering against the rain of clods and banner staves. In a quiet corner, craning to see, there is knot of public schoolboys: 'Break out the sabres, lads,' they cry as the mounted police go in. An American girl whirls round, nearly crying with tension: 'How *can* you be so stupid? It's fools like you that get people killed.'

The crowd impersonally spouts earth; the lumps go sailing towards the police lines as incessantly and mechanically as the lava from a volcano. Behind the roar there is an odd, insistent tap-tap of ball bearings fired from catapults against the Embassy windows. Some flew right over the building and broke windows in the mews behind – for which, as damage done by a riot, the police had to pay.

Reactions to the police handling of the event were on the whole favourable. The Home Secretary told the Commons that police casualties were 117, as against 45 demonstrators – a suspect figure, since many of the police casualties were minor, but had to be examined by a doctor in case of compensation for industrial injury, while demonstrators might have gone to any of half-a-dozen hospitals without explaining their part in the day's events. Even so, the implication was probably fair: that the police had taken as much of a beating as they had handed out.

They barely won. When the head of the march reached the Square, the Germans, in construction-site helmets, linked arms and charged in a hypnotising, swaying rush. They had trained against Berlin's *Schutzpolizei*: the first cordon melted before them. It seemed clear that the Metropolitan police with its present techniques and freedom of action could hardly handle anything rougher, yet Commander Lawlor, the officer in charge of such affairs, said to a *Guardian* reporter[1]: 'We would be very reluctant to curb any form of demonstration'[2], and, questioned about the use of more aggressive methods: 'Gas would never be contemplated in the context of a demonstration[3].'

An *Observer* leader writer helpfully contributed – wrongly, as it turned out – 'But whatever police attitudes are today, the political and emotional climate of the country may force them to change. Polarisation of political opinion is emerging. It was during the Fascist-Communists fights of the 1930s that the police were last faced with sustained public violence. Now the lack of definition between parliamentary political parties; the inability of existing machinery to solve the big problems; the many focal points for unrest – Vietnam, the wage freeze, student discontent, immigration and aggravated housing and employment situations – are combining to make the individual feel helpless. This summer it will be through public demonstration that these dissatisfied individuals will be seeking expression. Violence will be a certain keynote.'

One reason for the favourable public reaction was that the new public relations policy at Scotland Yard had begun to bite. The

---

[1] *Guardian,* 19 March 1968.

[2] Summing up the year's events, the Commissioner afterwards wrote, about the demonstrations: '... in spite of the threatened violence and the inconvenience these marches create, I would always support the right of peaceful demonstration. If this were limited, or curtailed, the ban would unite many of those who at the moment have opposing policies'. (*Report of the Commissioner of Police of the Metropolis, 1968,* p. 9).

[3] *Observer,* 24 March 1968.

Press were *helped* to cover the second demonstration – a profound change from the traditional police mistrust of journalists. In return it seems that at least one set of potentially damaging photographs was voluntarily suppressed by the papers.

An enormous influence was exerted by Granada Television's documentary on the march, which was made with some help from the Public Relations Branch. This lasted half-an-hour and was shown, by a minor miracle of technique, on Monday evening, barely twenty-four hours after the march finished. Instead of the cold, frozen photographs of students and policemen scuffling, with nothing to show which side had the right of it, this film made plain just what was involved for both sides, how patiently most of the police stood the shouting and the rushes. By the morning of the following Tuesday, thousands of letters began to arrive at Scotland Yard: letters from housewives, round-robins signed by whole streets, by the staffs of whole factories, from the engineers of a remote ITV transmitter who saw the film on their monitor screen.

For the third march, a 'return match' as some policemen saw it, in July 1968, twenty-three journalists were given conspicuous red tags by the police and allowed behind the cordon round the Embassy.

There was an air of anti-climax, and as the first head of the column appeared, rigorously shepherded by Communist stewards, the police commander, who had made such a fuss about letting any journalists in at all, relaxed and suddenly let another half-dozen pressmen through the cordon. The march filed past until the Maoist section came abreast of the square. They burst in half-way along the south side: a police cordon was quickly formed along the west end. The Maoists tore up bushes, pulled down leafy branches and tried to set fire to them. The police watched in bored amazement. A PC said: 'I bet the Viet Cong really appreciate that.'

One of the demonstrators came up to the line with a cut lip. He complained to an Inspector, who turned to a movie cameraman – in itself, something unthinkable a year before – 'There you are – you can see we didn't start the punch-up.' A PC said to the man: 'I'm not nicking anyone today, and don't you think it, chum. Tomorrow's my rest day.' All the time more policemen were being added to the north end of the cordon, extending it, so that after ten minutes' wait they all loped forward and physically pushed the Maoists back into the street.

As the two lines got closer they started throwing pennies and flints – which are not indigenous to Grosvenor Square. As the two groups solidified into a tight knot by the gap in the hedge, a dazed girl was spewed out of the scrum – a shock-headed boy fell down; for a second he was curled up with boots prodding at him. But the crowd was too dense for real kicking. Then it was all over. A youth, his face twisted in hate, was carried off by the march, screaming, 'Fascists'. Nothing happened, but it was emotionally disturbing: a lot of the police were pale, yawning with reaction.

As the demonstrators were driven back, the front row of police wrenched the banners and poles out of their hands and passed them back over their heads. Men behind quickly broke the staves over their knees and threw the pieces further back, so that they couldn't be used again as weapons. As the last Maoist was ejected, a fresh-faced boy said, 'Please Mr 499, could I have my flag back? Just the flag, not the stick.' It was torn off and thrown to him. 'Say "Thank you", then.' 'Thank you.' Parts of this group broke away from the main march and rampaged down Park Lane, smashing windows and the Sheik of Kuwait's car. They were finally dispersed outside Burlington House in Piccadilly. The *Daily Mirror* led next day with a photo of one solitary copper, his stick drawn, defying dozens of Maoists. It was another PR victory.

By the fourth demonstration, in October 1968, the police had settled on an entirely and conspicuously non-violent policy. This was in spite of an extraordinary press campaign, led by *The Times,* predicting a revolution. In consequence, public buildings and large offices were barricaded: the BBC built wooden walls round their studios, the *Daily Mirror* installed steel roller-blinds to cover their front doors and windows, the *Daily Express* hired forty Argyll and Sutherland Highlanders, and so on. The London School of Economics was taken over by the students as a command and recuperation centre – and it also established medical aid posts along the route. The police conceded them the school buildings.

In a broad sense the idea that the day would trigger a revolution was a canard: there could be no general, popular support for such a development. It was in the event a magnificent, if not actually very difficult, vindication of police pacifism. Fifty thousand people assembled at Charing Cross, marched east to the bottom of Fleet Street, back west to Trafalgar Square, Whitehall, and on to Hyde Park and Speakers' Corner. The police said that they would concede the street to the demonstrators, who could sit or lie down as long as they liked, and thus defused the commonest excuse for violence. There was no trouble on the main march, and only a breakaway group of Anarchists, at the most 5,000 people, tried to force their way into the American Embassy. Many of the police outside were sincerely frightened, for they had been warned to expect acid and firearms. When the first firework exploded, the serried helmets swayed like a field of poppies in a storm: the Anarchists pushed, the police gave way, and then nipped off the factious lump with a charge and a pincer movement, surrounding the troublemakers like an amoeba eating, and pushed them away down South Audley Street.

By dark the demonstrators had almost all gone; and those left linked arms with the police to sing *Auld Lang Syne* (it really happened). The next day the police were universally applauded: the *Daily Mirror* led its front page with the headline: *The Day the Police were Wonderful*. There was a perceptible air of cheerfulness and relief in the capital. The thousand arrests, the dead and maimed, the hate, the fear which people had expected had magically gone away. It was like a tiny Dunkirk.

A motion of praise for the police was tabled in the House of Commons and in consequence of it being carried unanimously, the Speaker sent this Resolution to the Commissioner:

"That this House wishes to congratulate all the police who were on duty in London on 27th October, 1968, for their efficiency, good discipline and tolerance under great provocation; requests Mr Speaker to send a letter of commendation on behalf of the whole House to all concerned especially thanking those who gave up their leave periods to be on duty; and, furthermore, wishes to place on record their admiration of the Chief Commissioner of the Metropolitan Police who in the interests of the liberty of all Her Majesty's subjects decided not to invoke his powers to ban the demonstration."

This was a most unusual honour. Moreover, both the *Guardian* and *Observer*, papers that can usually be expected to take a line critical of the establishment, were complimentary.

Mary McCarthy, imported by the *Sunday Times Magazine*[1] for the occasion, wrote, 'For the first time in history a massed police force practised "passive" resistance and it worked. Thus, if the police are brutal, as in Mayor Daley's Chicago, it is not from necessity, but from choice.' It was, of course, far from the first time. In 150 years' co-existence, the Metropolitan Police and the London crowd have evolved an organic, non-violent relationship. That is not to say that there haven't been violent clashes, but they have been relatively few, and they are far less frequent now than in the early days.

This relationship was strikingly demonstrated as the 1969 Commonwealth Prime Ministers' Conference opened. Dozens of national groups demonstrated simultaneously; representatives of both sides in the appalling Nigerian civil war were there, separated by a single line of police with their hands folded behind their backs. 'You could only see it in England,' remarked Mr Trudeau, Canada's Prime Minister. It is said that Britain has the best police force in the world, but we have good crowds too; one wonders how satisfied the ratepayers of Berlin or Paris would be with the Met's handling of violent mobs.

[1] 8 December 1968.

CHAPTER FIVE

Traffic Policing

The Traffic Department is a separate world of police. It has its own problems, its own organisation, boundaries, bases and radio control room, called, for some reason 'Oscar' (see below, p. 213). 'With the stroke of a pen,' I was told by one of the senior officers, 'It could be a separate force.'

Accident Car

It is a sheeting-wet summer evening. Wherever there is a light in the streets it shows the close, parallel bars of rain that break in clouds on the road. I am riding with a late-turn crew out of Barnes Garage in an accident car – one of the old police Wolseleys with POLICE in lights across the front, and a big loudspeaker on the roof. We drift slowly down to Hammersmith, and then back along the flyover, cruising a little faster than the suddenly law-abiding drivers and their wives swishing along in closed cars to spend an evening with their friends.

Then one pulls out in front and works up to fifty mph. This is only ten mph above the speed limit there, but he promises well. The police driver follows him judiciously, the needle on his outsize, accurate speedometer crawling up. We run behind him for a mile and a half; he has the air of a goer, but irritatingly fails either to take off or to notice us and slow down.

At the first traffic light we pull alongside. One expects some reaction when he sees who has been following his mad career, but he turns a bland, scholarly face to us. He wears spectacles: this crew have had a recent unhappy experience with the local magistrate and a short-sighted offender. It seems that the magistrate thought he was asking too much of a man to read his speedometer as well as drive, if he has glasses. They decide not to do him for speed.

'He'll come again; they always do,' says the observer. And the driver: 'It's amazing that he didn't see us. It's incredible really how people behave in cars. It was very foggy a month or so ago, and there'd been an accident on the M4 (a twenty-mile stretch of motorway leading into west London). I was putting out big MOTORWAY CLOSED signs across the far end, and a row of beacons across the road. I'd just finished, and I was getting back into the car, when I saw a big Jaguar off through the mist, picking his way between two beacons. I went over and asked him:

"Where are you off to, sir?" It was obvious that if I didn't stop him, he'd be away.

"To London."

"Can you read at all, sir?"

"Yes, of course, officer."

"Can you read that the motorway is closed, sir?"

"Well, I thought it would be all right." Can you believe it? Chummy isn't stupid, he's one of the leading barristers in one of the Inns of Court. But when people get into cars, they act like animals.'

On the radio there is the noise of an ambulance and its escort pelting up the Kingston Bypass. Oscar is offering the job of running it into central London. Two motorcycles take it and arrange to rendezvous at Roehampton. 'I escorted an ambulance once – Bournemouth to Great Ormond Street in one hour fifty-five minutes. That's *averaging* nearly sixty on a very crowded road,' said the driver. Unlike most policemen, Traffic Department men positively enjoy cars, motorcycles and the road, and will gossip for hours about engines or memorable runs. Thunderclouds overhead make the radio roar and crackle. Oscar says: 'There is a damage-only accident with allegations at Chancery Lane and a Hillman

Minx in altercation with a horse-trough, non-movable type. Any unit fancy this?'

It is a very quiet night. The breathalyser was then new enough to have stopped most of the drunken evening accidents; with no jobs to occupy the traffic police, the air is filled with desultory chat. Traffic Department has only a thousand men, all volunteers, who have known each other for years. They know the controllers of each shift by their first names. Messages are longer and less formal than Information Room's busy anonymity. Policemen who ask for advice sign off with a courtly: 'I'm most obliged to you,' to which Oscar replies: 'That's quite all right, Robbie, old son. We appreciate your efforts out there, we really do.' Our crew can recognise nameless voices in the dark; the marital plans or accomplished infidelities of half-a-dozen are sketched by the observer. 'Listen to Oscar, the station where it's all at,' he says.

At half-past ten we have to go to a street in Paddington where an old man was knocked down at the same hour ten days before. He died this morning. The Inspector in charge of the job needs more witnesses for the inquest, he wants the crew to make a broadcast 'This is *embarrassing*,' they say. They don't like to wake up all the sleeping children with their loudspeaker, to disturb the families settled round the tellies. But it has to be done. 'This is a police message. Will anyone who saw an accident . . .?' The voice goes rumbling and growling round the houses like the thunder above. We wait, but no one comes out. As we move away, a car crosses the street ahead of us. The driver recognises it as belonging to an expert housebreaker from his old subdivision, and sets off in chase. Quite a lot of time with policemen is spent following old criminal friends: now, as usual, we lose him.

The daytime accident car is much busier. Within a minute of leaving the garage, the crew get a job in a sleazy street behind the Portobello Road. On the way there we meet an ambulance dealing with another accident, a little girl knocked over by a sports car. This is a coloured area, and on a Saturday afternoon the children run all over the roads. We radio the location of this one to Oscar – they'll send a motorbike – and push on to ours. The police is to represent the state, to freeze the facts of the case in the amber of a report.

Our accident was in a long straight street with T-junctions at both ends and no turnings in between. A brand new Volkswagen is standing slightly askew in the middle of the road. A little girl had run out of her house, down the steps, across the pavement and onto the car's bumper with the accuracy of a missile. She had done the same thing six months before. The driver of the Volkswagen was going, he said, at about twenty-five miles an hour, or maybe less. The policemen measured the length of the skid marks – forty feet – with a tape measure, took their distance from the kerb and wrote it all down. Although a dozen people were sitting on doorsteps with a good view, no one had been looking in the right direction, and there were no witnesses.

We go to the hospital to write down the child's injuries. The ambulance crew which we met on the way are in Sister's office drinking tea and filling out their job-sheets. They and the policemen exchange names and addresses of victims. The mother of our girl is visible as a pair of pacing feet under the curtain of the accident cubicle. The motorbike policeman comes in to complete his report on the other accident. Ours is serious: a pierced stomach and a fractured skull. We finish our tea and get back on watch.

We have no jobs for half-an-hour, but, waiting in a crowd of cars for a green light at Notting Hill Gate, there are four in clear view with broken rear lights. The two policemen wind down their windows and start calling to the other drivers to get their lights mended. They smile nervously and shout back that indeed they will. 'If we stuck this lot on, we'd be off the road for an hour. Is that what the ratepayers want?' said the driver. 'This job is madness,' said the observer, 'there's literally a thousand different traffic offences you can commit. We need a briefcase to carry round all the laws, and before you turn round, you're bogged down in detail.'

The volume of legislation has grown so unwieldy that an instant radio-reference law library has been established in the Oscar control room; during working-hours a PC, who has made a study of the subject, is available to settle difficult problems. The observer tells a suede-sheep-skinned couple in a mauve sports car that they too have a broken rear light. 'Your accent goes all to pieces when you talk to the toffs,' the driver afterwards tells him unkindly.

Motorway Electronics

The next Saturday, a close, muggy day, I spend the afternoon at the M4 Motorway control room in Hounslow Police Station (now moved to the Heston Service Area, Bucks). A bored PC reads the afternoon away. Here the emergency roadside telephones terminate, he has his own radio transmitter to send motorway patrols to drivers' assistance, but most of the equipment deals with the two-mile long Chiswick flyover. An elaborate wall-map driven by a small computer, connected to sensing-loops in the road surface, signals traffic flows with winking amber lights. If a light shines steadily it means that traffic has stopped, and there must be an accident or a breakdown further up.

When everything is going well, motorways are empty strips of concrete with a few swishing cars; but when things go wrong, they quickly jam up. When the M4 was first opened, a mini ran out of petrol at the west end of the flyover; within minutes the motorway had to be closed at Slough, fifteen miles away. The constable's job is to wait for a light to glow steadily, then to see what is wrong on the road with his television cameras. He has three, mounted on high buildings, he can pan and zoom them with a little joystick on the desk. The picture shows on a monitor screen, and he can soon tell what services are needed: a breakdown truck to remove lifeless cars, or an accident car, or an ambulance or whatever.

He has also control of a series of illuminated gantries over the road, so that before a difficult situation gets any worse, he can close the motorway and organise diversions. At the time of my visit, supplements to the sensing-pads in the road surface were being tried out. A small radar set attached to one of the gantry legs showed the speeds of passing cars on a meter in the office: if they fall below that of the rush-hour crawl a bell would ring to signal mishap.

One of the duty PCs had pinned to the wall a stupid letter cut from the magazine *Autosport*:

> Sir,
> I would like to issue a warning to my fellow motorists who travel on the M4. There is a certain Sunbeam Tiger that is being used for the ungentlemanly practice of catching 70 mph speed limit exceeders. It has absolutely no identification, so the Metropolitan Police must be having great fun. I wonder if Rootes (the manufacturers) approve of their vehicle being used in this way?
>
> Yours sincerely,
> Christopher Chorly

By a nice British compromise, the enforcement car – visible just then as a white spot on the television screen – has nothing externally to show its police affiliation, but unlike the CID's nondescripts, carries two large policemen in uniform. Policemen can wear plain clothes to deal with criminals: when they catch motorists, who kill far more people, they must play the game by wearing uniform.

Another job of the Traffic Department is to remove 200 ill-parked cars every day to squalid pounds on unused scraps of land round London. The policemen who do this have developed an enviable expertise in getting into other people's locked cars, and are subjected to quite extraordinary abuse when the owners come to reclaim them. The department also escorts heavy loads, but since this is a job for three

motorcycles, leap-frogging slowly round the lorry, it was
not something of which much could be seen by a casual
visitor. Then, too, it operates seventeen Specially Equipped
Traffic Accident Cars (SETACS), big station-wagons crammed
with jacks, saws, release gear, blankets, road signs, whose
job is to release people trapped in nasty accidents, but which
are too full of equipment to take a passenger.

It is no criticism of this department that I found most of
its practical work rather boring. One is exposed to enormous
numbers of mechanical centaurs – not the most attractive
manifestations of modern man – who come to the official attention of the police only when they do something silly.
The traffic policeman spends most of his life reproving idiots;
unless he is fond of cars and motorcycles in themselves –
and many are – the job perhaps lacks the interest of other
branches of police work. But all those traffic men whom I
met were genuinely interested in their jobs, they were all
volunteers, and there was a particularly pleasant informal
and down-to-earth quality about relationships between the
ranks.

Traffic Study

Traffic policing only begins with the patrols. They are
a sort of poultice to be applied when something goes wrong.
Ideally, there should be nothing for them to do, because
the roads are so well-engineered that cars cannot collide and
all the drivers obey all the laws. Failing this ideal condition,
traffic patrols should merely sit beside the road so that the
largest possible number of drivers see them and are reminded
of the existence of the police. For instance, a Traffic Department Jaguar parked beside a main road reduces the average
speed of traffic by as much as five mph.

The Metropolitan Police have done some extremely interesting experiments on the effect of posting policemen at
difficult junctions. Because the same drivers tend to go through
them at the same time every day, a week's solid policing,

even if no more is done than just stand around, is claimed to produce a thirty per cent decrease in common driving faults, and that a strong enough impression is made on the centaurs' tiny minds for the improvement to last a week after the policing is withdrawn[1].

Drivers do not obey the law or the Highway Code nearly enough, and in consequence a large number of accidents result. In London there are some 55–60,000 Personal Injury (PI) accidents a year, including 700 deaths, and something like three times as many accidents involving damage only. These cost the community a formidable amount. A study by Dawson[2] concludes that, taking damage to machinery, loss of productivity, legal and police costs into account, urban accidents should be charged at the following tariff:

	Urban	Motorway
Fatal	£2,420	£7,850
Serious Injury	410	960
Slight Injury	125	480
Average PI	240	1,170
Damage	60	180

(Motorway accidents cost a great deal more because of the higher speeds and increased kinetic energies involved. These figures amply justify, for instance, the elaborate equipment described above at Chiswick, part of whose function is to prevent multiple pile-ups).

This table shows that PI accidents in London cost £22 millions and damage only £10 millions – together, half the cost of the *whole* Metropolitan police, or seven times the cost of the Traffic Department. So anything that the police can do to reduce accidents is effort and money well invested.

---

[1] The 'moral exemplar' role of the police, which, it is suggested below (p. 279), is in fact their main job in society, is particularly apparent in traffic work. So is the essential law-abidingness of people.

[2] Dawson, R. F. F., *Cost of Road Accidents in Great Britain*, Road Research Laboratory Report, LR79, MOT, 1967.

'Bar his Colt, there's nought alarming
To a *man*, in Burglar Jim,
But if us you can't be arming,
'Ow about *dis-arming him?*

AN UNEQUAL MATCH

[*Punch*, Oct. 8 1881]

LEFT: The problem of the unarmed policeman against the armed criminal has been with us a long time (by kind permission of *Punch*). RIGHT The armed policeman: a group of detectives about to search a house in Maida Vale for an armed gang (*United Press International Ltd*)

RUFFIANLY POLICEMAN

ABOUT TO PERPETRATE A BRUTAL AND DASTARDLY ASSAULT ON THE PEOPLE

[*Punch*, Aug. 11, 1866

Social attitudes towards the police change slowly. ABOVE: Compare this sympathy-arousing, middle-class view of the brave beleaguered bobby stemming the mob, with (RIGHT) an almost identical scene from a century later (photograph above by kind permission of *Punch*; photograph on right, as reproduced in the *Daily Mirror*, July 22, 1968)

In 1966 three unarmed detectives, the crew of a Q car, were senselessly murdered at Shepherd's Bush by a man whom they had stopped for questioning. This episode aroused enormous public sympathy, and reversed the tide of unpopularity which had been running against the police since the latter '50's. The top picture shows the Police Q car and two of the bodies at the scene of the shooting. The bottom picture shows the funeral of the three policemen (*Daily Express*)

Since the war, traffic accidents everywhere in Britain have tended to increase, though not nearly so fast as the number of cars on the road. However, in London, since the middle of the sixties, the number has fallen each year. This is mainly due to a reduced number of bicycles and motorbikes – the most accident-prone vehicles on the roads – but also to traffic engineering and good policing. But there is still scope for police effort.

Every day vehicles in London travel twenty million miles; there are 224 of them to every mile of road – as against sixty per mile in the rest of the country. Most main roads in London now carry almost their saturation volume of traffic all day – this means that there is little road left to accommodate drivers' mistakes, so every error means an accident. If traffic and accidents were evenly spread over London's 8,600 miles of road, the police task would be hopeless; fortunately (from the police point of view) seventy per cent of the accidents are concentrated in the A and B class roads which make up only seventeen per cent of the mileage. But even so, they cannot patrol all of these 1,600 miles of road.

To concentrate their efforts, they have instituted a system of Accident Intelligence. This begins with a record system kept locally, which identifies each stretch of road that has had ten or more accidents in six months. A pilot study done in 'T' Division (an area with the size and population of the city of Sheffield) shows that this criterion usually indicates something wrong with the road rather than with the drivers. A study is made, and often something can be done to reduce the danger.

In many cases the problem is something as simple and basic as two streets crossing. Though one doesn't realise it, this offers sixteen places where cars can hit each other, and eight where they can run over pedestrians. If one of the streets is made one-way, the collision points are reduced to nine and pedestrian points to six. If both are one-way, there are only three collision and four pedestrian points. One-way working greatly reduces accidents; it also increases road capacity because traffic is not held up by cars waiting to turn right. Studies of one-way schemes in central London show journey times cut by sixty to seventy per cent even though cars have to go further.

But not all traffic engineering is as simple. Accidents Intelligence investigations often show up obscure faults like traffic-light signals sometimes being hidden by double-decker buses, or a road sign combined with a little hill that

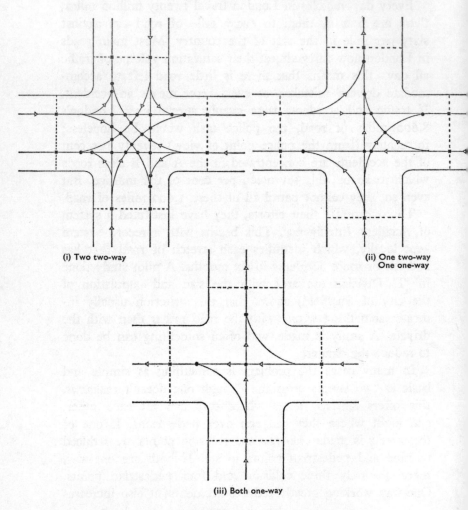

(i) Two two-way

(ii) One two-way
One one-way

(iii) Both one-way

**Points at which two vehicles can collide with each other
and pedestrians when two roads cross**

makes it impossible to see cars coming out of a side-turning, or a badly-sited street light. Since a quarter of all London's accidents involve pedestrians – we have no effective jay-walking law – many Accident Intelligence investigations recommend curbing them by building guard rails along the pavements. It is estimated that about ten per cent of the total number of accidents, costing some three million pounds a year, can be eliminated by tinkering with the road furniture, and police supervision at the right moments. The first 150 sites dealt with by this process showed twelve per cent reduction in accidents[1].

An interesting effect of traffic problems has been the increase in expertise within the police. As one senior administrator said, 'At the end of the war, traffic management hadn't become as technical as it has now, and we could say to a local authority, "The Commissioner cannot agree to the siting of a pedestrian-crossing at so-and-so street," and that was that. Nowadays they would laugh at us, and start talking traffic-flows. So we have had to learn the same language as County Hall and the Ministry. Some people think that the police have no real role in this sort of business, but I feel that, as the only agency that gets out on the street, watches what motorists actually do and talks to them after they've done it, we have an enormous fund of practical experience which is often needed to modify the engineers' elegant but sometimes impractical schemes.'

So, as one result of this involvement, there is a small department of self-taught policemen who specialise in the esoteric mathematics of traffic-flows and traffic-light programming. They see to it that County Hall's proposals make sense, and also give expert evidence about traffic-light phases when needed in court. Some traffic-light systems, like the linked set in Oxford Street, are extremely complicated.

But it has become apparent that it is not nearly enough to smooth off the edges of the road system, to refine traffic-flows and light-timings, to treat London's streets as a sort of

[1] *Report of the Commissioner of the Police of the Metropolis*, 1967.

pipe-system into which traffic pours itself insensately and at random. The whole business needs active control, which is being worked out on a large and rather obsolete computer, linked to road-sensors and traffic-lights all over Kensington, Chelsea, Fulham and Hammersmith. It is being used to develop complex programmes of traffic-light timing, which vary with the time of day, the kind of traffic, the season of the year, to make the best use of the road system.

At the control room on the first floor of Scotland Yard, the duty staff (jointly Ministry of Transport and Police) have a system of television cameras, like those at Chiswick, to watch danger points and alert them instantly to the cause of any hold-up. Before television, a traffic blockage would have to be investigated by a motorcyclist: it might take him ten minutes to get to it, and by then the jam would have spread two miles. When fully developed, the computer will be able to divert traffic automatically from a clogged road to a freer route. By 1971 it is hoped to extend the control system to the whole of inner London, using a new computer. It is estimated that if it increases journey speeds by a modest five per cent, the social profit will show a twenty per cent return on the capital invested. Even now the effect is noticeable enough for newspaper reporters to ring up within minutes of a computer breakdown, asking what has gone wrong.

The design of new traffic schemes, and arrangements to deal with temporary impediments caused by road works, are dealt with by four teams of half-a-dozen specialist policemen, one to each of the four districts. At the time of my visit to No 1 team, ninety-eight different jobs were in hand. Twenty were road resurfacing, twenty-six drainage and electricity and water works. Two local authority parking-meter schemes caused some work, because every painted line on the pavement and lamp-post notice had to be checked against the printed regulations. In the past the team had found as many as a hundred mistakes: each one could gain a prosecuted motorist an acquittal.

But railway bridges presented a more serious problem. British Rail, the year before, had found that a cast-iron bridge in the Midlands had developed a serious weakness: when they examined the several hundred others of the same design, it became apparent that the weakness was general. So all over London, as elsewhere, most of the railway bridges were being rebuilt – discreetly to avoid alarming the rail-travelling public. One of these, at Acton, involved remodelling eight road junctions so that traffic could be one-way over the bridge, to allow it to be rebuilt one half at a time, with a different scheme again at weekends to allow the whole bridge to be shut.

Another bridge, a tiny brick arch built in the eighteenth century to carry the Edgware Road across a stream, was being rebuilt in the same way, one half at a time. The traffic problem here was aggravated by a solid layer, under the whole road surface, of trunk telephone and television cables. A third job was the daily supervision of the temporary signs erected by contractors rebuilding the North Circular Road. Occasionally the police had to stop work on the road until better arrangements were made to protect cars and pedestrians.

Hackney Carriages

An interesting, but anomalous, responsibility of the Metropolitan Police is the licensing of London's cabs and cab drivers. Quarrels between cabbies and their passengers were so frequent in the early nineteenth century that the police acquired supervision as part of their general responsibility for good order in the street. It has been extended into a most thorough and beneficial scrutiny.

Interest in the cab starts with a prescription for the way in which it is to be built. It must be able to turn in one sweep between walls twenty-eight feet apart. When loaded with weights to represent the driver, passengers and luggage, it must not tip over if tilted forty degrees from the horizontal, it must be less than five foot nine inches wide and fifteen feet long, and when a passenger is sitting on the back seat, there must be a thirty-eight inch clearance under the roof, so that he may wear a top hat. There must be a screen between passengers and the driver with an opening not more than four and a half inches wide, so that if the passenger wants to hit him, he has to get out, and the driver can then drive away.

There are 7,500 cabs designed to the specifications of the police, they have to be taken out of service after ten years, and in between they are stringently tested at the Public Carriage Office in Islington once a year, with three spot checks by mobile teams in between. Any policeman can stop a defective cab and send it to be put right, even if it is no worse than dirty. Drivers are scrutinised as carefully. There are 12,000 of them, who have all passed an examination in the 'knowledge of London'.

Preparation for this takes at least eighteen months, during which time they are to be seen riding around on light-weight motor-cycles, memorising the streets. It involves knowing most of London's 40,000 streets, and at the examination candidates are expected to be able to reel off eighteen journeys from memory, knowing the names of all the streets on the shortest route, the one-ways, and the no-right-turns (there are several hundred, and many operate only during the day). The successful candidate may mistake five streets in eighteen journeys, but no more.

In addition, he has to pass a medical examination and have a fairly clean criminal record. Just how good it has to be depends on the Deputy Commissioner's decision, but broadly, a conviction for housebreaking ten years before the application would be no bar, while a sexual offence at any time would be, because women with children put themselves in the cabbie's hands. If a cab driver is convicted of a serious driving offence, like being drunk in charge, he will have his licence revoked for three years *after* he has served whatever disqualification the justices order.

CHAPTER SIX

Crime and Divisional CID

It was much easier to get on with the CID than with the Uniform branch. This was odd, because when the possibility of writing this book was first discussed with the Yard, it was generally assumed, taking into account the CID's known passion for secrecy and dislike of journalists, that they would prove a great stumbling-block. One reason was perhaps that I found their work and aims easy to understand; given that we had different end-products, my professional life and a detective's have a lot in common. We both deal in information, in finding out things, often from sources that are not very willing to reveal what they know, or indeed that they know anything. We both are lone workers, we rely on our own poor intelligence and abilities.

The end-product of the detective's job is easy to understand: given a known or suspected crime, he discovers who did it and ferrets out the evidence to prove it. It requires no great mental leap to put oneself in his shoes, though I was surprised how important to him was his ability to get on with people, to talk to them, to extract what they knew and to detect when they were lying, and how relatively unimportant were his powers of deduction and observation. A real-life detective more often acts as a clearing-house for complaints and information and as an organiser of prosecutions than as a Sherlock Holmes.

On the other hand, a uniform policeman's job is far more complex; the result of decades of compromise between the State and the people. It is a vast mass of negatives: no disorder in the street, no loafing-about, no Peeping Toms, no car accidents, no pairs of prostitutes, no complaints by Members of Parliament about parking, no complaints by anybody about anything. Not too much zeal and not too little; not too blind and not too vigilant. A uniform policeman's working life is directed towards dozens of small, often unwritten and conflicting goals: a detective's towards a few simple, straightforward ones. To generalise: a uniform policeman tries to keep things as they are; the detective tries to change them. One has many restraints and the other few: simply – for that reason perhaps – it was easier to understand the one than the other.

In this section I have tried to describe the daily lives of detectives at different levels, dealing with different levels of crime. Discussion of the factors that influence their behaviour is reserved for a later chapter. Detectives look different from ordinary people. Their faces are expressionless; they have trained themselves to give nothing away, and after some time I found that I was copying them. By making a conscious effort, one can disconnect the muscles round one's mouth that normally show feelings. In the difficult social situations of a detective's work, it felt reassuring, like a little bit of armour, to throw the person to whom one was talking on the defensive by giving him no clues about one's thoughts. On top of this, detectives' faces have an ominous glaze due to exhaustion.

CID talk, too, is different and hard to follow. They converse in a peculiarly disjointed way, often two or three strands run through each conversation. They say the same things several times, ask the same questions over and over again. This disjointedness is perhaps accounted for by the disjointedness of their lives. Their main job is interviewing witnesses and they must come and go as the witnesses will; but at any moment there might be a major murder hunt and they find themselves up for three days and nights searching every house in a dozen streets. They live in what would be for most people a constant state of crisis, and their mannerisms reflect this. Their fractured conversation makes it easier to conceal what they are thinking. They affect a deliberate absence of conventional response; they won't laugh at jokes, don't react the way one expects, take a longer or shorter time to reply than normal; their speech and mannerisms are full of defensive disconnections.

A favourite CID game is played on the telephone. The aim is to have as long a conversation as possible with a friend without revealing your identity. Or again: I was to meet a DI Jones at an East End station. I walked into the CID office and said interrogatively: 'DI Jones of C10?' The Sergeant sitting there affected to understand that *I* was DI Jones, although the real Inspector Jones had been talking to him five minutes before. The correct response was to imply that his judgement was weak: 'You can't really think so!'

In part, this attitude of compliance with whatever situation your interlocutor likes to set up is a result of the world of lies in which detectives move. A sound basic strategy is for them to pretend to believe all that they hear: while a denial will shut off the flow, passivity may produce something worth-while. As one young detective explained: 'You must never let the villains think that you don't know. One said to a mate of mine: "Let me off and I'll give you a good slaughter." He's stupid. "What's that?" he says, and the villain nearly changed his mind. *I* knew because I'd been told an hour before: it's a run-in for stolen lorries. The villain got six months and I got a slaughter.'

The CID office at Kensington police station is a big room, about twenty feet by fifty. It contains some thirty pale wooden desks: twenty face to face in a row down the centre and the rest in pairs by the window wall. At one end there is a small square office for the Detective Inspector. He keeps the door open unless he has a caller, in which case it is shut. Just in front of his door, at a slight angle denoting status, is the desk of the first-class Sergeant, who faces down the room so that he can keep an eye on the personnel. There are only a dozen typewriters, and they are continually being carried from desk to desk.

On a table at one end of the room there are three telephones and another in a sound-muffling hood. These come off the station switchboard downstairs. At the other end of the room there is a direct outside line with its own number, so that detectives can ring in quickly, and informants don't have to dial the give-away 1113 of a police station. These are the only telephones, so that there is often a crowd of people over and round the table making notes, fidgeting, waiting for each other to finish with the crime books which are kept on the table there.

The CID are not lavishly equipped. The room is decorated with notices, photographs and CRO files, which may not be shut away in a drawer in case they are urgently needed. On the walls there are a list of official interpreters; a District Fingerprint Officer's duty list, giving telephone numbers for night hours; a board with photographs and identikit pictures of wanted men – most of them scruffy and improbable-looking, Bruce Reynolds[1], the Great Train Robber, alone looking smooth and executive; a cross memo from the lab on the lax way in which vaginal swabs from dead women are being sent in; a big blue Minor Crime Book with thick covers, shut by a crank handle; Divisional Crime Information sheets hanging by the telephone; a list of persons in custody; a digest of crime in the district; a book for personal messages to the detectives, a book in which are entered all the houses searched; messages from provincial forces; two Grid Crime Books – like the Minor Crime Book – one for odd and one for even numbers; a CID night-duty list; a prisoners' antecedents book; a duty book in which DCs and Sergeants write where they intend to go when they go out (they have to repeat this downstairs for the benefit of the Uniform Superintendent who nominally has control over them); and another for TDCs.

Each officer has a diary in which he writes on the left-hand page where he actually went: 'Came on duty at 8.30, read Infos, Circulations and Police Orders. Proceeded on patrol until 9.30, then to West London Court until 11.50. Then to 1 Nowhere Road, N.1, *re* inquiry into larceny

[1] Later captured and tried.

gas meter. At 12.45 entered Nags Head public house to pur-
chase refreshment for informant. 1.15, proceeded on patrol,
stopped John Henry EVERSEDGE in Bryanston Square, re
movements, satisfactory . . .' As a control on officers' movements it is virtually useless. The important part is written
on the right-hand page: their expenses for the week. When the
Metropolitan Police accounts are audited, paper is pasted over
the left-hand page so that the auditors can't read the diary part.

In the back they put their arrests. Wednesday is diary
day, when they have to be read by the Chief Inspector of
the division: people bend to it, asking each other where
they were last Sunday. On the table by the telephone there
is a loose-leaf folder full of teleprinter messages, each in-
itialled by the DI and first-class sergeant. There are recent
police gazettes, Orders and Confidential Infos., all bound.
There is a portrait book of local thieves.

Life revolves round the Grid Crime Book. As crimes are
reported to the police – either direct by telephone, or by
a uniform crew after a 999 call – they are written in this
book, each one to a page, and numbered. Towards the end
of the year this book will have 1,700 pages in it. The DI reads
the entries and assigns crimes to officers by writing their
names against them. There are so many that every morning
the detectives run their eyes down their assignments, trying to guess which are the likely jobs, which are the jobs
that will get nowhere.

The DI checks every paper going out of the office for
spelling, accuracy and style. Detectives have three main
qualifications: ability to arrest people, ability to do their
paper work, and ability to give evidence in court. The first
two seldom go together, and the more active officers are
crucified by their typewriters. The DI at this moment is
sending back a legal aid form for the third time, with an
evil smile: 'You got the offence right last time, James; this
time you've left out that she's married.' He also keeps the
prisoners' property store under his control: the key lives
in his desk with three feet of chain and two pounds of lead

attached. 'Anyone who says: "I forgot I had it in my pocket" is well for it. Next to other people's wives, more good men have got into bother in this job over prisoners' property than anything else.'

A small, dapper man with a moustache and wavy, greying hair; he looks more like a brewer's executive than a policeman. He is exhausted: there was a suicide the night before just as his head touched the pillow, and he had to go in case it was murder. He assigns a DC to be my partner for the next three weeks simply by lifting up his head and yelling: 'Edwards, cum earh!'

Man management is so brutally Victorian in the CID that anyone unable to take it has left years ago (see p. 50). As one experienced sergeant put it: 'If a man can't get on with his governor, that's his fault. He's a failure as far as the Department goes.' At the same time, this master and man relationship is tempered by a real comradeship based on the equality of all detectives as investigating officers. Rather like air-line pilots, they all ply the same trade, they are all equals in that sense.

Edward 'cums earh' and is ordered to take me out. Happy, he leaves his hated typewriter, his tray full of dockets, burying the most sensitive at the bottom in case the DI rummages through it, shrugs himself into the short padded coat that young detectives wear for protection against cold and blows, and away we go. He is a tall lean young man with six years' service – that makes him about twenty-five. He has a long face, and a way of walking, leaning forward, with his lower jaw dropped. At first it makes him look worried and confused; then, when I know him better, he resembles a dangerous fish. We go to find a dip.

Patrolling

As he walks along Kensington High Street, he scans the faces of everyone coming the other way, particularly the young men. I find I am used to walking with my eyes on the ground to avoid the embarrassment of meeting others' eyes. At first I miss all sorts of things that he sees.

Catching pickpockets is one of the purest of police arts. It needs two in a team, for juridical as well as practical reasons. In a burglary, an independent witness, the householder, exists who can prove that there actually has been a crime, and the police, if they catch someone, are not just charging him with something made up out of their heads. But in pickpocketing, typically, the loser is completely unaware that anything has gone. He – or more likely she – cannot swear that they didn't lose their purse any time in the previous sixty minutes. Often, too, the dip has passed the purse on to one or two more members of his team; and in the minute between the dip and arrest the purse can have been gutted and thrown away. So it is police evidence against dip's evidence, and as routine the police work in pairs to corroborate each other.

Because of my inexperience, our chances today were not good. It was like going out with a Scottish gillie after stag: I would, metaphorically, be crashing through the heather and looking every way for the frightened creatures. Ron Edwards told me that he'd spent a year without any luck, then suddenly, like learning to ride a bicycle, it had clicked. He could suddenly see the 'shape' of a dip team at work – the formation they had to adopt, with two men at the front, one stealing, passing the purse behind the victim to the carrier, who passed it away down a tail of accomplices. Then, across the road, would be the inconspicuous look-out, watching for people as alert and watchful as himself.

Ron had learned to look for men crossing and re-crossing the side-roads, always against the press of people, so they would be carried away by the crowd before the theft was noticed. He learned to look for men at the front and back of bus queues; the one at the back would drive the queue forward, and the one at the front would turn round and go against the stream – sometimes downstairs from the top of the bus, harvesting as he went. He would try to spend two or three days continuously patrolling up and down, looking out for the same faces; waiting for the amorphous crowd to resolve itself.

It was a very odd sensation to be a hunter among this sleepy mass of people, Ron beside me, hungry as a piranha among shoals of fat fish, playing a game that none of those around us in Kensington High Street knew about.

After half an hour we went into a department store to get warm. Back through the shop, through a double rubber door into the bleak inward parts, and finally to the security office where a neat store detective with large brown eyes and excellent legs squeals at her boss: 'Mr P! Made the tea?' After this refreshing interlude we walked on to call at a block of flats where two pieces of antique furniture had been stolen from the common hall. A big pile of old *Queen* magazines stands on the floor where the thieves took them out of one of the chests. August 1957 is on the top; it has a cover photo showing an aristocratic girl with a round porcelain face and a bright red mouth; her skirt, ten years before the maxis, hangs well below the ears of the labrador squatting in the heather. The lady who lives in the ground floor flat comes out. She has no useful information, except the time within half an hour. She concludes: 'It makes me quite sick. They're obviously watching me. Well, I mean, any morning in our beds . . .!'

We say goodbye to our lunches and start checking the neighbours across the street, preferably spinsters in the bottom flats who might have seen the van that the thieves used. In fact there are three. They 'haven't taken their eyes off the street all morning', and they have seen nothing. A workman stacking tiles exactly across the road has seen nothing either: he looks vacuous and pleased with himself. We search round for the milkman – who hadn't been in the right spot – try the porter across the road, and having spent a fruitless hour go on to the next thing.

In the end, furniture-stealing occupied most of our time on this ground. What seemed to be happening was this: an antique dealer in Fulham, who was known to be something of a rascal, would go round calling on these flats, spying out the pieces standing in the halls. If he was challenged, he would say, quite accurately, he was a dealer looking for furniture to buy. He would then go home and send a couple of men out with a job sheet which would say: 'Collect oak chest from hall of Monster Mansions.' If they were challenged with the chest in their hands they would show the job sheet: if anyone traced them back to the dealer, he would say that he had a telephone order from someone who he assumed was the owner to remove the chest. He was terribly sorry for the mistake, he couldn't understand it.

Since they were seldom challenged, they would take the chest to a warehouse the police didn't know, then send them to antique dealers down in the country. He took care to have nothing stolen that was very distinctive, that could be recognised from a written description. It was extremely unlikely that he would be caught. The car which he drove and the van which his men drove were both known. I dug through the crime books at the station and made a map showing where and when they struck; we watched his home, we spent days and days in the sleet patrolling the likely places; yet nothing came of it all. It is one thing to know who is doing a crime, what it is, how it is done, what is to be stolen, what vehicles are going to be used, and quite another thing to catch him at it.

Partly this was due to a shortage of time and equipment: if we had had a couple of cars with Regional Crime Squad radios, or even personal radios, we could have followed the van about, but the only force which the police could spare was car-less Ron and his civilian assistant.

We spend the rest of the afternoon patrolling: slithering over the slush frozen into smooth little hills on the pavement. It seemed to me that we were very conspicuous: two large young men walking slowly, looking keenly about them, going nowhere. I put this to my companion. 'That's part of the point: you stand out as law, but the only people who notice are the villains. You watch their eyes because they are watching for you. I can smell them, I feel them in the pit of my stomach.' After a few days' practice, I saw what he meant: the ordinary pedestrian becomes almost invisible, but those who were up to no good flashed their unconcealable code of fear to us. They were too alert. However hard they tried to suppress it, their anxiety to spot us made them glow as if they were outlined in neon.

Charles Dickens, interviewing the entire Metropolitan Detective Police in 1850, asked: 'Whether in a place of public amusement, a thief knows an officer, and an officer knows a thief – supposing them, beforehand strangers to each other – because each recognises in the other, under all disguise, an inattention to what is going on, and a purpose that is not the purpose of being entertained?' And was told: 'Yes, that is exactly the way of it.' Of course, again, it was one thing to know who in the street had evil intentions, and quite another to catch him during the crucial few seconds of a crime.

These weeks of patrolling began to make me see the fascination of police work. They transformed the dull streets of the city where I live into a hunting-ground, made me see my fellow creatures in terms of the oldest and most exciting game: as predators and prey. It came as a surprise to feel the urgency even of mild chases like this, the stalking round corners, the dash round the back of a block, the pretended interest in door nameplates, the quick sideways glance. The outcome was uncertain enough to both sides to make it interesting: policemen have been shot, stabbed and beaten senseless playing this game, even in peaceful London; more often villains have gone to prison.

Two weeks before, Ron had caught a very good breaker, a grave elderly man in a bowler hat, dark jacket, pinstripe trousers, a gold watch-chain, a heavy expensive overcoat and a gleaming briefcase. When he stopped him with his vacant expression, the man reacted with controlled indignation. He would see this young man suffered for his impertinence. Appprehensive, Ron pressed him. The upshot was satisfactory: the briefcase contained a fine set of lock-picks, levers and jewellery. My attachment turned out to be very typical of police work: nothing like this happened at all.

Magistrates' Court

The next morning Ron had to be in court at ten: when I arrive at nine-fifteen, he is fussing around, scratching his papers together, angry because he had just heard that, while we were out the day before, the Aid on court duty had taken an arrest to court that should have been left for Ron. They were squabbling: 'It's so aggravating. I knew nothing about it. If I had had a chat with him, he'd have said he'd plead and he'd have stayed that way. He just had you over for a ninny. Said he'd plead, then when he got in the box he gave you a grin and said, "Not guilty". The bastard. I'll be writing for a whole day now, thanks to you. I *know* this lad – he'd have pleaded all right,' Ron said.

The trouble is that by his pleading 'Not guilty,' the case has been sent for trial at Sessions, presenting Ron with a mass of work. The deceitful accused has to be provided with legal aid at the expense of two reports, witnesses have to be organised, statements taken; all work that Ron hates and this time for no better outcome. The evidence is quite conclusive. But as so often, this villain prefers bail now to freedom at the other end of his sentence; he might well devote the weeks before his case comes up to more intensive crime.

So Ron is in a thoroughly bad mood. We set off with long strides through the morning air to West London Magistrates' Court, which stands in a side-street by Olympia, about twenty minutes' walk away. The crisp air and the exercise cheer him up, and the bustle of the court restores his temper. The square hall is already full of families, witnesses, policemen, the garish friends of prostitutes, mothers come to bail their sons out in anticipation of a remand. Detectives and uniform policemen and solicitors are talking urgently with their customers in corners, squatting on the floor with papers spread out on their knees. It is a sort of stock exchange of minor crime.

Courts are part of policemen's lives. They come two or three times a week, bringing their efforts for judgement. We have no one to talk to in the hall today, so we dive down the corridor to the gaoler's office – where a police sergeant, who knows Ron well, pulls the brass lever to open the wicket. We plunge further, hammer at the judas of the cell corridor to be let in, then wait again to get through the big steel gate in the square inner hall where the prisoners are kept.

If the front hall was archaic, the tangle of people sitting on the benches is like a Newgate print. Here is a long, lean young doctor doing *The Times* crossword: he wears an arrogant imperial beard, he was rioting drunk in the street last night. Next to him sits a disgruntled, smooth-faced, neat little man, with a blue cardigan under his tweed suit, and beyond, a pudgy-faced schoolboy in a blazer with his cap on his knee. A friend of Ron is dealing with them. They were arrested for mutual masturbation in a parked car in the middle of the afternoon. The crime is the boy's youth. The two erstwhile lovers sit side by side, paying no heed to each other. Neither looks very attractive. It is always surprising what Eros does for people.

This is an offence that has to be prosecuted by the Director of Public Prosecutions, whose solicitor now appears behind the grill. He is a tall, ambitious-looking young man with heavy glasses and a bulging briefcase. He is let in, bringing the boy's aunt in tow. He asks the boy if he'll give evidence against the man: the boy says he won't, and the DPP's man says, 'Let him go' to the gaoler. Within the minute he has vanished from the scene. The man, a chef in a big hotel, whose pots and pans are being handled by someone else, sits there unmoved.

The doctor finishes the last of the crossword, flips the paper over and starts reading the opera notices. His long legs stick out into the room so that the assistant gaoler has to stretch over them to see when our job is on. Next to him, two huge prison warders sit together with shiny handcuffs dripping out of their pockets. Their peaked caps bend up at the front like the *Wehrmacht's*: They have brought a man on remand for murder up from Brixton, but their writs run out in here. The CID dealing with the job have to take him into court and see that he doesn't fly away – as he seems quite likely to, because, from his cell down the corridor, where the remands in custody are kept, come screaming and the noise of kicking. It was louder before we arrived, but one of the screws took his shoes away.

The rest of the room is filled with three prostitutes, a woman in for neglecting her baby, half a dozen vagrants, drunks and people done for 'sus', quite a lot of CID, and a very pretty probation officer of the new sort, her skirts rather shorter than the prostitutes'. We hang our coats up in a little police office full of anxious people waiting for the direct line to CRO to check their prisoners' previous convictions. All over London at this moment, policemen are phoning from the courts on this last-minute errand, and the CRO switchboard is like a mad computer with flashing lights and its servants tearing up and down with CRO files.

After three-quarters of an hour, our case comes on. We wait at the starting-line, then shoot down the corridor. I sit on the bench in front of the populace – almost as strange-looking a collection as those in custody – and watch Ron with interest. He goes into the witness-box and spreads his papers out deliberately; scarcely an adult in real terms, here he is a figure of some importance. He asks the Magistrate to remand the case for further inquiries, and then the prisoner asks for bail.

Ron drops his jaw and looks at him, not in surprise, but like a large animal about to eat a small one as a matter of business. He turns to the Magistrate, saying in an immensely solid and convincing way: 'I object to bail, Your Worship, on the grounds that the offence may well be repeated.' The Magistrate looks over his glasses at the dock and asks what he has to say. The prisoner doesn't know this game, so the Magistrate explains: 'If you still want bail, the officer will have to tell me about your record, if you have one, so that when you come to trial the court may possibly be prejudiced.' The prisoner sees the drift, gets out that he doesn't object after all, and is led away again.

We get our things together and go round the corner for

a drink to celebrate not having been savaged by the Magistrate. Some of them are people of menace to police, cranky and bad-tempered, who throw lightning bolts in court. Their occasional indignant letters to the Commissioner about his younger minions' procedural shortcomings often produce severe depressions in the more sensitive policemen.

Housebreakings

Ron spends the afternoon slaving over his hated legal aid reports, so I go out with an amiable sergeant, a gentle man who was until a few years ago an officer in the Merchant Navy. He drives a little blue sports car and we whirl round on the never-ending tour of broken-into homes. The first is a flat high up in a new block. The loser is an old, old lady, haughty and alone; she lives in the quiet of leather-framed cabinet photographs of the dead, attended by a sixty-year-old maid. She wore two diamond rings to play bridge with friends on Tuesday; now it is Thursday and they are gone. Nothing else has been stolen or disturbed; that, the iron-framed windows, the absence of signs of entry, and the vigilant porter who stopped us downstairs, make us think that she's lost them somewhere in the flat. We spend half-an-hour looking under the beds and chairs, then give up.

Finished with her, we cross the road to a garden square and up long flights of stairs to a small, juvenile version of the flat which we have just left, where two working débutantes live. They were broken into and the place was ransacked – cameras stolen and jewellery gone. It was odd how soon one became callous about it: there would be no prints, no clues at all, nothing one could do. The Sergeant had listened to the same stories about how extraordinary it was that the thieves had missed the mink, or the Leica camera or the holiday money in a jam-jar, and always how, luckily, the loser had taken her pearl necklace or her sewing-machine to her mother's the night before, and how 'they must have been watching me for days'. In fact, burglars ring bells and bang on doors in a random way, knowing that if one house isn't empty with all its doors unlocked, another will be.

So we all sat in the rosy light of the table lamps and dusted the drink bottles for marks, while being given a little genteel refreshment out of the one at the back that hadn't been touched. The Sergeant's grey plastic box with the finger-print kit, the powders, tweezers and a huge Sherlock Holmes magnifying-glass put in for a joke, aroused great interest and made the girls feel that somebody was doing something for them. To make a convincing job of it, he had to take their fingerprints for elimination – if their marks turned up on the bottles it would be no great forensic discovery – and he had no cleanprint forms. He said he would come back with them, packed up and we trooped downstairs. 'I could get them up the nick and take their prints with ink, but that's really for slag. You don't want to get nice girls' hands dirty like that. When I go back I'll take them some flowers – I usually do that for the lady losers on the ground – it's very upsetting for them, being broken into, and it makes them feel somebody takes an interest.'

The messy business of ink and fingerprint forms would do for rubbish; nicely-brought up girls deserved a clean print and a bunch of flowers. The reason was not subser-vience. Policemen bitterly resent wealthy people who patron-ise them or who expect them to fetch parcels and open car doors, but they still represent the ideal that policing is all about. Theirs are the standards which the police are fighting to preserve; often they are more precious to policemen than they are to the people who live by them, because police see intimately what life is like without them. In some sense the stable, moneyed, well-behaved, neat, polite world of 'decent' people – often so suffocating to those born into it – is like a promised land at the top of Sisyphus' hill, towards which the police roll their boulder of arrests and prosecu-tions all their working-lives.

This Sergeant was a kind, gentle man. Far from being a red-faced thief-taker, he said that he would never be a great copper, but that in catching thieves he was doing something definitely useful: 'I don't like people taking other people's property. It upsets me.'

Executing a Brief

Two more days passed in patrolling with Ron: interesting, at times even exciting, and I began to get obsessed with the antique dealer. On the second evening, we met after supper, and I drove him across London to Lewisham, to look at a house which he intended to search. This was part of an involved job that had begun some time before. A couple of young men had gone into a shop in Kensington High Street with a cheque-book and a Barclaycard to buy a woman's suede coat. The shop-girl, more alert than most, took a suspicion to them and snatched the Barclaycard: they turned and left. She rang the police.

The area car, *Alpha one*, took the call, picked her up and cruised the back streets. Luckily they saw the two, chased them, and though they separated, one was cornered in a cul-de-sac. He was arrested, put in the car, jumped out again, was recaptured, and finally got to the nick. He was still carrying the brand-new suede coat in the bag of the shop where he bought it – a happy piece of evidence. The Q car went straight over to his house and searched it that evening, but found nothing. Next morning Ron got the job of untangling his frauds: with the aid of the cheque index at CRO, he discovered a sort of slug's trail of them round the West End. From the arrested boy's CRO file it became apparent that the whole family were villains.

On balance, Ron fancied the boy's elder brother, who had form for doping greyhounds, desertion, speeding and fraud, as the one who escaped; the arrested boy didn't, as he put it, 'seem to have the bottle for the job by himself'. The youngest brother had previous convictions – in fact, the family's pile of CRO dockets stood eight inches high. There was a photograph of him, but not, unfortunately, of the eldest. When I came in that morning, Ron was stapling down the Borstal photo of the youngest on to a sheet with photos of eight other young men that were kept in a box for the purpose: we strolled round to the shop to see if the girl could pick him out from among the irrelevant faces. She looked hard and couldn't. It made him more sure that the elder brother was the one.

The rest of the day was spent in complicated researches by telephone with the local council's rating department and the voters' list. Ron established that the address given in the latest CRO form was wrong, that the family had split up, the father and the daughter living in one place, the wife, the brothers and her lover living in the next street. After lunch Ron typed out two informations and set to work on two blank search warrants. He crossed out 'in the daytime', leaving 'by night', and crossed out 'and it appearing to me to be necessary, you are hearby authorised and empowered, having previously made known your authority and with such assistance as may be found necessary, to use force for the effect of such entry, whether by breaking open doors or otherwise' because, 'They'll let us in all right now their son's on bail, and it makes it that much more difficult to get a warrant if you leave "force" in'. He wrote 'property' after 'divers things to wit' that he wanted to search for, because, 'There's no point telling chummy what you're looking for. If you don't find it this time, he'll make damn sure you don't find it next.'

We find someone to drive us round to court, take the information to the Chief Clerk, who signs it, then to a minion who stamps it with a pro-forma for the Magistrate to sign, and then we go into the courtroom, whisper what we want to the court Inspector, and wait for a gap in the proceedings. After a chirrupy, bedraggled old lady tramp has been fined ten shillings for being drunk and incapable – 'I drink to kill the pain in me feet, your wushup' – Ron is motioned to the witness box. Being cautious, he goes right up to the Magistrate's desk and swears in a whisper that by Almighty God the information which he has given is the truth.

Courts are indecently public places, full, by their nature, of criminals; there is no point in broadcasting what he is going to do. That is one reason why policemen sometimes search without warrants. When he gets back to the nick, he should, to protect himself, in case the warrant gets snatched in the raid – and for some reason the record of it gets mislaid at the court – enter it in the Warrants Book, and get the DI to sign it on the back. He doesn't, again for a tactical reason based on habit, because although he means to execute the warrant that night, he might not be able. An Aid, or a uniform PC, anxious for a good arrest, might see the unexecuted entry, go over to the address, and bungle the business, or, more irritating still, succeed.

Towards ten we meet in the now dead CID office: Ron, cheerful and wolfish, a nice, solid West Country DC called John, and a quiet sergeant who has nothing else to do that evening. Ron rings Cannon Row to make a meet with the Q car – since they started the job, they can hardly be left out – but they have set out on patrol, so he rings Information Room to fix a meet with them by radio.

A couple of streets short of the objective, both cars pull up for a tactical conference. It is decided that, since one of the two houses has no phone, it is safe to raid them one at a time: those done first won't be able to get round to warn the others; if they go somewhere else, we may be able to follow them. Since the people in the arrested boy's house already know the Q car, it is agreed we shall do that one; so they will do the first. We park outside and watch the Q car crew steal away into the dark round the back of the house. In a minute they come back swearing. It has been empty for months. Ron's staff-work is sarcastically praised.

In a less-good temper, we go to the other house. The Q car parks round the corner. The street is a cul-de-sac. They agree to nab anyone coming down it if they hear shouting. The front door gives straight onto the street, so I am stood there with instructions to shout if anyone comes out; John can't speak to the family because he took the boy to court, so he goes down the alley to watch the back door. Ron and the Sergeant will execute the warrant. I borrow a torch from the Q car – a good heavy one – we put our coats on and slide off.

After the arranged minute's wait, we hear Ron banging at the side door. Gleams of light shoot out over our heads. We stand there, pressed against the brickwork, not to frighten anyone coming out. In the dark, when there's nothing to look at, you point your ears, and we could follow the progress of the search by the shouting getting louder and softer as they laced their way backwards and forwards across the house. 'You're dhronk, you're intoxicated, you're rude, you're aggressive', someone shouts in a bad-tempered Irish-Scots voice, a woman's, and we hear Ron's loud, flat reply: 'If you're not satisfied, Madam, ring the local Station and get someone over.'

When it seems unlikely that anyone will bolt, John goes off through the hoar-rimed grass to search a shed at the bottom. I look over a derelict car parked beside the house. The old childish pleasure of knifing through the dark with long torch beams is as strong as ever: the elation of having nerved oneself to argue with a complete stranger, and not having to do it, the cold air, the stars and the shouts from inside the house make me feel very cheerful.

Ron and the Sergeant leave amid bellows of rage and the slamming of the front door. They have found nothing: Ron's tactical assumption that the gear would have been hidden after the Q car search ten days before and the people might have now got careless, was ill-founded. If there had been anything there, they probably wouldn't have made such an indignant noise. As it was, the boy who was still on remand and probably expected the energy of the police prosecution to have a material effect on his future, follows his mother about, saying: 'Please, Ma, don't aggravate them. Please don't.'

By now, Ron is not in favour. For half the way back he defends his judgement with tedious repetition, and then sinks into a moody silence. In Bermondsey a Q car pulls up, objecting to two loads of large men on their ground in the middle of the night. There follows one of those odd police social occasions: people in the dark, leaning in at car windows, old acquaintances brushed up, introductions made. I transfer to our Q car to talk to the crew, one of them takes my place. It is 2.30 a.m. London is police land.

Some Arrests

The next day one of Ron's villains came to see him. Since the boy's on bail for larceny and Ron had arrested him, he asked me to come as a witness that the visit is nothing to do with bribery. The boy, a volatile, likeable young rogue, with hair standing out of an overgrown crew-cut and a cheap, smart suit, brought his pretty, blonde common-law wife. Their landlord wanted them and her three children out of the two rooms they inhabit. To get them out he had accused the boy of stealing £6 from the gas meter. This, the second of the two charges for which the boy was on bail, had already been sent for trial at Sessions, but then the landlord said that he would drop it if they left.

After a long, circuitous debate, conducted on the friendliest of terms, Ron observed: 'The aggravation of it. He verbals up my villains and then says *he*'ll let him off. I'm afraid he'll have to explain that to the bench at Sessions: they won't be best pleased.' The boy said: 'Ron, when we get in court, I've got to call you a liar on the first one – my solicitor says it's the only hope. No hard feelings?' Ron replied: 'If only I had a pound for every time I've been called a liar.'

It was odd, but impressive, that the boy came to see 'his' detective rather than a solicitor, or the Citizens' Advice Bureau, and that his detective found this the natural and proper thing. The fact that in a few weeks they would be confronting each other in the court room, that Ron would do his best to get the boy his fourth conviction, and the boy would do his best to discredit the police evidence, was quite irrelevant. This was accepted as part of the game played out for the benefit of society. The situation, in reality, was more like that between a doctor and his patient.

146

After court we went back to the nick and found, for once, nothing to do. We went to eat a delicious lunch in the BEA staff canteen where the police had an unofficial entrée. After a stroll round to look for the furniture thieves, we walked back to the nick again and found a message from two detectives from a northern division who had come to arrest a fraudsman on the ground; they wanted help and advice. We went to the address. There, in a basement flat, we found a scene of confusion in a baroque setting. There were Spanish iron filigree and purple-beaded lampshades, with two tweedy detectives and a miserable, thin, forty-year-old queer with dyed black hair mincing around tearfully among the proceeds of several years' fraud.

Their main quarry had flown out of the back door, over the garden wall and through a tiny estate of prefabs. Normally in a London street it wouldn't be possible to escape like this, and only the local CID would know the catch of these particular houses. Anyway, they had lost one, and were now taking their irritation out on the survivor by searching the entire flat. It made, one had to admit, an impressive sight. Suitcases full of shoes, blankets by the bundle, still done up in their cellophane, bedspreads, cases of men's toilet water, all, it appeared, got with stolen cheque-books and credit cards, and singularly useless-looking.

The detectives' direct questions discovered that the man who kept sinking into a chair, sniffling into his poodle's fur, earned his living by male prostitution, and had saved up £5,000 to buy a bungalow for his old age. While we were rummaging through all his tacky gear, trying to find what was bent and what was straight, the phone rang. Ron pulled the queer out of his chair and told him, menacingly and unarguably, to answer it. The queer's side of the conversation was tremulous and terse: 'No, dear, I'm not very well. No, I got a bit of bother. No, don't come round. No, not for a bit.'

Ron, with his ear crammed up against the man's head, could hear that the caller was asking for a rendezvous, so he grabbed the phone, put his hand over the mouthpiece and hissed: 'Say you'll go.' 'All right, then', said the dreary voice, 'I'll come over. Yes, I'll be an hour. All right, then. Goodbye, dear.' Ron snapped his finger on the button and asked who it was. 'My hairdresser. He often rings up to ask how I am.' To me, confused by this odd situation, it seemed quite likely, but Ron pressed him further: 'Which hairdresser is that? You said just now you had it dyed round the corner. Do you mean he rings up – just when you've got the law here? Don't aggravate me. That was your mate, wasn't it?' Quaveringly, he said that it was, ringing from *his* hairdresser's at Shepherd's Bush. Ron and one of the visitors drove off to nick him; the other and I sat down to watch our friend.

The detective was exhausted, he made no move when the poove got up and wandered about. He seemed to have cheered up, and offered us a drink, then went out to make some coffee. Feeling that I'd better live the part, I followed him to keep watch and then we sat to drink it. He asked if he could go to the lavatory. Again I followed. The evening was getting dark: in the basement it was all black and subdued reds. The three of us sat in silence, hardly able to see each other. The poove occasionally got up and pottered to and fro, then sat down again. It didn't seem necessary to follow him. After a long silence, the detective leapt up and ran to the back, shouting: 'The bugger's had it away!' I could have sworn he was still sitting opposite us in the dark – but he wasn't. He had flown out of the back window like his friend. I slunk back to the station, walking a mile and a half, feeling oddly raw, like a child that has done something silly and has been denied a treat, or hasn't worked hard enough and has failed an exam that he could easily have passed. At the station Ron was in a superior mood. He had handled his side of the affair with competence, and could now be sarcastic about the visitor's ineptitude. There was relief that I hadn't told the management what had happened. If it came out, the detective could have been thrown out of the department, or at the least, he would have lost a fortnight's pay. It was a serious business. I felt rather reduced by all this and inclined to slink off home.

Luckily, I stayed. It was now 7.30 p.m. and the CID office was empty but for the late relief – the gentle sergeant. Ron was downstairs having another talk with his cheque artist, when the sergeant began to run about calling out for someone to go and arrest a housebreaker. Ron agreed that he would go. John, who had gone with us to Bromley, came too. We got into his car and all went down to the bottom end of the ground, among the slag of Earl's Court, where crimes tend to be many and small and arrests easy.

The situation, Ron explained, was this: two men had been released from prison a month before – a Pole and a Hungarian. They took a room together in a hotel by Earl's Court tube station. The Pole was determined to go straight, but the Hungarian immediately started breaking again. Since he brought the spoils back to his room, the Pole was likely to be arrested and tried as a receiver. To protect himself, he had given information about the breaker, who was, at that moment, out at work. To salt the business, he seemed to have said in his poor English that the man was dangerous.

We found the hotel and double-parked – the uniform police knew the car. The room number was a low one, suggesting that it was on the ground or first floor, so we went into a hotel two doors down, through the building and out into the dark garden. I found my face was flushed; I was shaking with exhilaration and anticipation. The room we wanted gave on to a balcony. We agreed that Ron should risk being flung off it, while John and I went in the door. Having settled this, we crept into the hotel, past the thieves' room and upstairs – to see how the land lay.

On the floor above, a door was open; a striking blonde in a tight black dress was talking loudly and crossly to her boy-friend. She had just got home and found her room ransacked. She was impressed by our quick arrival – she must have rung the police station while we were on our way. Ron wrote down a quick description of the things which she had lost and we went back downstairs. We knocked on the breaker's door, but he was not there. The white-haired Pole was sitting on his bed in the sparse light. He jumped up and showed us the wardrobe filled with things which he said had been stolen. We quietened him: he was shouting with nervousness. We went into the next room: narrow, bleak, with two beds almost touching and fly-blown Spanish bullfight posters on the walls; a tiny electric heater smeared with burnt milk. There was a smell of inadequately laundered clothes and unwashed bodies. John stood by the door as patiently as a cow in a field; Ron went to the balcony and kept watch through the net curtains of the thief's room. I sat on the end of the bed and read *Reader's Digest*. The young Australian, whose room it was, looked at us with incurious eyes.

We seemed to wait for a long time. Once, the Pole started crashing about and Ron darted out to go in through the balcony window, but it was a false alarm. The other Australian came in. He said 'Police?', but we didn't introduce ourselves. After forty-five minutes – a very short wait in CID terms (it could have been six or ten hours) – there were noises next door. Ron looked in the window and signalled that we were on. John and I got up. I felt dazed with boredom and the heat and the knowledge that the man might be savage (it was in one of these hotels that Podola shot a CID man from the same station). I crowded out behind John. He knocked on the door and said very solemnly: 'I am a police officer. I have reason to believe that you have stolen property here.'

Ron stepped in through the balcony window, artistically draped in the long muslin curtain. He was relieved that he didn't have to fight on the balcony with its low railing and long drop in the dark. He started to shout at the Pole – he had to protect him from the Hungarian who must not guess who shopped him. The breaker is a small, alert, intelligent little man. About thirty-five, like many other good Hungarian villains, he came across at the Revolution, and they all have CRO numbers, beginning 56 or 57. John dealt with him, leaving his unexpected friend to Ron. He began to get out his own belongings, but then Ron stopped him and went through the rest himself. It must be harder than it looks to search a stranger, even a cooperative one. I could see that he was having to twist his hands to very odd angles to get into the man's pockets, even though this was something which he had done hundreds of times before.

He had, besides the usual things, a table knife with a strong springy blade – good for slipping Yale locks – a nail-file – although his nails were filthy – and a brand new screwdriver. He maintained stoutly that he'd 'bought it to mend my car, which is frozen up.'

'What sort of car?'

'A Black Wolseley.'

'What number?' I couldn't have thought of a number and neither could he.

'What are you going to *do* with the screwdriver?'

'Mend my car.'

Ron asked, rather cunningly: 'What are you actually going to unscrew to unfreeze it?' This was going too far. He turned and said: 'Please don't make fun of me, sir.' The conversation came to an end. His things were piled at one end of the bed; the other end was heaped with property which Ron had also found in the wardrobe. There was the radio lost by the girl upstairs – he had 'had it for years'. There, too, was a set of women's underclothes which 'belong to a friend in hospital'.

The Hungarian produced a horrid pen-stand out of his mac pocket. He said he 'bought it in a shop'. Then he said: 'No, I didn't. I got it from a negro in a café. I don't know his name.' Then, later, he said: 'No, I didn't. I took it as a security on a ten-bob loan. I don't know the man's name or where he lives.' He maintained stoutly that he had never been in trouble with the police before, and kept it up consistently. We had to admire him when his Criminal Record form showed fifteen previous convictions. He stood there silently. Then he started to tremble and, curiously, to rattle. The detectives traced the tiny noise to his left-hand pocket – which *he* had turned out. It contained a huge key-ring with thirty or forty different keys all ringing a tiny betraying carillon. Later on that night Ron and John turned his room over, and found yet another Hungarian in bed, naked but for an immense gold watch. Unbelievably, he said he bought it for five pounds, 'It must have been stolen.' So that made three arrests in as many hours.

An Unfortunate Manslaughter

It is a cold February morning in the Horseferry Road. The weather is drizzle inclining to sleet. I am to meet a detective superintendent from south of the river, at a post-mortem. Since it is part of his job to investigate murders on his division he is here at least once a week. A room, that most citizens pass through but few see, is as familiar to him as his own office. The mortuary looks like a quaint period tea-shop behind its neat fence and broad gate – to let hearses through. Inside there is a tiled front hall, with waiting-rooms and offices off it, and, deeper, a couple of big white-tile sheds lit by skylights. Each has a pair of crude operating tables with water-hoses hooked over the top. In the first shed the tables are empty but in the second there is a mass of people.

The most conspicuous are naked and quiet: a couple of very old ladies, waxily clean; their hands so relaxed by death they look like seals' flippers. There is a sad young man, his chest shows two half-moon scars where incipient breasts have been removed and a glass testicle recovered with interest by the pathologist is balanced on his stomach. His history shows hermaphroditism and schizophrenia; after several stays in mental hospitals and operations to confirm his masculinity, he has found a tranquillity which the doctors couldn't give him. Beside him lies the body of an elderly jeweller, crow-barred to death by a robbery team as he opened up his shop one morning the week before. His head is seared with crude black stitches where the surgeons tried to relieve the pressure on his brain. His anaesthetist, an extremely beautiful Indian lady, has come on her day off to try and establish what killed him in the end. Was it the brain injuries, or had he been hurt in some other way that they'd missed? She says: 'It's so annoying when you work hard for these people and they still die on you.'

A small crowd is gathered round the table at the far end. There are half-a-dozen massive, tweed-clad CID sergeants from a Scenes of Crime course at the Detective Training School, the pathologist in a white coat; a mortuary attendant and, in the corner away from the gruesome scene, the Detective Superintendent. The centre of attention is a toothy, middle-aged Irishman, a minor villain of those parts, who died in a fight at 3 a.m. that morning. The local CID people had been got out of bed thirty minutes later, and when the other half of the fight came to the hospital at six to inquire after his friend, he was arrested by the PC placed there for that purpose. He is now safely and co operatively in custody.

The question is, does he go on for murder or manslaughter? His story is that they were drinking in the dead man's fourth floor flat where, at about 2 a.m., the witty suggestion was made that he should be thrown out of the window. For his own safety, and on principle, he resented this. The dead man became menacing and started struggling; blows were exchanged; he got out a knife, which the survivor snatched from him, hit him again on the ear, and the victim then fell forward on the blade. It could be true, half-true or lies. The pathologist's report will tell a lot.

The pathologist's rubber-gloved hands have been holding down the corpse's lower lip so that the photographer could take a snap of the bruises inside the mouth. This confirms the prisoner's story that there had been a fight. Then the lights are packed up and the young civilian photographer retires to the corner. The students begin to shuffle away as the attendant – a solid young man with a striking orange brush-cut hair-do – rips the body straight up the middle. The knife makes a nasty gristly noise and the inexperienced instinctively cower back. A few chisel blows split the sternum to let the ribs spring apart. A pause while the grave old white-faced pathologist considers the knife-hole in the stomach wall, and then he carefully turns back the skin and starts to follow the track of the blade through the intestines, running a long piece of wire through the dozen or so holes.

After five minutes of this crochet work, he decides to take the blue-black innards out: swift dissection round the tongue and a man's entire internal equipment lifts out as one piece – as a mechanic miraculously takes the entire engine out of a car. The disturbed intestines release a most ominous smell. Anxious as they are not to seem cissies, the students are pressed back by it. The pathologist, peering over his half-glasses, remarks: 'The intelligent Scenes of Crime officer carries a fresh air spray.'

He and the attendant turn the heap of lights over and continue the search. So far the knife has touched nothing vital: it seems to have passed the aorta by a hair's-breadth and lodged its point in the backbone. They turn back to the now cavernous body and, after much peering, find a tiny nick on the spine. We all press forward to look but, not really liking to get right down to the problem, we only glance at what the imperious scalpel indicates.

Heaps of innards don't photograph well, so a picture is not attempted. The pathologist now turns his attention to the brain. The attendant, whistling lightly, brushes the corpse's hair into a parting across the head from ear to ear. He cuts along this – again the gristly noise – and folds the scalp forward over the rest of the head. The dead man now appears to be wearing a sort of grey-pink shiny hat with a black fur fringe down to his nose. The attendant gets out a big chromium-plated saw and cuts a groove through the bone from ear to ear, and another, parallel to where the dead man's collar would have been, but about three inches higher.

To make the second cut, he lifts the head and puts it on a wooden block. The dead man's chin presses on his chest and he smiles a slow, deep smile. A few blows from a chisel and the two cuts join. They enclose a sort of quarter-orange segment of bone which lifts off, revealing the brain underneath. A little separation and that comes out too. Usually it's a brownish-yellow inside its transparent covering, but this time the base is blackish with blood. The pathologist turns it over and finds the tiny broken vessel that killed the man. He leans on the corpse's knee and studies the brain slowly through a big magnifying-glass.

The Exhibits Officer, an unhappy DC, is shooed forward to collect little bottles of blood and urine and to take the hair samples that a proper murder inquiry demands. To get the blood, the attendant holds up an arm and caresses it while the DC holds a bottle under the vein inside the chest cavity, trying not to trail his jacket sleeves across the edges of the body.

The pathologist sections the brain with a bread-knife, flips the slices briskly over and then slides it all away. 'I shall report that this man died from subdural haemorrhage.' The Superintendent, not to be outdone, asks for an X-ray of the base of the skull in case there's a hair-line crack, and we push out past the next customer – an immense greeny-blue man with a vast baby face and ominous emerald shadings to his extremities. He gives off a deep organ note of smell that stirs one's innards strangely. He had died in his bed-sitter three weeks earlier, telling no one. As we crossed the road for brandies, I remembered where I'd read about him. Robert Graves met his brothers in Flanders in the first World War:

'After the first few days the corpses swelled and stank. I vomited more than once while superintending the carrying. Those we could not get in from the German wire continued to swell until the wall of the stomach collapsed, either naturally or when punctured by a bullet; a disgusting smell would float across. The colour of the dead faces changed from white to yellow-grey, to red, to purple, to green to black, to slimy.'[1]

After half-an-hour in the pub we pile into two cars and go round to the 'death flat'. It is four storeys up in a post-war council block, with big square dust-bins by the foot of the open windy stairs, and on each floor an open passage to each front door. Natives push past us, coming and going:

[1] Graves, Robert, *Goodbye to All That*, Cassell, 1957.

death and the police excite little interest. The girl-friend of the dead man lives there: she has a girl-friend of her own in bed with shock and a hangover. One says the dead man fell one way; the other, when she's woken out of her cocoon of blankets, says thickly that he fell the other way and hit his head on the fire-place. He didn't. The Exhibits Officer cleverly finds some spots of old dried blood on the wall, several feet from where the blows were allegedly struck and nothing to do with this case. The DI says, 'I like these simple cases as long as people don't complicate them.' He goes back to the sleeping girl and, squatting beside her mattress on the floor, he shakes her shoulder, 'Wake up, love, I've got another question to ask you.'

Back at the nick, the man is got up from the cells, sat down with the Superintendent and the DI in the quiet of the DI's office, where he makes a statement and is taken downstairs to be charged. His clothes have been taken for laboratory examination; wearing a large pair of overalls, he is paraded in front of the desk in the charge room. The Superintendent stands in front of the door in case he makes a bolt, but he stands quiet and shaken – a sad end to an evening's frolic. Since the actual cause of death was the blow to the ear, which wasn't intended to cause any real damage, he's charged with unlawful killing.

He stands trembling before the Station Sergeant while the DI gives his evidence. He and the Superintendent immediately make a note in their pocket-books of what he says on being charged – which is nothing at all. By now they feel protective towards the poor fellow: he saw his girl-friend off on the bus, went into a pub, met a mate, got invited to a party, got drunk, defended himself from being thrown out of the window – and crunch. What a way to spend a Thursday. But again it is as if there were a Victorian God with a ledger: his record in Northern Ireland shows several convictions for brawling. 'You're too apt to settle your problems with your fists, son,' remarks the DI, 'I expect your Ma said you'd come to a bad end.'

The Old Bailey

Court is where the policemen's work receives its proof. This is the market-place in which he sells his wares; the judge is the connoisseur who praises and blames. The ordinary citizen may have a decent respect for High Court Judges, but to policemen they are far more imposing figures. As evidence of the complete impartiality of Traffic Patrols when being rude to drivers, it is said that they had even insulted Judges: this was considered a singular circumstance.

Although in theory the police act as private citizens in bringing prosecutions, they have an uncitizenly close daily relationship with judges and magistrates. Although a criminal case is formally couched as a contest between the two sides, the police are also required to act as officers of the court, to reveal their witnesses, to investigate matters impartially; unlike the defence, they may not conceal evidence unfavourable to their case.

Historically too, police acted under the direction and supervision of magistrates and judges; this has not entirely vanished. A policeman who annoys one of these may expect a reprimand from the Commissioner. But it is not entirely the relationship between a superior and inferior. The courts depend for their existence on the efforts of the police to bring them prisoners and witnesses, while the police depend on the courts for justification, vindication and occasionally praise.

Going with policemen to Court and particularly to the Old Bailey[1], I often felt we weren't going to an institution of

[1] The English hierarchy of criminal courts: Magistrates' Court, Quarter Sessions, Assizes, Criminal Division, Court of Appeal, House of Lords. Criminal cases start in a Magistrates' Court and ninety-five per cent are heard completely there. The others, after a preliminary hearing which may be no more now than an exchange of witnesses' statements, are committed for trial by jury either to Quarter Sessions, before a panel of Magistrates, or to Assizes before a High Court Judge. London Assizes sit almost continuously at the Old Bailey. The two higher courts deal only with appeals, seldom hear evidence, and so rarely concern policemen.

the twentieth century, but to one of those tricky Greek oracles who, if propitiated with sacrifice and correctly worded prayer, would shower blessings on its votaries; but if caught on a bad day could be spiteful.

The Old Bailey is a building in the Victorian grandiose style, with enormous space allowed to the halls, off which there are rather smaller courts. The halls are mosaic and panelled, with pillars and obscure frescoes representing unfamiliar abstractions with ample figures. Witnesses, counsel, detectives[1], sit about in the hall or stand talking to each other, forced by the proportions of the scene into the composition of an architectural painting. Over the front door is carved *Fiat Justicia*, on the walls inside the telephone-box, the users have written their own messages: 'Public schoolboy, pretty face, even prettier arse, ring XYZ 0003, ask for Nikki,' and 'Fred's counsel is a fat wank.'

The halls are so ample that a couple of new courts have been carved out of them, miniaturised versions, executed in cream-painted hardboard, of the more majestic arenas. In the new courts, Judge, Jury, Counsel and prisoners loom on top of each other like toys in a cardboard box. The case in one of them involves the stabbing of one coloured Brixtonian by another. It is alleged that A, driving in the rain, saw Mrs B, a stranger, and offered her a lift. Within minutes he demanded a pound out of her handbag and said she had to sleep with him. Some months later he wrote to her and asked for several hundred pounds to buy a new car. If she had not given him the money, he would have had to tell her husband. Not surprisingly, he was stabbed by someone in the street. The husband and wife stand jointly charged with the assault.

Counsel for the defence, a brisk young man, is reading part of the letter. The Jamaican inflexion filters through his Etonian accent like broadcast through a thunderstorm; the

---

[1] Ten per cent of a detective's working-time is spent physically in Court and much of that waiting around to be called or cross-examined. Martin & Wilson, *op. cit.*, p. 178.

158

writer is making a moral point: 'The car (the one he picked her up in), I have my wife's money in it and good friends' too, and yet you accept to drive in it.' The motives of the people are complicated, yet the facts are simple. The only tactic for the defence is to nag at the police. After the stabbing the husband was put up for identification by the victim: counsel is wrangling with the Detective Sergeant who investigated the case. Both have played this game so often that they're making points against each other that mean nothing to the jury at all.

'No officer, you said there was a "surplus of coloured people on the parade". That's a funny word. Do you feel there are too many?' (a favourite defence line in cases with coloured defendants is that the police are colour-prejudiced). 'I actually said Jamaicans, not coloured; and I suppose surplus does mean too many, but that's not what I meant. My point was that in Brixton we have far more West Indians than African coloured people.'

The Sergeant is forty-ish, cool, a solid craftsman. He takes time to think out his answers, then refuses to repeat the phrasing of the barrister. Counsel is theatrical, loud, incisive, dangerous-sounding, but makes no headway. A knife is produced, alleged to have stabbed the prosecutor. Counsel: 'I am suggesting nothing sinister or improper, but there has been no dulling of the blade' (he suggests that the police have re-sharpened it). Perhaps the jury do think he's not suggesting anything improper. Who knows what is going on behind those blank faces? Then they come to the identification parade.

Counsel: 'Was there not a gap in the parade to which Mr Jones was waved by the police officer?'

'Definitely not, sir.' The jury do not get the point of this. Some minutes later:

Counsel: 'Let us be quite sure about this point. I don't want to trap you. He answered 'Yes' when you asked him to come to the station, not 'Yes, why not?' Pause while the Sergeant looks at his notes.

'Yes, why not.' The Judge breaks in.

'I'm afraid, Sergeant, we'll have to go through the rigmarole. I say "Sergeant! What are you reading from?" and you say "A notebook, my Lord." When we have all recovered from our surprise and horror, we say: "When did you make your notes?" and you tell us some plausible story, and I say "Oh, very well then, you may go on." Once in thirty-eight years I've seen a police officer caught out.' The Sergeant, encouraged, tells the court when and where he made his notes. Judge: 'You haven't been asked that yet, but I suppose it doesn't matter.'

A young constable, who had been the first to arrive at the scene of the stabbing, gives his evidence. He is obviously worried in case what he says happened differs in some minute detail from what the other police witnesses say – for instance that the victim's car was pointing north instead of south. Since the defence has nothing else to go on, they could build on a slip like that and make a monument of police fabrication and corruption.

The Detective Inspector is called, and examined. He has been sitting outside on a bench in the marble hall, wringing his hands together while back on his sub-division the cream of London's criminals ply their trade. Counsel nags away again about the parade: 'Was my client not the tallest, the oldest, the shortest, the ugliest, the only one wearing a hat?' In answer to each of his questions the Detective Inspector calmly repeats the standing orders for the conduct of identity parades as if there were no other way to describe the particular one in issue. It was held five months before; none of the policemen can remember the slightest thing about it.

Then the DI jumps a question and says: 'No, sir, Mr Jones was not pushed into a prepared gap in the parade.' Counsel, suddenly menacing: 'How did you know I was going to ask you that? Was it as a result of information you had received?' But the DI: 'No, sir, I have some experience of courts.'

CHAPTER SEVEN

Detectives at The Yard

Central

Necessity is polarising detective work into at least two levels, which are vaguely defined at the moment, but becoming more distinct. The first includes the greater volume of crime, probably represents in aggregate the greater social cost, but fragmented and often trivial. This is investigated by Divisional CID officers, whose operations are almost always *post facto*. They follow behind criminals, arresting the obvious ones, collecting evidence, and have, broadly speaking, a book-keeping function. As we see below, the number of arrests achieved by the efforts of the police alone is probably a small fraction of the total and almost negligible in comparison with the number of crimes committed[1]. Divisional detectives also have a subsidiary 'general practitioner' function in referring more specialised crime to more specialised agencies. Each Division contains five per cent of London's people, and its detective staff is necessarily concerned with events in and round it.

The second level of detective work is concerned either with specialised crimes of national significance like drug-trafficking or forgery, or crimes that are widespread over the MPD, like systematic cheque frauds. There are roughly a dozen specialist branches of the CID, each headed by a Detective Chief Superintendent. Of these the oldest is C1, 'Central'; in Dickens's day, the 'Detective Office', the historical core of the CID. It lives at Scotland Yard, and a conspicuous photostat in its Chief's office proclaims its interest in:

[1] See below, pp. 270–278.

Provincial Murder Investigations – Murders on the High Seas – Confidential Enquiries – Crime relating to, and inquiries for, Government Departments – Important Prosecutions undertaken by the DPP – International Crime – Extradition and Fugitive Offenders – Serious Crimes and those widespread over the MPD and in the country – Forgery of Banknotes and Coinage Offences – Commissions Rogatoire (formal statements taken from witnesses in England for use in foreign legal proceedings) – International Criminal Police Organisation – International Lotteries – Obscene Publications – Dangerous Drugs and Inspection of Chemists' Registers – Procuration and Sexual Offences (involved cases) – Involved Fraud – Multiple Cheque Frauds – Gaming Machines – Port Warnings – Charity Commission Inquiries – Monitoring of Television and Radio – American Express Travellers' Cheques – Prisoner's Property Office – Liaison with GPO Investigation Branch, SIB[1], American Embassy and Canadian High Commission, Ministry of Social Security and London Hospitals – Industrial Espionage – Bribery and Corruption – Restrictive Trade Practices – Union Ballot Rigging – Criminal Libel – Art Inquiries.

These functions are divided among ten squads, each run by a Detective Superintendent. This responsibility is more nominal than real, since these ten also form the Murder Squad, and each, with a First Class Sergeant from C1, is on a rota for instant call. On the average they are away six months of the year, so responsibility falls to their Chief Inspectors. But these unfortunates, like all other CID officers of the same rank, are largely occupied investigating complaints against policemen, so ultimately the squads are run by their Detective Inspectors.

Although C1 sounds interesting, their work is largely on paper, heavily supervised, and is probably rather duller than in divisions. The ten squads vary: No. 1 deals with Liaison and Administration, 2 with Obscene Publications and Art Inquiries, 3 with Interpol, 4 with Extradition, 5

[1] Special Investigation Branch of the British Army.

with Charities Commissions, Travellers' Cheques and Passport Offences, 6 with Involved Frauds and International Lotteries, 7 with Bank Note Forgeries and Counterfeit Coin, 8 with issuing Port Warnings and Internal Records, 9 with Criminal Libel, Voting Offences, Bribery, Industrial Espionage, Union Ballot Rigging, and 10 with Dangerous Drugs.

Obscene publications – the 'Dirty Squad' – is moderately amusing. It does a brisk business in dirty books, postcards, blue films and the newish development in London of magazines full of advertisements by 'broadminded couples' seeking 'more of the same'. It has a tiny projection-room where films captured in raids are run, because, before they can be used as evidence, some policeman has to be able to swear that they are obscene. On the folding screen, badly photographed, ill-looking people go endlessly through the old biological ritual.

The Drugs Squad is aimed principally at the importers and big dealers in narcotics, but necessarily it takes notice of addicts and casual drug-users because it has to work back from them. It maintains an 18,000-card, national index of everyone convicted of drug offences, together with useful bits of information like their friends, landlords, and the sources of their drugs. Every morning the Squad has a couple of messages from members of the public who have rung the Yard to report drug offences, but they get most of their information about big drug movements from professional criminals getting even with each other. Four unfortunate Sergeants in the Drug Squad spend their working lives going round every chemist in London, checking their books against their prescriptions, looking out for new addicts, forged prescriptions, unlocked dangerous drug cupboards. Their work is appallingly dull but is an essential deterrent to lax practices among pharmacists.

The Forgery Squad deals with perhaps no more than two or three separate forgeries a year: but each one may give rise to tens of thousands of notes, and each note, as it turns up across the country, generates a report by the local police that goes by way of C1 to the Bank of England. One recent current preoccupation was with a large issue of forged five-pound notes, whose backs were fairly good, particularly for colour, but whose fronts were less successful, so they were usually tendered, folded in half, in dark shops. On the underworld market they were worth wholesale about £1 each, a price which reflected the difficulty of getting rid of them. A big run of forged notes is a real problem for the monetary authority of any country, and sometimes has to be dealt with by recalling a complete denomination and printing a new design – as the Bank of Scotland had to do a few years ago.

The actual printing of forged notes is done quickly and secretly and, without information, it is almost impossible to catch people at it. But to some extent the business of a forger for profit is self-limiting. He cannot make a note that will reliably pass the routine scrutiny of a bank clerk. This means that as his efforts get around and are found by banks, they and tradesmen get suspicious. Notes generally come under close scrutiny, and if the forgeries are widespread people may refuse to accept the denomination at all. This means that a forger has to get rid of his notes quickly before people are alerted, and this in turn needs great effort from a lot of collaborators, and sharply reduces the profit of his efforts.

Perhaps a more rewarding sort of forgery is the 'home hobby' variety: the enthusiast who takes eleven five-pound notes, cuts a vertical slice, one eleventh of a note's width out of each one, in positions that march across the face of the note. Then he binds each note up with a wide piece of opaque tape, as if it had been torn and mended, and sticks the twelve strips together by the edges to make one new one. He relies on no one noticing either his conspicuously mended notes, or the lattice-work texture of his thirteenth one, or – and this is the snag – the fact that it has a different number at each end. It would be difficult for anyone to make and get rid of more than a couple a week: it is more an eccentric hobby than a threat to the integrity of the State. But a man convicted of this offence in 1968 was sentenced to eight years.

Coining used to be a common offence; now it is almost forgotten. 1952 half-crowns are so rare – King George VI died after only a few had been struck – that a good one fetches £2,000; ingenious people occasionally alter the date on a 1957 one. Sometimes, too, people cast lead coins for slot-machines; this is a stupid trick because a blank disc would work as well and would not be forgery. The forgery squad get out and do some active police work – in the spring and summer after my visit, as a result of information received, they arrested five teams complete with plates, and by August were very happy with themselves.

Much of the rest of C1 work is dealing with other people's paper. The Interpol Office, in particular, is awash with dockets: it acts as a sort of multilingual police post office, routing fifty or sixty messages a day: asking Spain to trace a British fraudsman, a request from Canada to find the relatives of an old lady who died there, a young boy missing from his home in Holland – has he gone to Gretna Green? A Swiss gentleman is in custody at Marylebone Lane – is anything known about him in Geneva?

The Interpol organisation refuses to deal with political problems. They wouldn't touch the spy Blake or the Nazi war criminals. As one officer put it: 'You have to be firm about political inquiries because if you don't, you find that whoever's got control of the police barracks in Awooloo Land is agitating through Interpol for extradition of all the opposition who live here.' Nor will it handle antecedent inquiries – if, for example, a Spaniard is found running with some good villains here in London, Interpol channels cannot be consulted to find his form. But Interpol meetings and the International Police Association encourage friendships, and doubtless someone can ring up old Juan in Barcelona to find out.

C1 is evidently a repository for homeless inquiries. It has over the years spawned a large number of other, now independent, departments, which rank as organisational equals:

C2 deals with case papers, correspondence, and searches in public records, in particular the Companies Register. In 1967 it did 6,000 searches there. C3 is the Finger-print Branch (see below p. 193) C4 Criminal Record Office, C5 CID administration, postings, instructions, commendations, complaints, discipline (and 'rubber heel'). C6 is the joint Metropolitan and City Police Company Fraud Branch, C7 the Detective Training School (see p. 50), C8 the Flying Squad, C9 The Metropolitan and Provincial Police Crime Branch – a joint office staffed by Met CID officers and an equal number of CID people drawn from Home County Forces. The object of the latter is to liaise between detectives in, say, Norfolk, investigating breakings when the criminals live in London. The existence of C9 saves a great deal of travelling and contact-making between provincial and London detectives. C10 is Stolen Vehicle Investigation Branch, a double offshoot, via the Flying Squad: and C11 is Criminal Intelligence. Of these squads most dealt either in paper, or were unwilling or unable to show me action, but two were interesting.

Ringers

C10 Branch inhabits a large garage behind the Tube station at Chalk Farm. Inside, on seven floors connected by ramps, there is nearly a mile of echoing concrete, littered with dusty cars, some in pieces, some so new that the paint and chrome are still protected. Here and there the subject of an investigation is spread out over the floor, complete to the last nut.

The function of this branch is to take cars that are suspected to be stolen, or, more often, made up of many stolen bits, and to prove rigorously where each bit came from, who owned it legitimately, and when and where it was stolen. The idea is that when the thief comes to court, he has something solid to face. This kind of thief is called a 'ringer' because he 'rings the changes' on stolen cars. C10's staff of forty-two consists equally of specialist vehicle-examiners --

detectives who have become expert in this intricate trade, and ordinary investigating officers who do three-year tours with the branch.

They have two sources of business: firstly, cars that are stopped by policemen in the street in London and are suspected to be stolen; and cars that have been crashed, junked, repaired and re-registered. The re-registration of wrecks used to be a fruitful source of car documents for ringers: they would buy a heap of scrap for a couple of pounds, keep the log-book, throw the car away, steal a car like it, re-number the engine and chassis, make up a new set of number-plates, and sell it as a legitimate car.

Then, when things got more difficult, they would steal several cars, cut them up, weld them back together in various proportions, so that even if this hybrid were suspected, it would be extremely difficult to identify with a particular stolen car. The ordinary divisional detective had a very small chance of hitting on a part which could be identified with a car which he knew to be stolen. Moreover, the more complicated the stolen car might be, the better chance the whole case had of being snarled up in court.

The jury, having to bear in mind a dynamo from here, a mudguard from there, seats from this place and engine from that, might give up in despair. It demands an organisation with a lot of time, space and expertise to sort out the confusion, to document the rung car so accurately that every part is traced through each of its legitimate owners to the final theft. C10 do not look for particular stolen cars; but given one that has been stolen it can prove to the satisfaction of a criminal court when and where it was stolen.

The attraction of car-ringing is obvious. Every street is lined with objects worth, on the average, £1,000. When stolen, these will have a resale value to the criminal of seventy to seventy-five per cent, against the fifteen per cent which he could expect to get on the products of a burglary. They are laughably easy to obtain and change. The cost in labour of stealing and ringing a car might be £100, leaving the organiser with a handsome profit. C10 has arrested ringers working in large, prosperous and apparently honest garages. A proportion of the staff were criminals, and the cars that were to be cut and redistributed were buried in a mass of legitimate business.

Apart from being dishonest, ringing produces dangerous cars. It is difficult enough to weld bits of three cars together invisibly; to make the result strong enough to drive is almost impossible. A Jaguar that broke in half on the M1 some years ago had been rung; there may have been many similar accidents. A ringer is often arrested because of one suspicious car, or because his agents are caught in the act of stealing. But investigation after arrest may produce evidence of many more stolen cars.

The Branch was formed from the Flying Squad in 1960, and in the early days it would get batches of 120 cars to investigate at a time. Now the life of a car-ringer is much shorter, and normally it gets only twenty cars following each arrest. While I was with them an investigation started. The evening before, one of the area cars, Delta 3, had taken an interest in two youths driving a Mini. They followed them, the Mini panicked and tried to speed away but was chased and caught. The boys were arrested for highway offences. They were searched in case they had stolen property – which would explain their attempt to escape – but, instead, one of them carried a list of cars that were stolen: types that would presumably fit an existing collection of log-books. Thus: 'Ford Zephyr 1965, dark blue'; 'Armstrong Siddeley Sapphire 1961, fawn and brown'; 'Vauxhall Victor 1966, maroon': While their room was being searched, a third boy walked in, who proved more co-operative. He led the area car to a yard in Shoreditch where the ringers worked. Three more men, busy when the police burst in, were arrested for receiving stolen property.

The bodies having been collected and the crime revealed, C10 was called in to probe the case. The Squad assigned to the job – half-a-dozen men under DI – met at the yard: a desolate space in the middle of a block of mean, deserted houses. The whole area was ripe for demolition; no one lived in the houses to overlook the ringers, no one outside could see what they were doing. All round the edges of the yard there were ten-foot-high heaps of burnt-out car bodies and tyres, garnished with an indescribable quantity of dirt, mud, rubbish and broken machinery.

In the middle was a Sunbeam Rapier, upside down, stripped of wheels and engine, red with rust, gutted by fire. Two days before it had been someone's shiny, comfortable car. The engine stood near it on a trolley; all the wires and pipes had been cut with an axe in the thieves' hurry to get it out. The odds and ends of genteel living, shaken out of stolen cars, were trodden into the oily mud. There lay a broken city umbrella, a law student's leather briefcase with, just legible through the seeped oil, his last set of lecture notes, and a guide book to the Cotswolds lying open at Bourton-on-the-Water.

The house which the ringers used was dirty. Each room was full of some standard car part – in one, Sunbeam gearboxes; in another Landrover panels; in a third, wheels and tyres. One room had makeshift bunks with blackened blankets, everywhere smelled of old urine and rotting food. In the front room there were brazen samples of the gang's specialities, hung on the wall as in a conventional car dealer's. Presumably they acted as suppliers to other ringers.

The dirt and wastefulness of criminality are overpowering. The C10 people change into overalls and gumboots to turn the place over: picking up every piece of the tons of rubbish, looking at it for serial numbers, keeping it if there are any, throwing it on the pile behind if not. In the middle of the yard there grows a collection of discarded number-plates, which, they hope, will lead directly to stolen cars by way of the Central Vehicle Index. But the thieves can hardly have been that stupid. It is a dirty way to spend two days.

169

The Squads

Large-scale theft is investigated in London by the Flying Squad, an eighty-strong team, unique to London, and by No 9 District Regional Crime Squad ('9 District' refers to the Home Office's national inspectorate organisation for coordinating police forces; each district of England has its own Regional Crime Squad). The Flying Squad and the Regional Crime Squads are roughly equivalent in organisation, intention and staffing. Flying Squad officers are all Metropolitan, Regional Crime squads made up of Metropolitan and City men and officers from neighbouring counties.

The Flying Squad, as the core of the CID, is an extremely conservative organisation. I had one very brief conversation with its then chief, and was allowed no further contact with it, so I can only describe it at second-hand by way of accounts from officers that I met elsewhere who had served in it. The Regional Crime Squads were more helpful. Their job is to deal solely with major robbery teams – the groups who specialise in banks and payroll snatches. Each squad would try to concentrate on one team at a time. They would cultivate informants, use what information was available from Criminal Intelligence, follow their men about until they knew who would be involved, what cars would be used, what the target was, when it would be attacked, and then they would do their best to lie in wait to arrest the team in action. Failing this, again using information from their informants or people recently arrested, they would chase stolen property or wanted men, trying to catch them before they finally sank into the ground.

A Regional Crime Squad officer's day tended to be long. He would often have to get up at four or five a.m. to be outside his suspect's house by six a.m., in time to see him move off for the day. Or he might be searching houses or making arrests at the policeman's favourite hour of 5 a.m., when the criminal's morale is lowest. Work in the middle of the day would be slack, if he was not in court; he would perhaps have informants to meet at lunchtime. In the evening, observations and meetings would keep him occupied until late at night.

Regional Crime Squad men use their own cars. These are fitted unobtrusively by the police with a radio – ideally a multi-channel set which can be tuned to any of the fifty British police wave-lengths, and a short-wave set that gives car-to-car communication over two or three miles, so that two or more cars can co-operate in following a suspect.

The Flying Squad and Regional Crime Squads between them provide a strike force with its own organisation and communications that can be out on the street within half an hour. The Flying Squad particularly is used as a 'go any-where, nick anyone' force. The Regional Crime Squads like to take longer over their jobs, to play them quietly and, at the end, make a clean sweep. The Flying Squad tradition is to hit quick and hard. Both systems have their points. In 1966–7, Flying Squad officers executed 1,590 search warrants. 378 of them were successful and produced the arrest of 469 people. Regional Crime Squad officers executed 'over 1,000' warrants and were concerned in the arrest of 914 people – 92 robbers, 140 breakers, 254 receivers, and 19 lorry-thieves[1].

Criminal Intelligence

One of the most interesting branches in the Metropolitan Police is C11, Criminal Intelligence. Although it was much discussed among policemen, I had small hopes of seeing anything of it and its work. However, when the time came, nobody could have been more agreeable and helpful.

In the days of small-scale, local crime, when the Metro-politan Police jelled and set, a detective's knowledge of crim-inals and his sources of information were his own private affair. They were his reputation and his livelihood. They still are. Unfortunately times have changed. Enormous in-

[1] *Report of the Commissioner of Police of the Metropolis*, 1967, pp. 75, 78.

creases since then in community size have diluted the available information about crime and criminals. Although each general-duty detective may have more information than his forebears in terms of quantity, it becomes scrappier and about more and more people. Unlike the scientist, he gets to know less and less about more and more.

The problem is aggravated by an organisational dilemma. The Metropolitan Police, like all other forces, keeps its detectives up to the mark by demanding, in an informal sort of way, a minimum number of arrests a year from them. I don't mean that there is a regulation which prescribes an acceptable score, but rather that a man doing investigations which ought to produce arrests is expected to show them, and senior officers have a shrewd idea how many a particular assignment should produce. But since, as it were, a detective's score in the police 'game' is his arrest total, he will keep all his sources of information to himself, because these enable him to earn praise and advancement. If everyone is encouraged to contribute information to the public pot, then scoring by arrests must be abandoned.

How then are detectives to be administered? If they haven't got to show arrests, some will perhaps spend their days wenching and drinking. It is a difficult problem to solve. At the moment both views prevail in different places, and were incidentally reflected by the way in which the departments treated me. *The Flying Squad,* old and conservative, would have nothing of me; *Criminal Intelligence,* new and progressive, welcomed me almost with open arms.

C11 is a brave and flourishing attempt to get policemen to share what they know. It deliberately has, unlike *Central* or the *Flying Squad,* an almost American public relations policy within the force. Every day tours of detectives come round its office, and, unthinkably a few years ago, even uniform police constables. The idea is that *everyone* has something to contribute, if it is extracted from them, and C11 is anxious for it all.

Again I suffered under the prohibition against seeing an

operation and arrest of a team – and the things that I did happen to see were not in themselves very extraordinary. But if one multiplies them by a hundred or so, and by six days of the week, it is evident that a lot is being found out; that the criminal's freedom of action, to strike where and when he likes, in whatever guise he chooses, is being eroded.

The staff of Criminal Intelligence consists of about forty people: four teams of five, each under a DI, each cover a district, and try to work on a couple of teams of thieves at once. The point of their operation is to collect and collate every possible scrap of information that they can about major criminals and their associates in London. At the time of my visit their card index had 7,000 names, though only 500 or so were formidable villains. Their information comes in two main channels: from 'snouts' – only experienced detectives are posted to C11, and each brings with him his carefully nurtured sources; and observation by themselves and other policemen.

The most trivial things are worth recording. A well-kept card on a villain should show what pub he uses, what he drinks, whom he drinks with, the colour of his wife's and his girl-friend's hair, his friends, where he meets them, what they talk about and so on. It is important to establish his basic habits: when he gets up, where he eats, what day of the week he goes to see his mother – if he does. Only against this is it possible to set out-of-the-ordinary behaviour. If he starts drinking in a pub in Hatton Garden, is this his normal habit, or is he planning a diamond robbery? Unless one knows what he usually does, one can't tell.

If a team is being plotted they will be under almost continuous observation. There is also a stream of random gossip from detectives about villains whom they know but aren't interested in, and now from the Unit Beat uniform police who have, as part of the new station organisation, an Intelligence Collator who passes on news about villains living on his ground.

A couple of examples show the usefulness of this kind

of observation. One day last year Epsom police rang up C11 to say that they had seen two well-known robbers driving a white Cortina, number ABC 123 D. This was recorded. Four months later, a bank was robbed. One witness saw the getaway car, and all he could say is that the car was white and the letters were 'ABC'. A search through the index suggested the Epsom car: this led to the two villains, and a quick visit to their homes found the money neatly stacked in piles.

At the trial of five men for another robbery, one of them, who hadn't been arrested at the scene, put up the defence that he had never met the other four in his life or even heard of them, and that, in short, he was being framed. When he had established all this, C11 was able to produce their Occurrence Book – a log of observations in chronological order, which makes better evidence than a card that could have been made up anytime – of two years before. This showed him living with the sister of the team's leader. He changed his story and said yes, he'd met the leader once; but an alibi is like virginity, when a bit's gone, it's all gone.

The atmosphere at C11 is pleasantly hectic: at the near end of the office a portable radio, with its aerial propped against a window-frame, relays Channel 6 and messages from an operation in progress somewhere out there through the picture window. Down the inside wall there's a mass of filing-cabinets and where they end – a long way away – a pin-board covered with glossy photographs. They look rather like the sort taken at conferences, but these, however, are good clandestine snaps of a villain's charabanc outing, taken when they stopped for a roadside crate of beer. All comers are invited to suggest identities. Several of the drinking heads have red crayon haloes, with their names and CRO numbers written in.

At that end, too, a plump, excited detective is trying to get a portable television set and vidoe-tape-recorder working to demonstrate to a group of visitors; but someone has lost a vital wire. Behind him is the door to the Chief Inspector's room, where an agitated conference is in progress. Another branch has had word of an impending sale of stolen bonds between elements of the underworld. A detective has been put in as the buyer, armed, to the Yard's apprehension, with £5,000 in used notes, and a police team is needed to watch the approach of the seller. Unfortunately no one in the branch responsible for the operation can identify the principal. Unwillingly, the DI of the team to which I am attached, who does know him, is drawn in as an observer.

Leaving the TV camera staring glassily at the office across the street, we leave precipitately in a scruffy blue Vauxhall. My new friends have no status in the operation, and hardly any idea what it's about, except that out of the morass of lunch-hour people and traffic in the Strand, we are expected to find a mysterious 'Big Fred'.

The operation has been mounted in such a hurry – the information about it only came in an hour before – that there has been no time to arrange proper meets or even a simple code for use over the air. So we blunder about trying to find the other detectives' car, which is supposed to be parked somewhere by the Law Courts. They come up on the air, and, in a voice loaded with suppressed meaning, tell us to meet them by 'The Statue'.

London is full of statues. We gaze round with irritation and nervousness, wondering which statue the fool means. Finally we see them and DI gets into their car for briefing. Ten minutes later he comes back, a shortish, brisk man whom one would take for a vigorous chartered accountant, rubbing his forehead in some perplexity. Fred is billed to be amongst us in fifteen minutes time. His current car, according to his C11 card, is a green Diamler – he also has a gold Maserati, but that is being repaired. This same operation was run, unsuccessfully, a few weeks before. It seems highly unlikely that Fred will turn up again, but the other branch swears that he will, and that he will park his car in an alley in Bush House. The DI and the Sergeant think this smacks of fairy tales, but for the moment their part is to watch and wait.

So we set to driving round the block. The situation is complicated by the snout who is also around. We don't know him and they won't tell us who he is. Common sense suggests that there will also be a carrier bringing the bonds to the hotel where the deal's going to happen, and perhaps a number of decoys as well. A man arrested the last time was quite obviously carrying a parcel of bonds in a brief-case. When he was searched at the nick, it turned out to be dirty shirts packed in a cardboard box. To complicate things, the snout might be the carrier, or a decoy, or not there at all, or even Fred himself if the plot has undreamt-of con-volutions. So we look for the green Daimler, whose number is now written on the dashboard in black crayon so that we shan't forget it. We rattle round and round in the traffic, peering all ways; I'm bouncing about in the back in a swamp of old macs, a couple of hats for quick inconspicuousness, and a parcel of baseball bats done up in a loose brown-paper parcel – just in case there is trouble.

After a couple of circuits I offer to get out and look up the side-streets in case he is parked there. Five minutes' hunting brings me round a corner very near the spot marked X and face to face with two villainous-looking youths, standing opposite each other – or looking over each other's shoulders. They have identical briefcases of the smart dull chrome-edged American sort. Are they the carriers? Or decoys? Or young executives waiting for their girl-friends? This business is, if nothing else, decidedly stimulating. It again feels odd to be hunting purposefully through this somnolent lunch-time crowd, one's adrenalin streaming round, the colours brighter, and a feeling of 'if only' – not daring to think that the green car will be there, but hoping all the same.

On the next corner a young man in a dark suit is standing with his hands in his pocket: he turns as I come up. He's a detective whom I know by sight, and he knows me, though we've never spoken. He must be one of the reserve that was coming from CO. We stare through each other, in a way which I sincerely hope isn't too conspicuously nonchalant.

Then, there the car is, in a side square, nearly where they expected it; though one digit's wrong in the registration. It feels marvellous to have found it. I stroll past it, peering, as one might, into a smart and desirable machine, and on up to the top of the cul-de-sac to look in a shop-window. Then I walk back. There's nothing in the car, and I meet the two policemen as they come round the corner. This cheers everyone up: conversation is freer over the air, because though Fred might have a radio tuned to police frequencies in the car, he is unlikely to be walking about with one.

Then next time round, the DI sees him and points him out – a stocky bear of a man in a loud check suit – and then turns round as if to look for something in the back of the car, because Fred knows him as well as he knows Fred. It would impede the deal if he were recognised.

There is now a considerable cast assembled for this mini-drama. Three car-loads of detectives, an over-excited journalist, a master villain, his henchman, a carrier, a snout – the most shadowy figure of all – and the detective alone in the hotel room nervously waiting for the irruption of some third gang, anxious to get the bonds and/or the money without having the trouble to pay for them. Before he set out he went microscopically through his clothes and removed every scrap of paper that could show him to be a policeman. Even so, apparently, he was not in a happy frame of mind. If he got beaten up and the money was stolen, he would have a lot of explaining to do.

At this the DI gets out, leaving the Sergeant and me to go once more round the block. The next time round he stops us and says the bonds are definitely in a brown-paper carrier-bag, and a middle-aged man with very thin blond hair going grey, wearing a blue mac, is carrying them. It is like a dream: under our eyes one of the detectives must have met the snout and got this information. It's all there, in the crowds that swirl up and down, if only we could read it. The DI goes off again on foot: the Sergeant and I continue.

Round the corner, there he is, standing on the edge of

the pavement with a worried frown. The thin hair, the blue mac, the brown carrier-bag – which even looks like a carrier-bag full of bonds: we can see the corners of the parcel push-ing out the sides. In fact he looks so like the carrier that it was ridiculous. We must have passed him five times already. The traffic stops and we pull up within touching distance. He is looking abstractedly over our roof. But *was* he the mug? Or were the two smart office boys carrying, or perhaps someone we hadn't seen? Did the bag hold washing in en-velope boxes – an odd way to carry laundry, but not crim-inal? Or was it the real stuff?

If it *was* the bonds, was he also the snout and therefore sacrosanct – or if he was just the carrier, would it be safe to arrest him? Probably he has only a couple of convictions for shoplifting; when he is charged in court with possessing £50,000 of stolen bonds he will say that the police planted them on him, and it will be difficult to prove otherwise. Even so, would it be better to let the bonds run and catch Fred sometime later? But if he is nicked now, at least a lot of stolen bonds would be out of play and wouldn't that be a good thing?

Anyway, while the Sergeant, as he afterwards explains, goes over these puzzling thoughts, without nearly enough information to guide him to a decision, even if he hadn't been in thick traffic with the car behind flashing its head-lights, the man in the blue mac walks away, crosses a side road and gets into a taxi which then turns left behind us. Because of the one-way system it takes us three or four min-utes to get round the block to catch up; when we do, the taxi, the bonds, Fred and his green Daimler, have all blown away.

'I wish to God we'd had the Squad here,' moans the DI when we pick him up. But we didn't. After a little of this, one begins to sympathise with the Flying Squad philosophy that cuts through these subtleties and arrests anyone who has broken the law and against whom any sort of charge can be made out, regardless of the consequences.

CHAPTER EIGHT

Detection and Prosecution

This chapter discusses various matters that affect the detective's trade. Up to this point in the book I have tried to describe things that I saw happen, doing my best to put myself and the reader in the policeman's shoes. But some of the topics here, like informants, I could never experience directly. Others, like the effect of the end of capital punishment, spread over considerable periods of time. This chapter largely recounts what I learned from detectives in many conversations, and is an attempt to put their point of view as I understood it.

Informants

A detective's job is to arrest criminals, and since he seldom is privileged to find them at work, he has to know whom to arrest. Classically, as the layman understands it, the detective is presented with a set of tenuous clues which, properly interpreted, point out the criminal from among a small group of suspects. This Agatha-Christie situation makes good fiction but bad reality; most thefts, for example, are committed by a dark-haired man, wearing gloves, who is five feet nine to five feet eleven tall and twenty to thirty years old.

The possible suspects in any one case run into hundreds of thousands. In real life, once a suspect is found, then the detective-story process of observation and deduction may prove his guilt in court – though his admission is far more likely to do so – but in general the two processes are com-

pletely independent. For instance, the late director of the
Metropolitan Police Forensic Science Laboratory could only
recall one instance of a criminal being found by scientific
evidence alone[1].

The detective has three broad channels of information
which lead him to arrests:

(i) Luck: a man is stopped in the street, he is wanted,
or he carries some criminal object – weapon, drugs, stolen
property.

(ii) Through police records: a crime is committed in a
particular way and Method Index, or the detective's experience, suggests a candidate. Or finger prints are found and
matched to a known criminal.

But these are relatively unimportant compared to:

(iii) Information – an informant, who may be a snout, tells
him whom to arrest.

It is rather disconcerting to discover that nine times out
of ten, when the police disappear into the undergrowth
after some spectacular crime and re-appear, apparently
miraculously, with a man who is 'helping them with their
inquiries', it is because some third party has told them for
whom to look. It takes, perhaps, some mental readjustment
to get from a smear of cigarette-ash to a phone call in the
middle of the morning as the main tool of the detective's
trade. But 'Acting on information received' is less easy than
it sounds. The business of acquiring and keeping snouts, of
dealing, like an old-fashioned market trader, in information –
shouting one piece to the world, hiding another under the
counter, destroying a third, trading a fourth to an old friend
for a particularly choice fifth bit – is not soon learnt.

It is also difficult to realise that people give the police information not so much because the police are brilliant inter-
rogators, or because people are public-spirited, but because
it suits their interests. Informants can be roughly divided

[1] See p. 201 below.

into two groups. The first consists of people who are apt to be arrested and give information to stave off the evil day, or who have already been arrested and hope to buy police forbearance.

In the second are people running free in the community who give information to the police to further their own ends. They may, rarely, be honest men, helping the police as good citizens should, or dishonest. In this case their motives may be to gain a reward, to enjoy revenge, or to eliminate a criminal rival. The essence of the detective's job is to create conditions in which people will *want* to tell him useful things.

The easier sort to understand is the informer who tells because he's been arrested, or has the threat hanging over him. A Regional Crime Squad Sergeant explains:

' "Help" informants – you can make them. We keep observation on a lot of blokes who are at it. You meet one on his own one night, and you say, "Hullo, John, I saw you the other night drinking with so and so." He says, "No you didn't". "Yes, I did, you know, you were in the Queen's Elbow and you were driving a grey Rover. You ought to get it taxed or you might be in bother." Well then your heart's in your mouth – will he bite? And he's nervous, he doesn't know how much you *do* know – he's probably been up to something. So finally he says, "What of it?", and you say, "We're interested in such and such", so after a bit he says, "OK I'll phone you." And so you get a bit further on.

'Then you've nicked chummy and he thinks "Christ, please help me!" He's thinking desperately round for something to tell you. I nicked this bloke in Notting Hill for doing a gas-meter. And he thinks the old thing to himself: "Help!" And it comes to him. He says that in half-an-hour there'll be a pedlar down the road delivering a parcel of drugs. I go down there: he's there and actually selling and I get the buyer as well. Good as gold, he was. My friend goes into court, and I just gave the facts – perhaps sometimes you nip round and see the Magistrate and explain and

he gets four months instead of six[1]. He's an example of someone who wasn't a real informant any more than fly in the
air; he did what he could because he thought he had to.'

Since the interval between committal and hearing in a
higher court may often be several months, non-objection
to the prisoner's request for bail during this period is a
valuable gift in police hands. Once a case comes to court
the police are unable to do much for an informant. But, of
course, since they determine how and whether it does come
to court, a frequent form of deal is to get someone involved
in a crime to turn what used to be called King's Evidence.
Although this concept smacks of piracy, it is as alive today
as it was in the days of Captain Kidd. It has its own logic
which works thus.

Suppose that 'A', 'B', 'C' and 'D' commit a crime and that
there are no witnesses (in the piracy situation the crews
of the captured ships are all dead; in the modern gang situation no independent witness is brave enough to talk). If all
four keep silent, then all are safe and will escape prosecution.
But A, for instance, cannot be sure that the other three will
keep quiet. They may, they may not.

His only *sure* way to safety is to buy freedom by giving
evidence against his friends. The same thought is likely to
occur to the others; with proper police handling, the
pre-trial period resolves itself into a race for the witness-
box. In effect the prosecutor, quite independent of the court,
decides who is to be convicted and who is to go free. So,
in the Richardson and Kray gang trials, many of the witnesses
were, by their own confessions in the witness-box, almost
as guilty as the men in the dock.

Hart, the twenty-six-year-old member of the Kray gang
who helped them murder McVittie and later gave evidence
against them, was a classic example of an informant – and

[1] This betrays a degree of generosity which one might not expect
from detectives, because approaching a Magistrate for this purpose
would be a serious disciplinary offence. So perhaps it does not
happen very often.

a witness – for help. He said under cross-examination that he made his statement implicating the Krays because 'I would be in a better position giving evidence than being in the dock charged with murder[1].'

Recently, the power of the policemen to help the accused in court has considerably diminished. Ten years ago the prosecuting officer read out the man's convictions, and since he probably had the CRO docket in his hand, no one else was able or likely to complain if he omitted a few. Or, on the other hand, if the man had been difficult in custody or the police felt the law wasn't going to deal adequately with him, they could tell the court about his depraved habits and in-corrigible character.

Today a list of convictions has to be countersigned *in advance* by the DI, and the form delivered to the Bench. But this is an example from a uniform superintendent of what can still be done. 'When I was out vicing I had this nice little snout up the West End. He never gave me any aggravation, but he did ponce off people and eventually it was his turn to go. He was a good lad and he decided to plead to it. When he got up in court the Magistrate asks for his convictions to be read out. When you heard them like that, all in a lump, it did seem bad. There wasn't much in the book he hadn't turned his hand to. And it was the Magist-rate's bad day.

'He said: "I'm afraid this is a very bad case. It looks like a long term to me." We were all aghast – Chummy nearly fell out of the dock with fright. So I had to think wildly for some-thing to say in the poor sod's favour, because this was far too much. All I could say was that I felt this time he'd make a real effort to reform; I thought he'd been led astray, and I thought it was worth taking a chance with him. So he got a year suspended, and he's been my best little informant since. Though, with that year hanging over him, and his not entirely straight way of life, he rather had to be.'

[1] Times Law Report, 21 January 1969.

The essence of it all is acquiring snouts. All detectives of any competence have them: an ex-Flying Squad Sergeant gave me a lecture on the subject. 'Informants are like mistresses. You have a very odd relationship with them. You can *never, never* tell anyone about them, you must protect them – from the law if you can, and always from other criminals. There has to be a lot of trust between you: you have to trust him, because it would be the easiest thing in the world for him to manoeuvre you into a position where you could get your head beaten in, or, more likely, where it seems *you're* up to some villainy. He has to trust you not to implicate him, not to let anyone ever guess he told you what you know.

'Another thing is that you've always got to come when he calls – you can't afford to go cold on him or he'll lose his ten per cent and look for a more energetic officer. All in all, it's so demanding that you can't run more than three good, professional snouts.'

A revenge informant is often a good one in major crime because with him the detective can reach right into the heart of a gang, to people who, having the actual loot in their hands, would not be interested in the ten per cent of its value offered by the insurance companies. The same Sergeant explained one way of setting about this: 'We had a whisper about a team going to do a certain pay van. When the time came we were all set in ambush, then we swooped according to plan. It was the usual foul-up and five got away. We knew them and picked three up.

'That left two unaccounted for, that we never saw again – one didn't matter, but the other was important. After the trial we went to see the boss of the team in Brixton Prison. He asked who tipped us off, and I said, "No, nothing could ever possibly get me to tell." He offered £1,000 to know, but I couldn't say, and we started talking about other things. I said, buttering him up a bit, he was a good bloke, it was a good job and it should have succeeded.

'Half an hour later, as we were going, I said, "There's

only one fault, I don't think you're a very good judge of character." "What's that?", he said, sharp, and I pretended I'd spoken out of turn and refused to say more.

'Well, with a bit of luck, that will make him think. He's five years to brood on it – why hadn't the fifth man got nicked? He didn't because we couldn't find him, but he doesn't know that. Maybe in 1974 I'll get a phone call from him ... you never know. And the blokes who got away – I might even get a call from them, thinking we could have found them if we'd wanted to.

'But revenge snouts can be very dangerous. The whisper could be using you to get rid of an underworld enemy or it could be a way of framing you. I nearly got caught in a trap like that. The whisper said that a man we particularly wanted would be in a certain room in a particular house at six p.m. We went round at five past, kicked the door in, and you wouldn't believe it. There was Chummy, looking puzzled, and with him there was, in the following order: a Luger with ammunition in boxes, and a brand-new set of cleaning-gear – so he couldn't say he'd picked it up in the street.

'Then there was a morsel of gelignite, fuse, tamping and detonators all neatly packed in a matchbox – a proper little safe-blower's kit. Next we had some very good stolen silver, set out on a table, and last of all, what made it really ridiculous, a lump of cannabis. We were startled, but no one looked more surprised than Chummy, coming here for some plausible reason and finding the place laid out like a Judge's inspection. Later on, when he started shouting, quite rightly, that he'd been framed, who did the finger get pointed at? Right. You take a lot of risk with a grudge informant.

'The third and most reliable sort of snout is the straightforward commercial variety. The world of crime is composed of all sorts of different people. Mainly there are thieves and dealers – we call them placers. The thieves are usually labourers, stupid people. They steal a lorry load of tuna fish, let's say, and then they wonder what to do with it. Let's call them 'A's.

'They ring up 'B', the placer. He's a man with wide contacts, ready cash, and a reputation for honesty. He probably lives in Golders Green and his neighbours think he's something in the City. So he is. He says, "Right, leave it parked in such and such a street, and I'll give you two grand tomorrow in the Nag's Head." He organises a team to unload the lorry, re-box the tins, and sells the parcel for £4,000 to 'C', who might be a supermarket operator. 'B' never goes near the stuff. 'B' can also shop 'C', to get ten per cent of the market value, which is probably another £1,000.

'This has a lot of advantages for 'B'. By becoming a snout he gets a certain amount of protection from the law. Then he has a legitimate source of income which he can spend openly and still sleep at night. What he gets for information also disguises the money he makes dealing. The disadvantage is that it pays 'B' to organise thefts, because he wins either way. In fact there's probably a good deal of crime done for the ten per cent.

'Of course there's danger in it for 'B'. If 'C' is clever he tells 'B' to leave the lorry on such-and-such a road and hints it's going to Battersea. But he takes it to Finchley, and if places in Battersea get turned over, 'B' shows out and gets his ears cut off. To counter this we go about in our usual flat-footed fashion, creating noise and confusion, searching places at random, and sooner or later it's "Oh Sergeant! Look, I've found six tons of tuna!" '

The informing business is organised round the man who does it for money. I spent many hours with detectives wondering, in between things happening, what sort of men their informants were. Said one: 'He's a bit of a gambler, a bit of a liar. He's imaginative – he's got to be to think he'll get anywhere in this business. It's in his interest to embroider the story, to make it juicy so we think we're on to something good here and go out and sweat for him.'

The paying-off of informants poses some problems, too.

Wisely, the police refuse to pay large sums simply for information or conviction. There is an Informants Fund, administered by the CID, but on the average it pays out £25, and the absolute maximum is £100. The major banks offer £1000 for information leading to the conviction of bank robbers. But the real money comes from the insurance companies, who pay a reward of ten per cent of the value of the stolen property recovered to the informant who led to it. One tenth seems a small reward, but in practice its leverage is considerable. The resale value of stolen goods is generally only a fraction of their market value. This fraction varies in proportion to identifiability – stolen whisky or cigarettes may fetch fifty to seventy-five per cent, stolen jewellery fifteen to thirty per cent.

Since most crimes involve more than one person, ten per cent of the market value becomes comparable to any individual's share. In the first case, this happens if there are five to seven people involved – as there may be, since distribution involves unloading some tons of merchandise; or if there are two to three people in the second case. Naturally, a criminal does not become a snout simply because one reward is larger than his share from one job. He has to think of his future. Giving information to the police will wreck his team, even if it does not harm him, and cuts off that source of criminal income. But even so, ten per cent is not too small to produce results.

This system incorporates an ethical safeguard. No reward is payable until an actual crime has been committed and real goods have been recovered, so there is less incentive for informants to frame underworld enemies. But payment by results poses the police with a difficult problem. Suppose they know – because a snout has told them – that a robbery team is going to make an attempt on a payroll van.

Now, it is obviously their duty to anticipate the attack and arrest the team as soon as it declares its intentions and a charge of attempted robbery can be made out, so that civilians in the van don't get hurt. But if the police do that, nothing is stolen, and the insurance company refuses to pay a reward. This discourages the informant – he may have put some months of work and risk into the job. Next time he may opt to join the robbery himself. This is hardly in society's interest.

Informants are a London detective's bread, butter and reputation. They are his personal property, and it is against CID ethics to try to identify a colleague's snout. Once during this voyage, I spent an amusing morning, listening, while an ill-informed Detective Superintendent tried to bully a certain informant's name out of a Detective Inspector.

Not only are informants a detective's reputation, they are often an expense to him. It is common to have to give them ten to twenty pounds to tide them over a dead patch – one DI estimated that year in and year out he spent seventy pounds out of his own pocket keeping his informants housed and fed. He'd tried deducting it as a business expense but, 'They wouldn't have it. No receipts, you see, can't be. I suppose they felt, if they did allow it, every CID officer in London would find he was spending a couple of hundred a year on snouts.'

On the other hand, since for every ten pieces of gossip relayed by snouts, one, through the perseverance and hard work of the police, is turned into an arrest, a recovery of stolen property, and an insurance pay-out, it would be amazing if the informant – who is probably snouting lest a worse fate should befall him – and the officer in the case didn't sometimes share the reward in a discreet and gentlemanly fashion. This would go far to explain the agonised jealousy which detectives feel over their snouts.

At first sight, bearing in mind how, in a sophisticated criminal society, informants are really the only way of finding out what is going on, it would seem worth spending much more money on them. One well-placed, well-rewarded informant might produce better results than a team of ten officers working for a year. On grounds of cost alone he would be worth £30,000. But the problem is one of ethical engineering. As soon as rewards get too big, they become ends in themselves.

The current rate for pure information, unsupported by goods, is so meagre that it is not worth framing people for it. The rate for stolen property, ten per cent of the value, is nicely set so that it is too low to make it worth buying, even at underworld rates, to plant on an enemy. But if sums like £30,000 were being offered for information to convict well-known criminals, the rush of would-be frame-up artists would be terrifying. Prosecutions based on evidence got in this way would be gossamer structures apt to collapse into scandal.

The actual paying of informants is simple. Once the stolen property has been recovered, the detective in charge of the case simply produces a man – usually one of the well-known Smiths – in the Loss Adjuster's office – says "This is the one who helped us with the Horridge job," the loss adjuster hands over ten per cent in used notes and that's that.

Plea of Guilty

Although the courts are central to the detective's life, he does not particularly want to have to fight his cases there. He prefers the accused to plead guilty, the procedure in court to be amiable and automatic. The layman tends, per-haps, to think of the typical trial as a contest, a forensic battle between good and evil. In reality, the situation is rather different. In terms of figures, non-guilty pleas are distinctly rare, and it becomes apparent that the smooth – or indeed any sort of – working of the police and the courts is com-pletely dependent on a high rate of guilty pleas[1].

The argument is this. The CID in London initiate some 70,000 prosecutions a year for indictable offences. All but three per cent are heard in Magistrates' Courts[2], and it is thought that ninety per cent or more of these are settled

[1] See also Skolnick J., *Justice Without Trial*, Wiley, 1966.
[2] *Time Spent Awaiting Trial*, Home Office, HMSO, 1960.

by a plea of guilty, though the exact figure is not known. In the higher courts – Sessions and Assizes – the rate of guilty pleas falls to seventy-five per cent, but even so, the police have only to fight some 7,000 odd cases a year. It is difficult to say how much work these cause. A recent study of police manpower was unable to separate the work involved in preparing cases from that needed to detect criminals[1] but it would not be unreasonable to say that every contested case involves a detective in an average of two weeks' extra work.

This is not surprising when one considers that he has to find and persuade witnesses, take two sets of statements from them – one for police use, one for committal proceedings – write a report on the case, complete some thirteen forms on the prisoner, complete legal aid forms, take charge of recovered property and eventually return it to the owners, appear three or four times in court to ask for remands. And against the large number of easy cases, one also has to set, say, the gang trials, which each occupied 100 detectives for over a year.

To see how the not-guilty plea rate affects detective's work load, let us suppose that the rate in *all* courts rises to twenty-five per cent. To cope with the extra work, some 200–400 more detectives are needed. Since none of these are forthcoming, each existing detective's work is increased by one-seventh to one-third. Bearing in mind that detectives in London already work 116 hours a week,[2] it is evident that a *small* increase in the not-guilty plea rate imposes a very *large* burden on them.

This analysis is so crude that it can only illustrate a qualitative relationship. It is none the less real for that. One might imagine that, as in all living systems, some sort of dynamic equilibrium exists, that the actual level of not-guilty pleas is set by a process of give and take, of tacit bargaining be-

[1] Martin and Wilson, *The Police: A Study in Manpower*, Heinemann, London, 1969, p. 147.
[2] Martin and Wilson. *op. cit.*

tween accuser and accused – which the courts abet. It is almost too much to dignify this process with the name 'negotiation'. Experienced criminals and experienced detectives know the factors involved so well that there is probably seldom any need for formal, verbal bargaining, but the understood object is to find a level at which the seriousness of the charge, the punishment to be expected, the burden on the detective, balance out to produce a solution acceptable to all parties, expressed as a guilty plea[1].

The elaboration of the law means that almost any criminal action can be 'interpreted' to the court as one of several named crimes. Thus a man arrested for attacking another could be charged with either attempted murder, causing grievous bodily harm, or common assault. Each is easier for the detective to prove, but each carries a lower sentence. He might feel doubtful about attempted murder, but confident of proving grievous bodily harm, and ask the prisoner to plead guilty to that. The prisoner, on the other hand, might feel that it was too good a bargain as it stood. He might insist on being paid something extra in the small change of these negotiations – that the detective should speak well of his character. So perhaps a deal is made.

From the layman's point of view, an unexpected corollary of the high guilty plea rate is that the *contested* trial which we have come to know from innumerable representations in courtroom dramas, on film and television, is completely atypical. In the vast majority of cases, the real trial is conducted privately and informally between the detective and the accused in the privacy of a cell, or crouched in the court hall; the decision which they come to is then quickly rubber-stamped by the court, whose only real function is to pass sentence. Some courts encourage this by tacitly giving lower sentences to those who co-operate. The bonus can be impressive – one of the Great Train Robbers who pleaded guilty got fifteen years as against his colleagues' thirty.

[1] See the detective quoted on p. 238 for an explicit personal explanation of this process.

Even when the charge is of murder, the 'trial' following a plea of guilty consists of no more than a brief résumé of the circumstances of the offence and the passing of sentence. In less serious cases the whole business can literally be over in five minutes. One begins to see why it is important to policemen that their villains should plead. The investigation has often been hard enough work and the large amount extra needed to ensure conviction is to them so much unnecessary effort. In the long run, every plea of not guilty is a threat to the detective's precariously balanced workload.

Then the detective's *amour-propre* is involved. A guilty plea recognises the rightness of his case, the soundness of his judgement. The detective knows that the man is guilty – or else he wouldn't have arrested him – and a guilty plea shows a proper recognition of the fact. It gives the detective the initiative in their dealings, he can be lenient, agree to bail, put in a good word – they become to some extent collaborators. The detective is as much a prisoner of the judicial process as the man he arrests. A guilty plea unties his hands, and helps create a good relationship between them.

As well as saving him a great deal of physical work, the guilty plea relieves him of a lot of worry and thought. His witnesses may be weak – perhaps a feeble-minded girl, the victim, is his only witness of a sexual assault. She could be useless in cross-examination. It is like entering a horse for a race, and being given the blue rosette before you've saddled up.

Also, a plea pulls down the curtain on all past transactions. No questions can arise about the information that led to the arrest, about the arrest itself. There can be no complaints about the arresting officer's behaviour and no haggling over the Judges' Rules.

CHAPTER NINE

The Police Memory

Finger-prints

The first and fundamental difficulty in police information handling is to tie information contained in, say, a Criminal Record File about a given person to the correct body at large in the community. Without some indisputable link, CRO's two and a quarter million files would be useless, and criminals anonymous ghosts. The link is finger-printing, and the accident that makes modern policing possible is that humans have hairless fingers and palms.

The ridges that make up finger (and palm, toe, sole) prints are formed by 'elevated parallel rows of sweat gland orifices, and are laid down at an early stage in foetal life, probably by the tenth week[1]. The cause of their complicated patterns is unknown, but it seems that at first the ridges take the shortest paths over the embryonic skin, encircling the fingers and the pads that are present on the limb buds. As the hands and feet grow, so the patterns become distorted in various arbitrary ways. Even so, there is some logic to it. There are two basic finger-print patterns: loops, where the lines turn through two right angles, and triradii, the triangled pattern formed when three sets of parallel lines brush against each other.

It seems that, if a body of any simple shape – that is, without holes in it like a Hepworth sculpture – has parallel lines running over it, these two basic patterns must appear in defined numbers. For instance, the mathematician Littlewood[2] imagines the business of brushing a spherical dog;

[1] Penrose, L. D., British Medical Journal, 11 May 1968, 2: 321.
[2] Littlewood, J. E., A Mathematician's Miscellany, London, 1953.

he points out that there must be either four loops like a tennis ball, or two crowns, like those formed by lines of longitude on the earth at the poles.

Penrose shows that, if one thinks of a single limb, a simple rule connects the numbers of nails, triradii and loops. It is also becoming understood that finger-print abnormalities are linked to certain chromosomal oddities. Since a high proportion of these people are found in prison, due perhaps to their general unfitness for life, the rather wild claim has been made that criminality is genetically determined and can be diagnosed by finger-printing[1].

Such refinements are of little interest to the police. As far as they are concerned, finger-prints exist, each person's is unique, and the problem is to classify them. Although the individuality of finger-prints was recognised as early as 1684 by Nehemia Grew, they were useless as a means of identification until some way of sorting them had been invented. Galton, in 1892, stimulated research by pointing out that the patterns are unique and stay the same throughout life; Henry[2], then serving in the Bengal Police, invented a system of filing the prints of both hands in enough categories to keep even a very large collection in small enough bundles to make routine searching possible.

To the layman, Henry's system appears to be one of the most obscure inventions of the human mind. For his primary classification one looks only for whorls (two loops head to tail, making an oval, or race-track formation). Their appearance on any finger is scored thus:

16 points for each one on right thumb or right forefinger
8 for each one on right middle or ring fingers
4 for each one on right little finger or left thumb
2 for each one on left forefinger or left middle
1 for left ring or little finger.

---

[1] See Price, W. H., et al., Lancet, 12 March 1966, pp. 565; and Court Brown, W. M., et al., British Medical Journal, 11 May 1968, pp. 325.

[2] Sir Edward Henry, later Commissioner of the Metropolitan Police.

A fraction is then constructed by adding the scores for the right thumb, right middle, left fore and ring + 1 and dividing the total by the sum of the scores of the other fingers + 1. Arbitrary as this sounds, it works well, because it gives most weight and therefore most spread in the classification to the marks made by the right thumb, fore and middle fingers, the ones most often used in crime. Henry's secondary classification scores the patterns on the forefingers, his tertiary those on the rest[1].

The Main Collection is housed on half a floor of the Tower Block at New Scotland Yard. It is kept in neatly-made, Victorian wooden cabinets standing in rows, which contrast oddly with the stainless-steel and plate-glass walls. Each cabinet has, on its dozen shelves, bundles of foolscap finger-print forms bound in five-hundreds between cardboard covers.

The routine business of the Main Collection is to confirm the identities of the thousand odd people who are arrested in the United Kingdom every day. Their finger-prints have all been taken at police stations, and the forms are sent to Scotland Yard – from stations in London and the Home counties they arrive at or before dawn the next day; from the provinces they come by post and may take a day or two in transit.

The first check is by name, date of birth and height in a two-million-card rotary index in the middle of the room. About half of the people arrested have previous convictions, and their CRO numbers are shown on the cards. It is then easy to find their last finger-print form, check that the prints on the old and new forms are identical and draw the correct CRO file.

The other five hundred are more laborious and less rewarding. Four hundred and fifty of them, on the average, genuinely have no previous convictions, but hiding among them are the other fifty who do have, but who have given false names. Simply to find them, the whole five hundred

[1] Cherrill, Frederick R., *The Finger-print System at Scotland Yard*, HMSO, London, 1954.

forms have to be classified and searched. This involves one set of officers working out the Henry Classification for each set of prints – which takes them no longer than to add up a short bill – then the form is passed to a searcher who ploughs through the four thousand or so forms in the appropriate part of the collection, in the slim hope that one will match, giving him an 'ident'.

Because the Main Collection's classification depends on all ten fingers, it is seldom able to identify a criminal from the one or two marks he may leave at the scene of his crime. However, if there are three or four clear marks with an unusual pattern it may be possible to make allowances for the unknown fingers and make a successful search. Or, if there is only one mark but the crime is a serious one, the whole collection of two million forms will be searched. In the ordinary run of things about three Main Collection searches are done a week.

Once or twice a year, in London, a criminal leaves such a clear and complete set of marks that it is simple to search straight away for him in the Main Collection. More often, though, he leaves the smudged marks of only one or two fingers. The business of interpreting these is dealt with by another department of C3, the Scenes of Crime Section.

The worker here has several difficult problems to deal with. The first is the quality of his raw material. When a man is finger-printed at a police station, his fingers are rolled over the paper, making an exact, clear copy of every detail. At the scene of crime, if he leaves any marks at all, they are likely to be from only the tips of one or two fingers. The area of contact may easily omit the distinctive patterns that show on the form, and if he has been gripping hard, the pressure will spread his finger so that the mark is bigger than the print. It may also bring low-lying ridges into contact with the surface, completely altering the pattern. Marks left after light and heavy contacts can seem to have been made by different fingers.

To add to the searcher's problems, he has no automatic

way of telling which finger made a particular mark. He has
to guess from the size and shape of the object how the criminal held it. Then he has to ask whether the marks he has
could have been made by the criminal, and only the criminal.
Not many crimes are done with the hands – housebreaking,
lorry theft, robbery, rape, arson are the main ones. Many
others that would seem promising candidates are hopeless
from the start because the criminal could have 'legitimate
access'. Thus, it proves nothing about a shop assistant suspected of stealing cash to find her finger-prints on the till.

'What we want is four fingers, upside down in a bunch
under the window sill. He has to be a housebreaker,' observed the young finger-print officer with whom I spent
a morning, as he settled himself and his cards under a bright
light. He sat at one of half-a-dozen long desks, among a
couple of dozen colleagues; clipped to his lamp was a notice:
"Reynolds' first law of identification: the number of idents
is inversely proportional to the amount of chat." He was
a technological, dedicated young man who had worked his
way to this job after three years in the Main Collection. To
begin his work, he had a pile of finger-print forms from
people arrested the day before in his part of London. He
would first check these against recent scenes of crime marks,
which he had in the form of little cards bearing out negative
photographs of finger-prints, each card marked with the
date and the appropriate crime-book number.

The first man was arrested at Willesden Green, and is
a suspected burglar. So he searched all the marks from Q
Division. This produced nothing. Since ninety-five per cent
of burglaries are done within fifteen miles of the burglar's
home, he got out the cards for the divisions around the
man's home. 'I'm looking for a whorl on the right thumb
with a bifurcation to the right, two ridges below the delta,
and a little lake three below that and to the left. There's a
loop in the mid-finger (he has marks from what he thinks
are right fore and mid fingers) so that limits the search'
(i.e. any form with a classification lower than eight is out).

He has a street map of London with Scenes of Crime marked on it, because burglars tend to work one street one day and another the next, and gets out the marks from nearby jobs to compare them.

He flips through the cards almost faster than I can focus on them, doing about 100 in fifteen minutes, and then, having found nothing, inverts his method of working. He selects one new Scene of Crime mark and compares it with the Section's files of known housebreakers. These are xeroxed copies of the bottom parts of finger-print forms – straight contact prints, comparable with those left in real life. He takes care to select a full-bodied mark with plenty of detail. 'The only point of this game is to win, to get an ident. This means you don't want to spend too much time searching, and you want to be reasonably sure you've got a good enough mark to be able to identify it and then prove the identification in court.'

If part of the skill of Scenes of Crime searching is to start with a good mark, the other half is in clever filing of the reference-collection. For example, seventy per cent of housebreakers convicted for the first time are never convicted again – either because they become more cunning, or because they reform. So their forms are only kept long enough for other offences committed before arrest to come to light. He searched these recent arrests first. Then he searched the collection of wanted men and prison escapers because they often have to steal to eat. After that, he turned to the 9,000 housebreakers' prints filed in various subtle ways.

If in the past these men had committed crimes on one of the twenty-two divisions, they are filed under it, if they worked on two or more divisions, they are filed in one of the four district bundles, if on two districts, then in either the north or south London bundles, and if they have worked everywhere in the Metropolis they go in the all-London bundle. Which bundle the searcher chooses depends on his intuition and skill. He looks at the size and location of the crime, and tries to guess the size and location of the criminal.

While a steady plodding mind does well in the Main Collection, here the risk-taker succeeds better.

Each of the toiling searchers finds, perhaps, two idents a week. For them it is like finding diamonds. When it happens, the lucky one takes the form and the photograph of the mark to one of the Chief Inspectors who sit in a room of their own with a finger-print comparator – a device that enlarges both patterns and throws them onto a screen. Their job is to satisfy themselves that the mark and print are indeed identical.

This requires a close examination of the minute peculiarities of the ridges, which can only be seen under magnification. Here a ridge suddenly ends, there breaks into two round a lake, and so on. One square centimetre of one finger contains enough detail to identify a man uniquely, but before two prints can be said in court to be the same, sixteen matching peculiarities must be found. Then big photographs are made for the jury with rings drawn round each one of the sixteen points, and lines to join the similarities.

The raw material for Scenes of Crime searching, the photographs of marks, are provided by a dozen District Finger-print Officers, who are retired policemen, or, more often now, civilians promoted from within C3. Their job is to examine anything which a detective thinks may have been touched by a criminal. They dust bottles, cars, window-ledges with their traditional camel-hair brushes and mercury and chalk powder. They photograph the result with a simple, electronic-flash camera that automatically produces a print the same size as the mark. The rest of their job is to promote the virtues of finger-print detection throughout the Force, for the use of even so well-established a scientific method as this is by no means general.

The foregoing is an inadequate description of an office that employs 250 highly trained specialists, and has in its eighty years developed a lore, science and world-wide reputation all of its own. But at the time of writing it was undergoing a profound change. The Henry System was being almost abandoned, and a new computer-based classification introduced. Since the machine works so much more quickly than humans, a more thorough classification can be used than would be practicable with manual searching.

It will still be necessary to classify each print by hand, but a simple number will be assigned to each finger corresponding to the type of pattern on it. Some patterns, too, are measurable – by, say, the number of ridges between the centre of a whorl and its triradii: these ridge-counts go in as well. Altogether the classification can put each finger into one of 703 different compartments, and therefore the whole two hands into one of 10^{703} compartments.

The computer's memory will store these classifications as a string of numbers together with the man's name and CRO number, which leads immediately to his finger-print form. A trial section of the collection was reclassified for the computer: instead of the 4,000 forms which the average search involves, the computer will generally throw out ten candidates. The worst computer case yet showed 117 possibles. This system will do a lot to raise the speed and accuracy of searching, and will also make it possible to search a single print through the Main Collection, often giving a much improved service to the most minor housebreaking.

Although a single print can only be placed in one of 703 groups, and on the average a single print search will throw out some 30,000 suggestions, it will be possible to refine this a great deal by asking the computer to select only suspects who live in a particular place, or are within certain age limits – for instance, people breaking into a youth club are apt to be fourteen to sixteen years old.

The system should be working by the time that this book is published, but it still involves a good deal of manual effort. The total automation of finger-printing, where one hands a Scene of Crime mark to the computer and waits for the criminal's name and address to be printed out, is a long way away. In theory, the problem is not difficult. One makes a hologram of the mark (an optical transformation of the image which, as it were, distributes all the characteristics of the image all over itself) and compares it in turn with the holograms of all the stored prints. When they match, the villain is found.

Unfortunately the eye is a great deal better at this job than the computer. The machine can't tell which way up marks should be, it is confused by missing pieces, it is misled by bits of dirt or old marks underneath. Then the mark may be distorted by movement of the finger that made it, or by too much pressure. At the time of writing the Home Office had five research contracts out on this problem, worth £300,000, spread over four years[1]. No breakthrough is expected in less than a decade.

Forensic Science

Forensic science fits into this chapter because of its functional similarity with the bulk of finger-print work. The forensic scientist seldom, in fact, detects criminals. But as the Main Finger-print Collection proves the identity of suspects who have already been arrested, so forensic science can prove or disprove guilt. Suspects are seldom found by forensic analysis alone. In the vast majority of cases the work of the laboratory plays its part in the whole investigative machine: police effort in the field produces evidence for the laboratory to examine, and questions for it to answer; armed with the answers, the police can advance a step further. A rare example, in which scientific evidence almost on its own found a criminal, was described by the late Director of the Metropolitan Police Forensic Science Laboratory. A woman in the West Country woke up to find a man in her bedroom. She shrieked and he ran away. In the morning she discovered a strange pair of trousers on the floor. Examination showed scraps of nimonic alloy in the turnups, a metal mostly used to make jet engine rotor-blades: the man was found working a lathe in a nearby jet engine factory[2].

[1] First report from the Committee on the Estimates, Session 1966–7, *Police*, 1966, p. 17.
[2] Walls, H. J., *Forensic Science*, Sweet and Maxwell, London, 1967.

Partly this is because few crimes lend themselves to scientific analysis. In London only two per cent of all crimes are referred to the Laboratory. The distribution of 15,000 handled between 1962 and 1964 was[1]:

	per cent
Driving under the influence of drink	43.9
Dangerous drugs, identifying samples	11.8
Housebreaking	10.5
Sex	8.8
Larceny	5.9
Assaults and wounding	2.8
Arson, malicious damage	2.7
Road accidents	2.5
Murder, manslaughter	2.1
Poison	2.0
Robbery	1.7
Abortion	.9
Forgery, coining	.5
Other	3.9

The drink, drugs and sex cases, that together make up sixty-four per cent of all those dealt with, involve routine chemical examinations – for alcohol, for cannabis or heroin, for human semen on women's clothes.

In ninety-five per cent of his work, a forensic scientist will be asked a 'closed' question: are samples A and B identical? For instance, is the paint on the accused's jemmy identical with the paint on the victim's front door? Or he is asked to compare a sample with some known substance: (in a case of suspected arson) is there petrol at the scene of the fire? If the answer is yes, this leads to another closed question: is this petrol the same as that in a tin in the suspect's garage?

Recent years have given the forensic scientist some impressive equipment. The dogma of old-fashioned chemical analysis is now almost replaced by powerful new techniques of gas chromatography, mass and infra-red spectrometry,

[1] Walls, *op. cit.*

which make it possible to identify hundreds of components in the most minute samples. Each batch of petrol distilled, for instance, differs from every other, and gas chromatographic analysis gives as much identifying information about each as there is in a finger-print.

Almost too much information is now available. If a body were found murdered, with a tiny piece of coal in the wound, it would in principle be possible, by doing a pollen survey of British coal-pits, to identify the seam from which the fragment came, and then to trace it through distributors, perhaps to the house where it was delivered. Yet this raises formidable problems of cost-effectiveness. Such an expensive job might be worth doing in a murder case, but then suppose a man being prosecuted for stealing coal demanded the same service to prove that he had bought the stuff? Could the nation afford even a thousand cases like it a year?

New techniques, too, give a very much better means of identifying people. There are now five to six different systems of blood-grouping in use, as well as the familiar A, B and O. Most of these were developed in the Metropolitan Police Laboratory. Using them all, one could assign a stain to five per cent of the population in the worst case, to one in ten million at the best. There is a new method of identifying hair by exposing it to neutron radiation in a reactor for half an hour, and then measuring the energy of gamma radiation given off by the different decaying radioactive elements. This technique was recently able to demonstrate Napoleon's murder by arsenic. Human voices can be identified to the satisfaction of the courts by analysing the sound of spoken test words into their component frequencies.

None of these methods of identification, blood, hair, and voice, is as certain as finger-printing, but if they were all available at once, the probabilities multiplied together could give almost certainty. But to set against these advances, as forensic science becomes more sophisticated, gives more sensitive consideration to a wider range of possibilities, so it becomes vastly more expensive. And its results tend to be stated more often in terms of probabilities than certainties.

Instead of saying, with Victorian dogmatism, 'The blood-stain on the knife came from the murdered man, and no other', the scientist now has to say in court that the probability is, say, 10,000 to one that it did. It is common for defence counsel to be 'unable to understand' such statements as: 'The relative concentration of alcohol in blood and urine is as five to four', in the hope that the jury too will decide that the evidence is all far too technical for them to follow.

There is little point in trying to give a comprehensive account of forensic science here even if space allowed it. As Walls, quoted above, says, 'Forensic science is like couch grass – it infests a large area untidily and parasitically. It cannot be discussed without much arbitrary classification,' and the reader is referred to his up-to-date and thorough book.

Criminal Record Office

The Criminal Record Office has often been mentioned in this and other chapters, because it affects many aspects of policing. It is in a sense the memory of the Force, the information-store that correlates the efforts of individual policemen into something far more effective than anything that they could achieve alone.

CRO is simply an office, all over one floor of Scotland Yard, which keeps the national criminal records. Access is restricted to those who work or have business there. There are three million folders in row after row of green metal filing racks: pastel-coloured files, leaning softly against each other like a shabby fungus that grows faster and faster. Ladies in neat royal blue nylon dustcoats serve the stacks with mounds of files where the hardest-working people in London control the insensate operation.

They keep track of the 25,000 files out at any one moment in Scotland Yard and the 184 police stations, they route 5,000 files a day from one office to another. Clanking round the whole floor is a ceiling-railway bearing boxes of yet more files. It is a deluge of paper as stunning to the senses as a big waterfall; and it is odd to think that, if the English decided tonight to commit no more crime, within a week the flow would slacken, within a month many of these three hundred people would be doing nothing, within six months it would all be quiet, just several hundred tons of paper slumping a fraction lower each year on its metal shelves.

The Criminal Record Office, says a little handbook issued to all policemen, is a national registry of crimes, and a *Who's Who* of their perpetrators, a means of enabling new crimes to be traced to old criminals and old criminals to be recognised with certainty when arrested.' A CRO file is only started for serious crime – theft, violence, sexual offences – though once in being, it may well record subsequent minor convictions for parking, drunkenness, or breach of the peace.

Each file contains a form that describes the criminal at his last conviction. This, by a process of summation, includes all his previous convictions, gives something of his life-story, perhaps a photograph if he has been to prison, and a good deal of other material which may or may not be accurate and/or useful. This is the basic material of criminal investigation. When a policeman has it in his hand, he knows more or less with whom he is dealing. But CRO offers several other services.

In the centre of the floor there is a bank of pale-green telephone consoles, where detectives wait for calls from their colleagues in the street. A red light shines, a flicked toggle-switch releases a harsh police voice, which requests a search done on an Arthur George Mullen, born on 16 March 1928, and who is five foot ten or so. The listening detective is satisfied that this is a genuine policeman, as is evident from his rhythmic, confident delivery and his putting the details of the message in the right order. He has to be sure because sometimes, in the past, people have got hold of the confidential CRO number, pretended to be policemen and asked for their enemies' convictions.

He puts the headset down and goes to search in the filed slips of the CRO nominal index for Mullen, Mullin,

Mullins, Mullens, Arthur George, George Arthur, and then for Arthur Mullen GEORGE, and Mullen George ARTHUR and all the other combinations. In fact the nominal index shows a George Arthur Mullin born 16.3.21, 5' 10". He goes back to the desk, tells the PC to hang on and sends a girl for the file. Then he searches the 80,000 cards of deserters, and escapers from prisons and mental hospitals, and a few missing persons – either young people or those who are mad or ill (but the Wanted Index gives no help to people looking for lost spouses or debtors). As it happened, the George Arthur Mullin was in prison, and had no connection with PC Bambridge's customer.

In another corner of the same room, the Cheque Index, a relatively new department, keeps a record of all the cheque frauds reported to the police, filed by bank, branch and cheque-book number. Little help in detection, this index exists to bring home all a fraudsman's crimes when he is eventually caught – as seventy-five per cent are. It holds 40,000 cards, and each one corresponds to a cheque book stolen in the last five years and used to buy goods. The day of my visit a man had been arrested for murder, and confessed to 500 cheque frauds on the side. He could only remember the false names which he had used, so a detective was going laboriously through the Wanted Index after the names, in order to be directed to the cards recording the frauds.

Further along, at the end of a busy corridor, is a more interesting part of CRO, the Method Index. Originally, this recorded the trade marks of artists in burglary, who would use the same polished technique time after time. Now that breaking is becoming more varied, and specialists tend to perambulate, being used by different teams for different jobs, the Method Index is losing some of its original usefulness. But it has blossomed out in other directions. It files criminals under some 800 headings. Under *Larceny Dwelling*, for example, there are sub-sections: 'enters by acquaintance of servant, by imposture of electricity official, by . . .' Under *Fraud* there are sub-headings: 'character assumed, sort of person deceived, sort of proceeds – food and lodging, money, goods.' There is a little index of nick-names – very useful if a group is disturbed and as they run, one shouts "See you at Izzy's". It has names, 'Iggy, Hunch-back Charlie, Horse, Hoppy Taff (a one-legged Welshman), Jewzie, Jesus Christ (a hippy).

There are entries for deformities and habits. One card, pulled at random, describes a man who keeps a dog, bites his finger-nails, habitually confesses to murder, takes his boots off in the house and eats a meal, speaks of life in the army, uses the word 'redundant' a lot – all characteristics that are hard to disguise. Next to him, a fraudsman who poses as a Harley Street surgeon, and has actually operated on his patients in hospitals.

Again, by the time this is published, most of the Index will have been transferred to punched cards for eventual inclusion in the CRO computer. Half of it had been done when I saw it: a detective came in asking for a bald-headed, Jewish-looking fraudsman, born between 1926 and 1929 and about five foot ten tall. The sorting-machine whirred through an armful of cards and threw out two suggestions. In 1967 the Index had 5,000 such inquiries, and made 4,000 suggestions which produced 694 clear-ups or arrests, which, in police terms, is a good return for the work of four men.

Part of Method Index, but housed in another small room on the same floor, is the Witness Photo Albums, the 'rogues gallery'. Eye-witnesses of crimes are shown those books of anonymous portraits which contain the appropriate sort of criminals, and, on the off chance, everyone is shown the 'wanted men' album. The pictures vary in quality. Some are wedding-portraits, or taken from company reports or trade papers. These are mostly of fraudsmen, who look calm among the harassed riff-raff whose portraits had been taken in prison. Albums entertain 4,000 witnesses a year who hope they can reconcile the image stored in their brains with one of the hundreds on paper: in 1967 they had 600 identifications.

Next door is the Murder Index, a permanent liaison office with whatever murder squads are at work. Their main occupation when I was there was with the Cannock Chase murder. Several small girls living in the Walsall area of Birmingham had been raped and strangled. Because sex criminals tend to do the same thing over and over again, the police had searched 120,000 CRO files. The murder squad dealing with the case had interviewed 50,000 males between twenty-one and fifty living in Walsall, and checked each for a criminal record. After nearly two years' exhaustive work the murderer was caught and convicted. He had been a prime suspect almost from the first. Interviewed twice by the police, he had been shielded by his wife's false alibi; on the third visit she abandoned him.

Across the corridor in a large open office there is the Property Index, yards of card index, recording every sort of thing that can possibly be stolen. Running the eye along the top drawers, 'Cows, Firearms, Greyhounds, Inks, Mattresses, Pens, Pencils, Pins, Shirts, Water tanks.' There is an index of things that are numbered and have been stolen: television sets, air-compressors, cranes, binoculars; everything except cars, which are recorded in the Central Vehicle Index. Rather like the cheque index, this one exists mainly to prove the guilt of persons found in possession of stolen property, and to trace the proper owners.

To the visitor, and perhaps to the reader, the essential function of CRO may be obscure. In a small number of cases it identifies criminals by showing that they have committed similar crimes before, or it suggests suspects who may be identified by witnesses, finger-prints or some other means. More often, when a policeman has a suspect, it will tell him whether he is wanted, or whether he has previous convictions and is worth looking at closer. And, when a man is finally convicted, it proves his previous convictions to the court, thus, so policemen hope, securing to him the punishment which he deserves.

Communications

A store of criminal information, however large and efficiently filed, is of little use unless items from it can be quickly transmitted. This ability to communicate is perhaps the second major distinction between a police force and a crowd of law-enforcement officers, though at the moment it is not as good in London as is technically possible or as the police would like.

Rapid communication is by means of a fairly elaborate frequency-modulated radio system. There are eight channels in use, grouped around the 100 mcs band. Each channel uses two frequencies, one for cars to talk inwards, one for control to broadcast outwards. This second frequency also re-broadcasts the inward-coming messages, so that every car on the channel knows everything that is going on, and every car can serve, if necessary, as a control. So it is the practice that the first vehicle to arrive at the scene of a major disaster acts as the local control, taking over the channel until a properly-equipped mobile police station comes up.

The radio system is run from the Information Room at Scotland Yard, where there are two transmitters; four more ranged round the edges of London are connected to it by land-lines. None of these handles all eight channels, so that good reception depends on the channel used and the position of the car. The first four channels are allocated for ordinary operational use to the four districts.

Channels five and six are good anywhere in London, and are used for non-urgent messages transferred from one of the four operational channels, and for Central operations – Flying Squad, Criminal Intelligence, C1, photographers and laboratory vans. On special occasions of public rejoicing or demonstration, one of these channels is often used to co-ordinate police operations, working from the Urgent Communications Room (see below). Channels seven and eight are used for traffic control – seven covers the centre of London which is mostly patrolled by motorcyclists, and eight the perimeter.

At any moment there are some 3–400 police vehicles on the air; at busy times the operational channels are often overloaded. Much as the police would like, and could use, extra frequencies, they have to compete with other public utilities, such as the Gas and Electricity Boards. Denser local cover given by the personal radio system is superimposed on this network. The personal radio covers the MPD by sub-divisions, so that policemen on the street can talk straight to their home station.

Each little set has up to a dozen portable transceivers and a maximum of three base stations, all transmitting the same signal. For perfect coverage some sub-divisions should have as many as six base stations, but it would be too expensive to lease the control lines from the GPO. The system operates much as the car radios; messages are sent and received on different frequencies, but incoming messages are re-broadcast so that everyone can hear all. The system is designed to be informal so that policemen can chat away, passing on scraps of information as easily on the street as they can in the station canteen.

Several models of personal radio were being tried out during my visit. They were all one-piece transceivers slung on a canvas harness. The aerials were woven into the straps, so that the whole set could be worn under a jacket. The microphone-speaker worn on the lapel is the only visible part, and that can be put in a pocket (the City of London, and some other forces, prefer a two-piece set, each part of which is small enough to fit into an ordinary pocket).

Theoretically, a two-way portable radio set working at a frequency which filters through city buildings has been possible for decades. The Brighton Police experimented with such a system before World War Two, but with radio components the size they were, the set was too heavy to carry comfortably, and the necessarily long aerial made the policeman look like a Martian. Only recently, with the mass production of transistors and radio components in subminiature sizes, has it been possible to make a small, cheap, powerful and reliable set. Cheap, that is, in police terms. Each set costs about £150.

The station sets are no great problem. They can be as powerful as is necessary, but even with aerials placed as high as possible, in city streets, with many steel-framed buildings that soak up radio signals, the range over which the portable sets can be heard is only about three miles.

In Divisions, where 'Unit Beat' policing is operated (see p. 58) and patrolling PCs drive small cars, the personal radio-net works exactly like the main radio, able to send cars to urgent calls. In some places the two systems seem almost in competition: citizens in the outer reaches of London are finding that they get a quicker emergency service by ringing the local station and getting their problem passed by radio to a patrolling Panda car, than by ringing 999 for an Area car.

The two systems correspond to the fact that even urgent information coming into the police machine differs widely in the distribution it needs. Children throwing stones off a railway bridge and a major train disaster both need immediate attention, but the news of the first needs to be broadcast over a far smaller area than the second. The trouble is that any piece of information may arrive anywhere; news of the children may come into Information Room on a 999 call; the train wreck may be discovered by a walking PC.

The City of Birmingham, a rather more diffuse place than London, has solved the problem by scrapping its central control to which all 999 calls used to go. Instead, they are now routed to the local station, which directs a Panda car to the scene. It is claimed that reaction time to urgent calls is down to ninety seconds by day, and sixty seconds by night.

But the centre of London is too dense to have uncoordinated Panda cars rushing about, and it takes time and telephones to transfer information from one system to the other: to get news from a sub-division to Information Room or send it back. So a link is being developed. Information Room will be able, by broadcasting a code signal, to capture a particular sub-division's set automatically, and link it to whatever is going forward on the main channel.

If a bank is robbed in Fulham High Street, the Information Room controller will be able to press a button to capture the personal radio set at Fulham Police Station. His messages, and the re-broadcast incoming messages from cars, go out not only to all the cars in West London, but also to all the PCs with personal radio in Fulham. There may be one standing just round the corner. If there is, he may be able to broadcast to everyone a description of the raiders.

The same sort of link is being established with neighbouring county forces, so that London cars and county cars, operating on different radio systems, will be able to talk directly through to each other.

At Scotland Yard the radio system is controlled from three rooms. Information Room deals with crime calls; Central Traffic Control, called for some reason 'Oscar', deals only with traffic; and the Urgent Communications Room duplicates the equipment in the other two, but is only used for State occasions, major demonstrations or disasters, thus separating quantities of extra work from routine business.

In the Information Room four principal controllers each run one of the district channels. Each has a radio panel, a telephone headset, and a map of London's police boundaries. He takes incoming 999 calls from people in trouble, and broadcasts the results on the appropriate channel. At his left hand, he has a Fleet Indicator Board, a set of buttons with letters and numbers let into the desk. If a car is needed on 'A' Division, he presses button A, and the numbers of the cars available light up. If he selects Alpha One One he presses button 11, and it goes out, showing any of the other controllers, who want an 'A' Division car, that this one is busy. This panel is connected to a small computer in the next room whose job it is to keep track of the cars on the road, whether they are busy or waiting for work.

There are other subsidiary controllers, and up to the middle of the room, between the two rows of consoles, runs a set of moving belts to carry messages from the controllers to the Central Vehicle Index at the top of the room. Here a small, sweating team tends 30,000 cards, each one representing a car of interest to the police. Every day 200 cars are towed away by police removal teams for improper parking, and before midnight 196 unhappy owners have rung up to be referred to the appropriate pound. 200 cars are stolen, whose owners likewise telephone, and all but three are recovered within twenty-four hours.

Here are cards for cars that failed to stop when ordered, cars belonging to wanted men that should be stopped if seen, cars belonging to men of interest to Criminal Intelligence that should *not* be stopped, and the ordinary-looking cars used by the police themselves. All over London policemen are radioing in CVI checks, at the rate of one a minute, waiting in their cars, bouncing along behind their suspects for the radio to come up with the answer to their questions.

Information Room acts as a large message-handling centre. Oscar next door is much more a control, whose Duty Officer devises policies and executes them. The day on which I visited it, a bus had run into a bridge in the East End of London. The duty Inspector had projected the street map of the area on the a screen at the end of the room, and with magnetic symbols, and cards showing the height of all the bridges, was working out new routes for double-decker buses. As soon as he had decided what to do, instructions were radioed to a sign van that was already on the move. Within half an hour a complete new traffic system had been established.

When the second traffic-handling computer is installed, a rather more powerful machine than that which at present controls West London, it may be possible to programme it with bridge heights and other basic traffic data, so that it can work out new traffic patterns automatically. At the moment Oscar keeps plans prepared for this sort of emergency and much graver ones: an air crash on central London, a radio-active leak, flooding of the Thames, all typed out in folders, ready to go.

But day to day, its business is much more with traffic-flows and traffic accidents. It has thirty motorcyclists patrolling the danger spots in the West End – Hyde Park Corner, Marble Arch, Victoria – because if one jams, the freezing spreads implacably outwards at five miles an hour, and it may take hours before traffic is flowing as quickly as before.

Less urgent communications are handled by a new tele-printer system that links all the police stations in London to Scotland Yard and so to each other. Messages come in from any station as punched tape. This can be fed back into an automatic tape-reader which retransmits it to any combin-ation of other stations – the immediate neighbours of the originator, all stations of the division, or the district, or all stations in London. It seems a lot of machinery to report, as it often does, that someone's dog is lost.

Scotland Yard can also speak directly to its customers, by courtesy of the BBC. Oscar, like other police traffic con-trols throughout the country, can have bulletins broadcast at any time on the BBC's Radio One, the pop programme to which drivers tend to listen. This gives warning of traffic congestion, road-works, ice, fog and snow. There is a small studio suite in the Urgent Communications Room, from which, each day, the Yard's press bureau broadcasts a two-minute crime programme on Radio Four, called *Scotland Yard Calling*.

Response to this has brought about the arrest of murderers, the identification of dead bodies, the finding of lost children, the recovery of stolen lorries, furs, china, paintings and furniture. It is claimed that sixty-two per cent of the cases mentioned produce a useful response[1].

Security

Most transistor radios can pick up some of Information Room's broadcasts, and it would not be difficult to modify a set to receive transmissions from a portable police radio.

[1] *Report of the Commissioner of the Police for the Metropolis*, 1968, p. 39.

But although police radio seems an insecure medium, before anything expensive is done about it, it is necessary to consider how often it carries sensitive messages. In fact, on ordinary days, there might be only a few seconds of confidential traffic, and that on only one channel; one of the Regional Crime Squads, for instance, swooping on a team of robbers. This sort of traffic can be, and in properly planned operations is, made secure by the use of simple codes.

For instance, the criminals and the cars which they are expected to use can be given code names. Colours can be coded, too: 'orange' for blue, and so on. Number plates of unanticipated cars can be coded by going one down or two up, so that CDF 579 G would become EFH 791 I (two up from nine being one). To a cryptologist this would all be laughably simple, but the criminal's problem is to crack it on the move, within minutes. The difficulty is getting policemen to take the necessary trouble.

Technical solutions are also possible. Police radios can easily be modified to broadcast high voice tones as low ones, and vice-versa, but it is just as easy for the criminal to modify his set as well, and indeed the unaided ear can learn to interpret such messages. A subtler protection, employed on certain London channels used occasionally by the Flying Squad, is to turn off the re-broadcast of incoming messages, so that the listener with a transistor radio gets only half the story, and to switch the frequencies used at short intervals, so that the listener finds the signal fading erratically. Again, an expert with a sensitive set would find this easy to deal with, but it is probably good enough to baffle a keyed-up amateur fiddling with a portable in the back of a car who is at the same time trying to watch out for the physical presence of the police.

Complete security can be provided by fitting receivers and transmitters with military-style digital scramblers whose codes can be varied by the hour among thousands of possibilities. Even the theft of a police car, its radio and scrambler complete is then of little help. But these machines cost between

£500 and £1000 each, or at least three times the price of the radio, and perhaps as much as the car. It is difficult at the moment to justify the need.

A solution along a different line is being considered by the Home Office. Each car would have a miniature teleprinter installed to type out messages on the move[1]. Since teleprinter transmission involves digital coding anyway, security is no extra problem. The system would fit very neatly with the proposed police computer, because messages in and out would not have to be sent by voice and 'translated' on to a typewriter. The operator of a cruising police car, for instance, could amuse himself by typing the numbers of the cars that he passes into the computer, which could instantly tell him those stolen or wanted. This may be in action by 1972.

More serious than overhearing is the possibility of jamming police broadcasts. It is significant that a car full of jamming equipment was stopped and confiscated in London on the evening of the October 1968 anti-Vietnam demonstration. If it had been used intelligently, it could have been disrupting to police organisation. Although complete jamming of all channels all over London would need a very large transmitter indeed, which could be easily located, local jamming on one or two channels would not be difficult, and if done by mobile transmitter, very hard to stop.

It is possible to counter the threat, but only by spending money. Teleprinter would probably be harder to jam than voice, but what the police need for complete confidence is a number of alternative wavelengths. At the moment their needs appear to come low on the Government priority list of radio-users.

Computers

The Main Fingerprint collection (see above) is obviously a good place to employ a computer. But the rapidly increasing quantity and complexity of police records in general,

[1] In America it is already possible to buy commercial sets of this kind.

and the realisation of what improvements could be made in the fight against crime if more of the information that already exists in the police machine were available to PCs on the street, have suggested that half-a-dozen other sets of records should be put on machines. It is not surprising that the Home Office is devoting a good deal of thought to the problems and possibilities.

Broadly speaking, the proposals seem to be these, though at the time of writing no definite decision had been made. To complement the fingerprint collection, the essentials of the Criminal Records files would be put on computer, together with a nation-wide facsimile transmission service for finger-prints and photographs. The result would be that if a man were arrested, say, in the Lake District, within half-an-hour his photographs and finger-prints could be taken and transmitted to the Criminal Record computer centre. There the finger-prints could be classified, and searched on the finger-print computer. Within a minute or two he could be positively identified as a CRO man – a man with a record – his previous convictions printed out, and the information sent back to the Lake District within five more minutes.

Functionally, apart from compressing what might take two days into less than an hour, this is no different from today's method of identification. But there are two advantages. It cuts down the criminal's time initiative – he decides where he will go, what he will do and the police have to follow behind. Each delay in the detection process gives him valuable time to cover his tracks, and to dispose of evidence and stolen property. In Miami the police introduced a simple punched card register of housebreakers. Simply by reducing delay in identification, it is said to have increased their clear-up rate by a handsome amount.

In the same way it would be some help to have a national stolen-property index or computer, so that a television set, taken in Glasgow, could be positively identified in London even before it could physically arrive there. At the moment stolen-property indexes are local, and a thief who steals things of moderate value and moves them to another city has little chance of being detected. But at the moment this is low on the queue of computer priorities. The Central Vehicle Index likewise needs a computer, because the sheer number of stolen cars makes any routine sharing of information between forces impossible.

At the moment, for instance, it may take eight days for the theft of a car in St Albans, thirty miles from London, to be notified to Scotland Yard. In that time a PC may have found it suspicious, checked it with CVI and had no indication that it was stolen. It would also be helpful to know instantly about drivers who have been disqualified or who have suspended sentences. For simplicity, to take advantage of the new communications system that would be necessary, the Wanted Index would also go on computer, though there would be little other advantage over today's quick service by telephone.

Then it would be useful to have a Prison Computer, not only to help the Home Office run a firm that houses 30,000 people in 110 institutions, farms, 10,000 acres and produces £6 million worth of goods a year. The police/prison problem is that no one knows, from minute to minute, who is actually locked up in prison and who is outside. With the spread of parole, leave and hostel schemes, many men capable of serious offences are loose in the community, and though few of them actually commit crime, the few that do are very difficult to detect simply because they are assumed to be in prison and are not considered as suspects. So this computer would book every prisoner in and out of every prison, and would be able to say instantly whether a particular man could or could not have committed a particular crime. The Metropolitan Police traffic ticket-computer was, by the end of 1968, keeping a daily tally of people in prison.

The Ministry of Transport need a computer to keep track of vehicle licensing, the results of various roadworthiness tests, and to keep the accounts for road-pricing schemes if they are introduced. This too would be useful to tell the police instantly who owns a car involved in an accident or used in a crime. At the moment, for instance, to find out during the night who owns a car registered with some small county councils means ringing up the local police station, which sends a man round to the registry with a key; he lets himself in, does the search, locks up, bicycles back to the police station and telephones the result.

The importance of quick car-ownership information was shown by the Shepherd's Bush killing of three policemen in 1967. A witness took the number of the van which the killers were driving: before the owner of the van could drop his friends and get to his home the police were there waiting for him.

The Metropolitan Police have already installed two computers; one to look after the million or so traffic tickets that are issued each year and to do pay and statistics for the Force, the other experimentally in conjunction with the Ministry of Transport to gauge traffic flows and control the traffic lights to the best advantage in Kensington, Fulham, Chelsea and Hammersmith.

The final, and in some ways the most interesting, computer application is in Criminal Intelligence. This would not, at the moment, justify using a separate machine, so it is due to share the Traffic Ticket computer for an experimental period. The necessary programmes are being designed by a team in the Autonomics Division at the National Physical Laboratory, Teddington. This same division has done a great deal of work on the translation of language by computers, and in getting machines to read ordinary print – both problems that have a lot in common with extracting the best from police records.

The aim is to write a computer programme that is simple and fun to use. Detectives should get into the habit of sitting down with it and playing their hunches, trying out this question and that. This involves a compromise between writing a very expensive programme that understands colloquial English (to make the machine understand that 'Albert is

Anna's wife', means the same as 'Anna is the wife of Albert', takes three man-weeks of programming) and a simple programme that policemen will find hard to adapt to.

The first task is nothing very remarkable; just to file C11's information on 7,000 criminals under some twenty basic headings. So a detective might ask it to print out a list of blue or black 3.4 Jaguar cars because a witness saw someone in such a car studying a bank, or a list of criminals called 'Steve.'

The second task begins to exploit the full possibilities of the information stored by offering real cross-index sorting. A detective could ask it for 'the names and addresses of left-handed, sandy-haired men, five foot eight to five foot ten, living in or near Stockwell who have some female belonging wife, aunt, daughter, mistress – called Elsie, who lives in a house with a three in the number and likes to drive sports cars.' The computer deals with this problem by going through each index in turn to find the man or men, if any, who satisfy all these criteria.

Doing the job the easy way means that it starts with, say, hair colour, rejects all but sandy-haired men, then tries these on the height list, rejects those that are too short or too tall, and so goes on with the list of possibles getting smaller each time. The trouble is that a mistake at any stage invalidates the whole. One really wants a programme that compares *all* the lists with *all* the others, and prints out not only the hits, but also, ideally, the near-misses. Thus, there might be no one who fitted all the clues in this example, but there might be someone who did if the female belonging was called 'Elly.' Or there might be three men with 'fair' rather than 'sandy' hair who all live near Stockwell.

To be any use, the computer must allow for the vagaries of witnesses, and the uncertainties of what may be no more than scraps of gossip. It sounds easy enough, but this real cross-index sorting involves a vast amount of work, that increases as the *cube* of the amount of information stored. So, while C11's files double each year – as they have since it started – the work involved in getting the best out of them increases *eightfold* annually. Obviously, no manual system could cope. This is why CRO with three million files can still be usefully run by hand, while C11 with only 7,000 cannot.

The usefulness of the Criminal Intelligence computer might be extended by getting it to monitor the associations of known criminals. Every night, every day, the surveillance goes on. Information about criminals comes in more or less at random, and there will be more and more of it as more policemen are encouraged to pass morsels on. If the computer is programmed to make a note of who has been drinking with whom, it may remember that over the last few months:

A has been seen with B C E K Y
B „   „   „   „ A C K L O
C „   „   „   „ A B D K M O

and cross-sorting shows that A, B D, K and O are some sort of gang and that Y, M, D, L and E are hangers-on, though they would be interesting if they had special skills as car-drivers, safe-blowers, alarm-system disorganisers. If it is a new group, the computer rings a bell to warn its masters. An extension of this programme could draw on the Prison Computer to follow the development of gangs in prisons by noting who shared a cell with whom; who exercised together, who worked together.

Interestingly, no similar development seems to be planned in America, the home of the computer. There are apparently two reasons: an outcry is expected from people interested in Civil Liberties, and there is too great a risk of corrupt policemen inserting false information to protect their criminal friends.

In the second phase of police computer development, it seems logical that all these machines should work together, to exploit every contact between the police and the public. This would be getting back to the ideal village policeman situation, where the whole force's information is stored in one head. Only this time the 'head' will be electronic. For instance, some time in 1975, a PC in London might stop a car going through a red light. The licence-plate agrees with the age of the car, the driver has a clean driving licence, but his manner is slightly odd. The driver gives his name as John McHenery, born 13.3.31; he appears to be 6' 0" tall. Also in the car there is a German girl, Ilse Weber, and another man, Robert Norris. In the boot of the car there is an electric typewriter. The PC radios their description and the numbers of the car and typewriter to Information Room, where the information is typed into the computer.

Within thirty seconds the print-out begins and is radioed back: the car was stolen an hour before in Hertfordshire, the typewriter was obtained by a cheque fraud two years before in Glasgow, John McHenery was disqualified from driving at Belfast, and appears identical with Henry McJohn, born 13.3.35, wanted since for robbery with violence in Newcastle-on-Tyne. Weber has overstayed her entry permit, Norris is the pseudonym of a man being quietly investigated by the Fraud Squad; the officer in the case has been informed and the PC is to let Norris go. And the legitimate owner of the car has an unpaid parking ticket.

At the moment all this information might be available in the police system, but it would be unobtainable by the PC in less than a week or two, even if he managed to make the connection with the more obscure items. At the moment he might have to use his powers of arrest on suspicion, and he might often be wrong.

This inverse link bewteen quick, certain information and the need to use arbitrary powers of arrest has a bearing on the obvious sequel to computerisation: the possibility of finger-printing the entire population and giving everyone a tamper-proof identity card. This would, for instance, practically put a stop to crimes of fraud, because people would be unable to masquerade, to hide their identities. But there are serious problems involved, which probably could not be cheaply solved at the present stage of computer development.

One for instance is that rough identification, which limits the field of possibility in CRO's nominal index, is done by height, and from birth to death, people's heights vary a great deal. It works with criminals because most active criminals are people in their early and middle adult lives, when their heights are more or less constant. But there is little doubt that a workable system could be installed within fifteen to twenty years. Given that, it would be possible for the government to merge all its national and local records: health, tax, welfare, rates, even travel bookings by state-owned airways.

Furthermore, there is the unpleasant prediction of Kahn and Wiener[1], 'A capability for listening and recording temporarily, or even permanently, can be made very inexpensive. One can imagine the legal or illegal magnetic or other recording of an appreciable percentage of the telephone conversations that take place (for that matter, the same techniques could be applied to "bugged" conversations in bars, restaurants, offices and so on). It would then be feasible to scan these conversations rapidly by means of a high speed computer – at least for key phrases – and then record such conversations that meet some criteria for special interest or placement in a more permanent file for further investigation – or just to keep a record. For simple computers the criteria could be certain words – underworld jargon, obscenities, or words such as "kill", "subvert", "revolution", "Black Power", "organise", "oppose", or more sophisticated combinations!'

If one imagines this ability – and what governments could resist it, if it was cheap and discreet enough – coupled with a national 'voice-print' file which would identify anonymous speakers, added to all the other personal information available, it is apparent that one would have little freedom left. It is sobering to realise how much our present liberty depends on the sheer inefficiency of the government machine. Policemen, when talking about this potential state of affairs, say, logically, that the honest man has no need to worry, and they are more or less right. But it is the slight inaccuracy that alarms; for 'honest' one should read, 'Government approved'.

[1] Kahn, Herman, and Wiener, Anthony J., *The Year 2000*, Macmillan, New York, 1968, p. 97.

CHAPTER TEN

Complaints Against the Police, Misbehaviour and Corruption

A major safeguard of civil liberty in any democratic country is the existence of machinery to deal with complaints about police. In England, the machinery is the police force itself, governed by the 1964 Police Act. This provides that a chief officer must record every complaint made by members of the public and cause it to be investigated. He may, and must if directed by the Secretary of State, ask the Chief Officer of another force for an investigating officer, and when he receives the report he must, unless he is satisfied that no criminal offence has been committed by a policeman, send the papers to the Director of Public Prosecutions, who is responsible for prosecution[1]. Though this is a considerable improvement on the old system, which allowed too much latitude to the police force, it is a cumbersome procedure.

In 1968, 3,641 complaints were made against London policemen by three thousand people. About 200 or six point four per cent turned out to be well-founded. Five hundred complaints came from motorists who were told that they were going to be reported for traffic offences, and 372 from motorists who were not reported. Nearly a thousand complaints were withdrawn before they could be investigated. The 1962 Royal Commission on the Police found:

'In sixty-eight per cent of the complaints, the police were alleged to have exceeded their duty in some way. The total of sixty-eight per cent was made up of complaints of in-

[1] Police Act 1964, s. 49.

civility (twenty-eight per cent) excessive use of police powers (twenty-five per cent), and actual physical violence or assault (fifteen per cent). In most of the remaining thirty-two per cent of complaints the police were said to have fallen short of their duty, for instance by failing to give help to motorists in trouble, or by delay in arriving at the scene of a crime or accident. A small proportion of complaints against the police arose out of their traffic duties.'

During my visits I was constantly coming across complaints being investigated – and even on one occasion interrogated about one.

A few examples (in order to preserve the confidentiality that everyone who complains about the police is entitled to enjoy, these examples were made up for me by senior officers out of their recent experience): A police constable reported that a vagrant woman whom he had arrested on the street had complained that he had assaulted her sexually in the van. After three days' investigation it turned out that he had never been alone with her, and that in fact the assault had been done seven years before by 'a big man with ginger hair and bushy eye-brows'. When she had remembered that, she withdrew the complaint.

A lorry-driver, arrested in Holloway for obstruction, complained a month after the event that someone unknown had stolen a half-used packet of cigarettes out of his cab while the lorry was parked in the station yard. A detective chief inspector, interviewed him, interviewed the policeman on duty at the time, wrote a six-page report, and then went to get the man's signature on the final statement. He said: 'My solicitor says I'm not to talk to you, go away, forget all about it.'

Not all complaints are as trivial as these. A rather more serious problem arose in something like the following manner. An Indian couple moved into a flat near Battersea Park, by arrangement with the caretaker of the block. Unfortunately, when the landlord found out, he told them to go. He had promised the flat to someone else, and the caretaker had no right to let it. They refused to move and the landlord went to see them. An argument began; the Indian offered a cheque to pay the rent in advance, but this failed to soothe things. Eventually the police were called in to break up the row.

An area car attended, and two of the crew went upstairs. One said, correctly, he thought it was a civil dispute and nothing to do with the police. The Indian said that he was a police inspector from Calcutta, he knew his law, and he had a right to the flat. The other policeman decided he was a trespasser (whom the police can evict if asked to by the owner of the property) and unfortunately said: 'If you're a police inspector, why don't you get your hair cut?'

The Indian then complained about his rudeness. A form was served on the PC saying who had complained against him, and that the complaint was of 'rude and aggressive behaviour'. He was warned, by an already printed postscript on the form, that he need say nothing, but he might, if he wanted, make a statement – either verbal or written.

A chief inspector at another station found the docket on his desk, with the curt note: 'You are Investigating Officer.' He then had to take a statement from the complainant, the accused PC and the three witnesses: the housekeeper, the landlord and the other PC. He wrote a report in which he summarised the evidence which each person could give, their reliability as witnesses, their willingness to appear at a disciplinary hearing. The Indian was reading for his Bar finals and wasn't keen to come to a hearing, so the Chief Superintendent in his minute to the report recommended that he give the PC a dressing-down and then apologise personally to the complainant. This went to the Commissioner's office for approval and was carried out. By the time the file was closed it contained over a hundred sheets of paper and was nearly two inches thick.

If the Indian had been willing to give evidence, he would have told his story to a disciplinary board convened by the Chief Superintendent of the division. When he had given his evidence, he would have been invited to stay, with the other witnesses to watch the remainder of the case, and hear the Chief Superintendent's decision. They would be asked to leave before punishment was imposed.

The Chief Superintendent who synthesised the facts of this case for me said that, in his experience, eighty per cent of people who made complaints did so in a fit of bad temper, and were quite happy to let the whole thing go when they had had an explanation and had cooled down. He felt that few complainants were left unsatisfied. Generally I got the impression that complaints are thoroughly investigated, and the best evidence of this was the wholesome dread most constables have of investigations.

Even so, there are two major faults with the present system. The first is felt only by the police. It is far *too* rigorous, it imposes the same massive procedure on every complaint, however trivial. People in bad tempers are always going to police stations and shouting about parking, or the way PC 49 spoke to their young Jimmy. Very often a few soothing words from the man at the desk could send them away happy, but he applies them at his peril. He must record the complaint: police and temper are then caught up in the machinery which must grind through a set number of laborious and expensive revolutions before either party can escape.

The other fault is felt by the citizen. I quite believe that the vast majority of the people who complain are satisfied by the investigation. The police would say that is all that matters, no one else has any interest. This is not so: society is always an interested third party, and if one accepts the suggestion made below (p. 280) that an appearance of good behaviour is a major part of the police 'product', then the present system of investigating complaints in secret leaves a great deal to be desired. It is not even in the interests of the police, because the hundreds of cases which show policemen behaving perfectly properly, and the tens of cases that show them erring and properly dealt with, are hidden. Only the most squalid scandals come to light, and then in the eruptions of Royal Commissions[1]. The onlooker has the false security of one living by a dormant volcano. A proposal for a new procedure may be found in Appendix 1.

Investigation

It is often supposed that the police hold back when investigating their own people. In the Mars-Jones case they did, but this in many ways was exceptional. On the contrary, policemen are usually investigated with a ruthlessness that is seldom seen in ordinary criminal cases. Indeed, when there are bad relationships between the CID and the Uniform Branches, this is almost always at the bottom of them.

The resentment of the Uniform Branch is succinctly summarised by Victor Meek, a retired inspector in the Metropolitan Police, who writes:

'... any complaint of crime against a police officer must be dealt with by the CID (thus bringing a uniform enemy of whatever rank within reach at the cost of an unstamped anonymous letter) and that complaints against the CID must be dealt with by CID (thus defeating any counter-attack)[2].

Meek is extreme, but he sums up a real sentiment, which a uniform inspector, drawing on the *Lord of the Rings* for an image, confessed: 'The CID are the Nazgul; they are the most disciplined, tough, loyal – to each other – body in Britain. They *are* the Metropolitan Police, and quite frankly, they frighten me.'

[1] For an example, the reader is referred to the *Mars-Jones Enquiry*, HMSO, 1964, Cmnd 2526, a fascinating document in its own right, but too long to summarise here. It deals with a whole range of police disciplinary problems: Uniform/CID jealousy, having to twist the facts of an arrest to fit police regulations, pressure on Aids to produce arrests, planting of weapons, anonymity of informants, police cohesion in time of trouble, and the inability of the police to give reasons to justify their illegal acts.

[2] Meek, V., *This Coppering Lark*, Duckworth, 1963, p. 9.

Investigations of alleged police criminality occupy a good deal of police effort. In London there are about sixty Chief Inspectors who spend much of their time on this – a thankless task that can rarely be endured for more than a couple of years. There is said to be a secret 'rubber heel' department, with its own vehicles and communications that keeps observation on suspect policemen: the whisper 'rubber heel's on the ground' causes a flutter in the most innocent blue-jacketed breast.

Complaints as a Tactical Move

The very willingness of the police to listen to complaints and to investigate them vigorously gives the criminal a weapon – often used to short-circuit an active and about-to-be successful detective. The technique is simple. The criminal takes the trouble to find out where the detective was, by himself, for half-an-hour on any particular day. He then sends a couple of henchmen into a police station to say that the detective met them there and demanded such-and-such a sum of money not to fit them up with a crime. However odd the story is, the police must investigate it, and the first step is often to suspend the detective from duty. This gives the criminal time to remove evidence, to bribe or intimidate witnesses. A couple of such accusations, even if neither has any real credibility, might force the police to move the officer to a different area.

A recent tactical use of a complaint occurred in this way: A team of robbers were being tried at the Old Bailey. One of them, 'A', called an alibi witness, 'B', a man of apparently good character and no previous convictions. The police first heard of him when he stepped into the witness-box to say that 'A' was with him, watching television, on the day of the crime. He remembered it because his mother had come to Sunday lunch and it was the day before his niece's birthday. They were discussing a present for her, and 'A' offered to get one too.

'B' was very convincing, but not quite enough, and the jury hung (this was before Criminal Law Act, 1967). Before the retrial came on, the police had had time to take an interest in 'B'. Observation showed that he was involved with several robbery teams, and as a bonus to the investigation three men were arrested with £2,000 worth of stolen property. One of these three was 'C'.

The police continued to observe 'B', who unfortunately realised that he was being followed. He became alarmed and therefore got 'C', now committed for trial, but out on bail and apparently sensitive to police pressure, to be ready to say that one of the detectives involved in the case told him to steal a lorry and then to deliver it to 'B', so that 'B' could be arrested. 'B' wrote to Scotland Yard complaining about this dastardly stratagem, so that when and if he had been arrested, he had a weapon already aimed at the detective investigating him.

To complicate the situation, the detectives investigating the complaint could not tell the detectives prosecuting 'C' what they were doing, because this allegation might have come out at 'C's trial, and the forewarning would have prejudiced 'C's defence. But at 'C's trial it soon became obvious that he would be convicted and out of 'B's power. His one desire became to be left alone to serve his sentence in peace. In particular, if the police managed to make a case out against 'B', he didn't want to be involved.

So he sent his counsel to tell the detective in charge of the case that he wanted to withdraw his statement in support of 'B's complaint. Delighted as the police would have been to forget it, the detective had to point out that 'C's withdrawal might disclose offences of perjury, criminal libel and wasting police time, and he would therefore have to make a statement under caution. 'C' and his counsel were both taken aback. In the end he signed a declaration that he would not give evidence at a disciplinary inquiry. This virtually, but unsatisfactorily, withdrew the complaint.

As a weapon against this sort of manoeuvre, the Criminal

Law Act 1967, S. 5(2), creates a new offence of wasting police time by giving false information. Prosecutions have to be by or with the consent of the DPP, and there is a reluctance to use the section except in flagrant cases. In the first nine months of this Act, the Metropolitan Police initiated half-a-dozen prosecutions, most of them against people who said they had been robbed to disguise their loss or embezzlement of other people's money.

Misbehaviour and Corruption

Whenever power is given to a person, whether by the State or a group of people, corruption becomes possible; he can either use that power for the good of its donors or for himself. When we think of power given to many people over long periods of time, we can say that inevitably there will be some degree of corruption in some people. When one examines power systems for this fault, one must make the same assumption as an examiner of aircraft accidents: that if the mechanical arrangements allow a mistake to be made, then sooner or later it will happen, notwithstanding the good intention of all concerned.

There are roughly four categories of purely police mis-behaviour: in ascending order of seriousness one might rate them: abuse of their legal powers, using violence against prisoners, manufacturing evidence, and taking bribes.

Short Cuts

Because policing is such an artificial concept, policemen are often caught between contradictory impulses: they have a general duty to fight crime, but on many particular occasions law or practice prevents them doing the obvious, useful thing. A pretty example, now corrected by the Theft Act of 1969, was the lack of power to arrest someone obtaining goods on false pretences during 'Larceny Act day' – between six a.m. and nine p.m. A policeman called to a shop where such a customer was being held was confronted with a dilemma.

As a detective explained it: 'Here's Chummy in the shop with a funny cheque-book in his hand. Are you seriously going to say "Excuse me, sir, what is your address? I shall have to obtain a warrant from the Magistrate and come round tomorrow to arrest you." You just grab his collar – and the court doesn't inquire how you came by him[1].'

Or in general, as a uniform superintendent explained: 'If you went by the rules the clear-up rate would be down from twenty-five per cent to two per cent. Sometimes you have to pull someone and take him down the nick to clear your mind: but in fact you have no power to arrest him. So many crime arrests are made on hunch – the way someone looks, behaves, and there's really no "reasonable grounds" for suspicion. But if police could convict anyone they liked, C11 would just work through their lists of top criminals and major crime would come to an end – we could all go home.'

The most striking police abuse is their invention of a power of detention, which they like to think is half-way between liberty and arrest. In most police stations there is a 'Detention Room', which is rather more comfortable than a cell, where people are held. The 1929 Royal Commission on Police Powers and Procedure noted that the murderer Voisin was held four days for inquiries before he was charged, and the then practice in London was, if a burglary had been committed and the Method Index showed twelve likely suspects, to 'detain' them all for inquiries until the culprit became apparent. The Commission remarked this was wrong both in principle and in practice, but the practice continues.

After one particularly brutal robbery which occurred during my visit, teams of detectives were sent at 5 a.m. on three successive mornings to arrest all Method Index's candidates. Detention, on this grand scale, as well as in the everyday

[1] In some cases it was possible to justify the arrest by 'reasonably suspecting' that the cheque-book had been stolen.

business of policing, persists, because people seldom complain. They are held for a few hours, but when they are let go, they are so relieved they quite willingly sign a statement to say they came voluntarily and were satisfied with their treatment. And who else is a better judge? And some, at least, of the public believe in this power of detention.

For example, the barmaid at the Blind Beggar pub, who courageously gave evidence about Ronald Kray's murder of Cornell, was one. When she was asked by Defence Counsel at the Krays' trial in 1969 why she had refused to look for the killer in a police line-up in 1966, she said she didn't believe the Krays had been arrested. 'They'd just been taken in for questioning – not arrested or charged', and that this intermediate state of detention didn't make it safe for her to speak.

Of course, detention often justifies itself: a man who could not 'reasonably' be suspected, and so legally arrested, may, once he is in the police station, and gets the measure of the opposition, make a statement that incriminates himself or lets out enough information for further inquiries that prove his guilt. But occasionally it goes wrong; although the police claim, as I was told by a straight-faced detective superintendent, that the power to detain has never been tested in the House of Lords, the Solicitor to the Metropolitan Police settles such claims out of court, because, of all abuses, none is so easy to detect or prove.

Other frequently taken short cuts arise out of the difficulty of search. Fundamentally, private houses and business buildings are inviolate. Although the police can get warrants to search for stolen property, dangerous drugs, explosives, or material under the Official Secrets Act, there is no power to search for the evidence that would justify swearing out such warrants. To offset this, the police assume a common law right to search the homes of people who have been arrested. This is so taken for granted – and in fact so necessary – that it is seldom disputed.

233

The Woolf Inquiry[1] found that 'Detective Sergeant Bell decided that he was going to search the premises where Mr Woolf lived in order to see whether there was any further quantity of hemp there, and he told Mr Woolf that he proposed to do so. He had taken possession of Mr Woolf's keys from among his personal belongings and he asked him whether these were the keys of his premises and as to the location of his room at 21 Bourne Terrace. Detective Sergeant Bell did not, at any time, ask Mr Woolf's permission to search the premises, though he asserted that he had his implied permission from the fact that Mr Woolf gave him information without dissent as to the location of his premises.'

This is probably a fair description of a transaction that is played out a hundred or so times every night in London. Unless an arrested man definitely and loudly refuses to have his home searched, the police will go ahead and do it anyway. There are sensible reasons why he should agree. If he doesn't, he will be refused bail by the Station Sergeant, so he cannot go home and destroy evidence that might be revealed by a search with a warrant in the morning. If he still refuses, he has to realise that uniformed constables will be posted front and back, both to prevent anything leaving the house, and for the edification of his neighbours and the press.

Less legitimately the man is told, 'If we have to wake up the Magistrate to get a warrant at this time of night – well, he might be a bit aggravated and remember your name in the morning' and a detective explained further, 'If he still refuses you, just go ahead and kick the door down. He can sue you for trespass. But lawyers aren't keen – they're just interested in the criminal legal-aid money, not civil actions. Generally you don't have to worry unless he's acquitted.'

The Woolf Inquiry found that the prisoner's objection to a search 'was not allowed to be an obstacle', and continues[2]

[1] *Report of Inquiry into the Action of the Metropolitan Police in relation to the Case of Mr Herman Woolf*, HMSO, Cmnd 2319, para 49.
[2] *Ibid.*, para 106–107.

'... I do not feel that, unless or until Legislature sees fit to alter the law so as to permit the searching of premises without either the consent of the occupier or a warrant, unlawful searches should be countenanced. If the police require greater powers in this respect, the remedy is with the Legislature.' But neither the Criminal Law Act 1967 nor the Criminal Justice Act 1967, both of which appear to have been suitable vehicles, carries this power.

With the majority of small criminals there is no great problem and no great injustice done. Occasionally, with more powerful people, this inability to search for evidence is an unmistakeable fault. For instance, a large fraud was recently performed here and in Germany; then the managers fled abroad leaving all the evidence in two trunks full of papers, locked up in a furniture-store in London. Without a look at the papers, the police could not get a warrant for arrest – which would justify seizing the papers; and without a warrant, the firm who ran the furniture-store did not dare risk a civil action by letting the police have the trunks.

But practical problems of arrest and search are seldom acute, mainly because the criminal courts refuse to reject prisoners or evidence simply because they have been obtained by breaches of the civil law. Much is left to the discretion of the Judge, who has a general power to dismiss evidence which he feels is unfair to the accused. A more general problem, which worried a large majority of the policemen that I met, both uniformed and CID, is posed by the Judges' Rules[1]. The effect of these is broadly to prevent the prisoner saying anything to incriminate himself unless he sincerely and voluntarily wants to do so. Almost every time the prisoner opens his mouth to tell the police something, they must warn him to shut up, using the hallowed phrase: 'You are not obliged to say anything unless you wish to do so, but what you say may be put in writing and given in evidence.'

Historically the Rules are a result of the widespread capital penalties of the last century, when every possible trick

[1] Reproduced in Appendix 2.

was practised by the courts, to alleviate the horrors of the gallows. One of these was to gag the prisoner, to prevent him hanging himself through stupidly admitting to his crime. As a result, we are left with a set of rules that are, though pretty in theory, unworkable in practice.

A uniform superintendent put the police position pithily: 'I don't see any moral problem in getting a man to tell you what he has done. He's best placed to know, and if it's against the law he shouldn't have done it. If it isn't, he's nothing to hide.'

The 1929 Royal Commission (the last to examine working police practice) exercised itself with this problem; noting realistically that, if the prisoner had committed a crime, he would anyway be on his guard; if he had not, no caution was needed, and he should be encouraged to talk to clear himself. Lord Devlin deals with the problems of the caution in his *The Criminal Prosecution in England.*

He points out that the police bring much of their agonising over the Judges' Rules on themselves. They are not nearly as restrictive as they appear. Though the prisoner has the right to demand the rejection of an involuntary confession, he has no such right over evidence obtained in breach of the Judges' Rules. The Judge has a discretion to admit or reject the evidence as he thinks fit. ' ... The essence of the thing is that the Judge must be satisfied that some unfair or oppressive use has been made of police power[1].'

But it doesn't appear to the police like this. 'Lawyer-like tendencies flourish among the police to an even greater extent than they do at the Bar or on the Bench. The Police have sometimes seemed to treat the Judges' Rules as if they were a drill manual ... It is the general habit of police never to admit to the slightest departure from correctness[2].' The key word there is 'admit'. The police, as a disciplined body,

[1] Lord Devlin, *The Criminal Prosecution in England,* OUP, 1960, p. 57.
[2] *Ibid.,* p. 39.

are not happy with generalised advice. What they like is a hard and fast, black and white, code of instructions. Once a procedure has been written down, especially by so august a body as the Judges, they like to appear to follow it to the letter. This makes administration and court procedure easy. It is all very well for judges and lawyers – professional arguers – to look on the Judges' Rules as being . . . 'laid down as rules of guidance in matter of principle and not to be literally construed.' In court, the police do not want to become involved in prolonged wrangles about the general fairness of their treatment of the accused. Any such dispute must hurt them because the prosecution's case is expected to be perfect. They want a set of regulations that they can obey, or appear to obey, to the letter. Then there can be no argument.

In practice of course, the Judges' Rules are not obeyed to the letter. But the police, although they may have been perfectly fair, and 'made no oppressive use of police power', feel that they cannot admit this, if only because their own instructions tell them to obey the Rules. So many arrests involve at least one lie: 'I then informed him he was arrested and cautioned him.' One wonders how many prisoners realise that the glib word 'cautioned' implies the rigmarole of 'you are not obliged, etc.' How many realise that in the ordinary way they should be cautioned a minimum of two times and possibly three or more? How many who realise all this, need to be cautioned at all?

So in court: 'A number of what the police officer regards as ritualistic questions will be asked by counsel for the defence which call for only the appropriate ritualistic responses. It is a form of equivocation rather than perjury: it is as if the police officer by his denial were saying: "You know as well as I do that you have no business to be asking me questions of this sort; you know that I cannot possibly admit to even the slightest deviation from the prescription of the drill manual[1]." '

This is a bad business, forcing policemen to risk their

[1] *Ibid.,* p. 43.

careers not for their own benefit, but simply to do the job which society has given them. It means they always have a slightly sore conscience: when the temptation to do worse arises, they are already that much nearer the precipice. If workable (even slightly restrictive) Judges' Rules were offered the police, it is likely that they would fall into them with a sigh of relief, with considerable improvement to their general moral position.

Violence

Physical violence against prisoners is not a real problem among the police in England. There are grave practical difficulties in encouraging prisoners to talk by the threat of a beating. They are only in police hands for a short time – often only a few hours. If they are marked, they can complain convincingly in court the next morning. An allegation of violence – being a criminal offence – will be taken seriously by a criminal court, even if trespass is not.

As we saw above, in one sense the prisoner often has the upper hand, because, by refusing to plead guilty, he can condemn the detective to a great deal of work. So it is often in the policeman's interest to treat his prisoners reasonably, to use fair words to negotiate a plea of guilty rather than blows to force one. It would anyway be rather pointless to threaten a prisoner with violence to get him to plead guilty, because after his appearance in court, he is either released or immediately remanded to prison; in either case he is out of the detective's reach. And also, as we saw earlier, the short period of interrogation in police hands is a key moment in establishing rapport for intelligence purposes with the underworld. A policeman often wants to leave a criminal feeling fairly treated, so that he has no emotional reason to stop him becoming an informant later.

The atmosphere is perhaps more apt to be conspiratorial than violent. As one experienced detective sergeant said: 'You're supposed to report all conversations with the prisoner – well, who does? This is your moment. I have long chats with them about all sorts of things. He might have someone he wants to hand the poison to – if I treat him right he could ring up when he gets out. I'll willingly do deals if he'll be a man and plead – it saves me days of desk-work, writing reports, doing legal-aid forms, rounding up witnesses, going to court every week until the trial comes up – and I'll not put in the poison about him when I'm asked. This may sound very shocking, but what's more use to society: me tied down for a couple of weeks getting him a couple of months more on his sentence, or the whole thing over in a day, a happy informant, me out catching more thieves, and perhaps a string of arrests in the future?'

Then the police are elaborately organised to put further discouragements in the way of the potential assaulter. Though the arrest is often made by the CID, they have to give the prisoner to the Uniform Branch for custody in the station, where he is the responsibility of the Station Sergeant. His job has nothing to do with detection and prosecution. Any successes in that line are nothing to him. He has to make sure that the arrest was legally possible and that some evidence exists to justify it. That being established his – and the uniform gaoler's – one fervent desire is a happy prisoner.

Frank Elmes, known for his articles in the *Police Review*, who served thirty years in the Dorset Constabulary, writes (in a letter to the author): 'A complaint of police corruption in dealing with prisoners either is confined to the arresting officer(s) or involves a conspiracy among a number of officers whose personal interests (the preservation of their jobs and pensions) are in direct opposition to the development of a conspiracy. It would be absurd to claim, "It could never happen". It is accurate to say, "It is not likely to happen in circumstances where responsibilities are properly spread." '

Prisoners do get assaulted, it is true. Very often this is because when a man is arrested, the amount of violence used is up to him. If he is in a state of high excitement, mania, drunkenness, he will lash out and hardly notice what he is doing. To the policeman it's just a job. If he gets hurt it's time in hospital, time wasted. C. H. Rolph puts what seems a representative view:

'In twenty-five years of police experience I never came across an example of police violence to prisoners who did not initiate the violence themselves. If I were the policeman in charge of a prisoner who seemed likely to resort to violence I should resort to it first.' But afterwards the prisoner will forget his own mood, and (in isolation) remember the vigour of the police restraint.

The few exceptions may be prisoners who have earlier killed or injured policemen. A Regional Crime Squad officer on a man he had nearly arrested: 'There he stood with a plastic lemon in each hand full of ammonia: "OK, copper," he says, "come and get me," so I did and he squirted ammonia right in both eyes. I thought I was a St Dunstan's case. I'd like ten minutes with the lad when he's nicked.'

But while the Judges' Rules present problems every day, violence even in this modest form does not. Whatever their inclinations, most policemen let the temptation go by. We are in any case moving out of a period when it was natural for every man to be able to protect himself with his fists, when blows fairly exchanged were considered part of the normal currency of society. The illustration (see plates) of Bloody Sunday shows several stout constables trading fisticuffs with city louts, and doubtless no one thought the worse of it.

I am told by a policeman who served there that, until recent years, constables drafted to H Division – the dock area – were expected to fight some local champion in their first week. If they didn't, they would never after command respect. The idea that a policeman should never hit anyone, or if he does, only under necessity, and the risk of an inquiry afterwards, is very recent.

Assaults by the police on the public seem, interestingly, to follow the temper of police/public relationships. Thus, the number of complaints of assault found substantiated during the recent years of police unpopularity, 1958–62, was 11 a year, against an average of 3.8 for all the other years since the end of the last war.

Fitting Up

The next most serious problem is that of manufacturing evidence. Lord Devlin summarised the findings of the 1929 Commission: 'They found no credible evidence of confessions being obtained by violence or the threat of violence; but they found a volume of responsible evidence which it was impossible to ignore, suggesting the use of such devices for extracting statements as keeping a suspect in suspense – keeping him waiting for a long period, constant repetition of the same question, bluffing assertion that all the facts are known anyway, that a clean breast will enable them to make things easy at the trial and so on. They had no evidence of any disposition on the part of the police to trump up vague charges or to press for the conviction of people whom they believed to be innocent, but there was a disposition generally to strain the evidence against someone genuinely believed to be guilty. It is *probable that a similar conspectus of responsible opinion today would reach a similar conclusion,* though it might perhaps note a steady, if slight, improvement as the years have gone by[1].'

From conversations with many police officers who are worried by this problem, I would agree entirely with the opinions of these two distinguished authorities. I felt that there was no other issue that so worried policemen as the need 'to strain the evidence against someone genuinely believed to be guilty'. Bearing in mind the difficulty of proving anything in court, and the cunning of experienced criminals, they often felt that it was their clear duty to make sure that men they knew to be guilty were convicted. One can sympathise with this, but the outsider will have his doubts. How

[1] Devlin, *op. cit.,* p. 45, author's italics.

often does it happen, how sure can one be that the people who get framed *are* guilty – if a court cannot decide, how can a policeman *know* their guilt? There are obviously no statistics on these points; one has to proceed by narrative evidence.

This is the sort of problem that exercises them. I was riding one night with a crew in South London. We got a call at midnight to a smelly little urinal behind a pub where two Irishmen were said to have robbed a queer. His face was cut and dirty; he was very excited and indignant, but still coherent. We found his diary, pen and wallet flung down in the urine gutter. The Irishmen skulking outside admitted that they had hit him because he had made an indecent proposition, but they denied taking his things or his money, which couldn't be found, although three car crews spent half-an-hour looking for it.

There seemed no doubt about the robbery, but since the victim had convictions for homosexual offences in the past, his evidence would probably be discredited in court. It was very unlikely that the Irishmen would be convicted, and the CID probably would not even try. But if nothing happened to them, it would be plain licence for every Irish labourer in the area to beat up and rob homosexuals. This possibility personally offended the policemen involved because even homosexuals have rights. 'Some play hockey and some play golf,' observed a sergeant, 'It doesn't mean you're outside the law,' – and because it could involve them in a lot of fruitless work.

In the event, I have no idea what happened. The Irishmen were taken off by another crew and I neither saw nor heard any more about them. But thinking it over afterwards, it seemed to me that this is perhaps the sort of case where a conviction might justifiably be 'helped'. This is a good example of the sort of case in which the police know someone's guilty, but are unable to prove it.

In some form or other policemen probably help prosecutions quite often; though in terms of the number of crimes committed the occasions must be rare. How else can one explain the Metropolitan Police's low clear-up rate of twenty-five per cent? Robert Mark, now Deputy Commissioner, wrote when Chief Constable of Leicester: 'As a practical policeman of fairly long service, I will also agree that the incidence of such perjury is not necessarily to be assessed by reference to the number of prosecutions. I accept that there may be occasions on which an experienced policeman may endeavour to take a short cut in preparing evidence against a person of whose guilt he is – rightly or wrongly – convinced. If instances of this kind do occur, common sense suggests that they will relate almost entirely to the known criminal, whose protestations are unlikely to carry much weight and whose previous experience builds up a not improper resistance to the procedure by which ordinary criminal investigation is governed[1].'

One young detective told me: 'If I thought there was a one per cent chance he hadn't done it, I wouldn't screw him down. But let's face it; if stories weren't given a nudge along, the crime situation would be out of hand.' And a Flying Squad man: 'I'm not naïve, but I don't really believe that an honest little man going to work in the morning is going to get borrowed and handed, let's say, a load of stolen silver. People do get fixed up, but they're always good villains.'

How do people get fixed up? The simplest way is to invent a 'verbal' statement made on arrest admitting his guilt. A police definition: Counsel: 'Officer, do you know what a "verbal" is?' 'Yes, sir, a verbal is what a man says when I arrest him, that he afterwards denies in court on the advice of his counsel.'

Or a policeman can swear he saw the accused doing this and that – trying car door-handles, stretching out a hand towards ladies' handbags. Or the police can plant drugs or stolen property or offensive weapons. Or the neatest way is to plant some subtle forensic sign, then leave the laboratory to find it and give its unimpeachable story in court. The

[1] Mark, Robert, *The Lawyer*, 6, No. 3, p. 42.

trouble is that, where fixing up is possible, it is always in the accused's interest to suggest that it happened, so that cases which depend mainly on police evidence often descend into a welter of cross-accusations, with no hope of ever finding out the truth.

The necessity to protect informants complicates the police position. They may have acted perfectly fairly, but be unable to say so. Suppose a doorman rings a station with information that drugs are hidden in the lavatory of the club where he works. The police go and find them, and the owner, naturally, says that they were planted. It is, after all, his only defence. The fact of the message confirms the police story, but they are unable to use it because (a) the message itself is hearsay evidence; (b) it would expose their inform-ant. So in practice, in court, they have to invoke the hearsay rule against themselves with the formula 'Acting on in-formation received' which the defence will often allege means acting out of spite.

Although the manufacture of evidence means that a good many criminals are convicted who would otherwise be running loose (Lord Devlin pertinently observes: 'It is easy for lawyers to say that it is better for ninety-nine guilty men to be acquitted than for one innocent to be convicted; but to those in daily contact with the ninety-nine and who see at close quarters the harm that they do the maxim has less appeal"), it also means that a lot more policemen have a lot more on their consciences; they are a lot nearer the precipice, and occasionally some are caught, with spectacular and damaging publicity.

The most celebrated recent case involved Sergeant Chal-lenor of West End Central who was detected planting a half-brick on a demonstrator against the Greek Monarchy. Before that, he had spectacularly cleared Soho of protection gangs, as was suggested at the inquiry on his conduct, by wholesale planting of evidence. Nevertheless, he is re-garded, I found, by some policemen as something near to a saint: one who was sacrificed on the altar of hypocrisy

[1] Lord Devlin, *op. cit.*

because he did the job which he was given in the only way that it could be done. His admirers only regretted that he had involved three young Aids in his downfall – they felt that he should have taken the affair on his own back[1].

One detective chief inspector felt strongly enough to say: 'Society didn't *deserve* a man like Challenor. He did his utmost for them, and they sent him to a mad-house[2].' But Challenor's half-brick was quite exceptional, and for every officer who approved of his dedication, another was disgusted by the grossness of the plant. To replace evidence that the accused has destroyed, to describe what actually happened but which the policeman didn't actually see, is one thing; to fetch a stranger out of the crowd and give him a brick is quite another.

'Helping' the evidence to some extent or other is forced on policemen by the defects of the criminal law. In another field, that of public order, it is forced on him by society's denial of any general weapon for controlling a mob. In law, a policeman face-to-face with a crowd or mob is, until the situation becomes a riot, face-to-face with all the individual members. He can only take action against those members who commit offences. The theory is admirable, but it ignores the nature of an unruly crowd. It is not just a lot of individuals; it is to some extent big, stupid, sometimes vicious, animal. The policeman needs some general weapon to impress the whole beast.

In other countries the police have hoses or guns: here they have not, and they have to make do with their power of arrest. But naturally the person nearest to the policeman, the only one that he *can* physically arrest, is not the one swearing, kicking, throwing pennies or fireworks. But having arrested the ones whom he can reach, he and they are enmeshed in the machinery of justice: he has to accuse them of an arrestable offence. Sometimes he must invent it.

[1] See *The Challenor Enquiry*, HMSO, 1955, Cmnd 2735.
[2] There was in fact no doubt about Challenor's condition. He was diagnosed as schizophrenic and committed to a mental hospital.

Hence, for instance, Mervyn Jones in the *New States-man*[1]: 'Meanwhile, a man who was arrested in Grosvenor Square – and, by some slip-up, acquitted – has laid a complaint against the policeman concerned. Allegedly, this officer spoke of his intention to "invent half-truths when giving evidence" and "suggested that this was common practice". Well, you could have knocked me down with a truncheon! What happens is that, having arrested someone because he was in their way, the police have to think of something to charge him with. The Magistrate will normally accept their story in preference to his; and, to make things easier, they can get pleas of guilty by threatening and "withdrawing" more serious charges. I vividly remember being nicked during a CND demonstration and charged with assaulting Constable (let's say) Smith. As I was leaving Cannon Row after being bailed, I heard a young policeman addressed as Smith. I'd never seen him before in my life, but I thought it only polite to say: "How do you do? I'm charged with assaulting you." He responded with an amiable smile. Of course, it was his turn to get some practice in giving evidence; his performance lacked, but resulted in, conviction.'

Bribery

Wriggling around the safeguards of the law, thumping a prisoner to make him collect his thoughts, manufacturing a fragment of evidence, are all things which policemen deplore, but which are done – when they are done – for the good of the Force and society. When one gets over the initial social difficulty, policemen are often willing, and sometimes anxious, to discuss these moral problems. But bribery goes outside this communal, almost justifiable, wrong-doing, into a more private and more secret area. It is rather like masturbation in a Victorian public school – denounced in public and evasively discussed even in private.

The very fact that bribery is hardly discussed is, I think,

[1] 29 March 1968.

quite strong evidence that it is almost as rare among the Metropolitan Police as its senior officers claim. Any general wrong-doing creates a conspiracy: the individuals concerned do not do it *as* individuals; they are driven together for moral and practical support. A visitor like myself presents a problem. But Skolnick, who spent two years with police departments in America, going about with active officers as I did, writes:

'It is, incidentally, not very difficult to find out whether the police take graft in a city. If the researcher approaches police as someone who, in effect, has worked in another police department, he finds that they will reveal themselves. There is, however, *little* revelation involved. In Eastville (an East Coast Police Force) for example, graft is routine. The police realise that a social researcher or a reporter (as contrasted with a legal investigator who wants names and dates and places) can easily learn about the general pattern ... So long as the policeman trusts the researcher to protect his anonymity, the policeman has little to fear[1].'

Any individual policeman who spoke frankly to someone like Skolnick or me about a *general* misdeed in *general* terms was quite safe. Even if we decided to 'come clean' all we could report is that, 'Sergeant X says that he has known of this and that going on.' He could always deny it; without names and dates there can be no serious investigation. In any case, the researcher is very unlikely to do such a thing, because general confidences are as useful to him as particular ones (more so, in some cases), and the trust of the Police Force is far more valuable than the *réclame* of a single exposure. This is well understood by policemen, who tend to put a high value on their confidences.

To return from credibility to corruption. When Skolnick talks about graft, he means something which is, broadly speaking, unknown in England, because the basic amusements, drinking, betting, sex and drugs, are legally available in modest quantities. But in those states which have out-

[1] Skolnick, *op. cit.*

lawed them, these necessary businesses can only proceed by buying protection from the police. This basic economic relationship spreads until every crime has a price, and offices within the Police Force are bought and sold like commissions in the eighteenth-century army.

We must distinguish from bribery the traditional practices that favour policemen, increasing their effective wages by ten per cent to twenty per cent. On every division there are garages that do repairs for policemen at three-quarters of the normal price. There are shops happy to pass on goods at wholesale prices. There are restaurants that will give a beat man a meal, the coffee-stalls that pass over a brimming cup, pubs that leave a pint out on the back window-sill.

One night I enjoyed a lavish dinner from the kitchen of one of the best restaurants in London: the manager had been told to make himself 'agreeable' to the police, and so the crew I was with used to drop in some nights for a banquet. 'Mumping' is as old as policing. It has its pros and cons – one can look at it as a small tax paid directly by people who deal with the general public, and so call more often on the police for help. It creates those bonds of intimacy between citizens and policemen that are generally recognised to be desirable.

Many odd bits of information are doubtless exchanged over not-strictly-legal cups of tea. But it can go further: cheap repairs in a garage are one thing, accepting a commission for sending breakdowns there would be a disciplinary offence. And in all these transactions the policeman puts himself at risk. Although many policemen mump to some extent, and no great harm comes of it, it is illegal and they are by that much in the trader's power.

Graft doesn't happen, mumping does, but neither is bribery proper. Here the relationship is between a few successful and well-off criminals and a few well-placed detectives. One tends to imagine a lot of money is paid to beat a rap: but what may happen far more often is a smaller amount is paid to reduce a charge, or not to oppose bail, or most often for information that makes it possible never to be arrested. Half-a-dozen such transactions could earn a detective £1,000 in old notes over a year; he would pay no tax and they could effectively double his income without doing great violence to his conscience or causing the least risk of discovery.

Although real bribery happens on few occasions, criminals will say it happens far more often. There are several reasons for this: both psychological and practical. Allegations of bribery are a sort of mental armour; they denigrate the criminal's chief enemy, the policeman. Whenever he says, 'You'd sooner find a flying pig than a straight law,' it is mental balm to him, a spell against the dragons out in the night. Often criminals can contrive events to look as if they have successfully bribed policemen; this increases their status.

A detective superintendent says: 'It's always in a villain's interest to put about that he's able to bung coppers. What happens is this. You go and see a car-dealer about a stolen car. You haven't a hope of proving it on him, but, to show the flag and go through the motions, you take a statement. He says he doesn't know nothing about it; you try and scare him, and that's all there is to it. But when you've gone his mates say: "Cor, how did you odds that one?" He spreads his hands out and looks modest, "Well, it cost me fifty, but it's worth it."

'The villain now becomes a much more important person. He owns a bent law, and this creates happy situations later on, when some friend of a friend gets nicked. The phone rings and there's chummy saying, what was the name of that DI you bunged? Of course, he can't say, but for another fifty, cash in hand, he'll see what can be done. After a pause, he reports to the friends that the DI is sorry, it's all gone much too far. "Your mate is well in bother. But he says he'll try and see the poison doesn't go in at the trial." And of course, the fifty pounds doesn't come back.'

In the hands of a gangster, a reputation for bribing policemen is a powerful weapon. He puts it about that anything

said to the police about him gets back within the day. True
or false, this short-circuits opposition, because those who
are too weak to hurt him by force dare not hurt him by de-
nunciation. This was one of the great resources of the Richardson gang, and had such a powerful effect on those round
them that one man whom they'd beaten up, in hospital
with broken ribs, burns and lacerations, ran out into the
streets in February in his pyjamas rather than stay to talk
with two detectives who had called on him. Even if it is
false, this is a difficult tactic for the police to counter, because it involves proving a negative – and not an academic
negative, but one of the most painful importance to would-
be informants.

But any investigation into bribery and collusion is unlikely
to succeed. Any criminal at large who has a policeman in
his power (or who knows of a policeman in a friend's power)
is unlikely to sacrifice him – who knows when he might be
needed? And who else need know anything about it?

The transactions between them are very transient, impossible to catch, impossible to prove. Bribery seldom comes
to light except in two special circumstances: (i) when the
police do a deal and then, as the case comes on, want more
money: (ii) when a criminal gets much more severe sentence
than he expected, and then complains about his friends who
have tempered prosecutions in the past.

I want to emphasise again that even the severest critics
of the Metropolitan Police do not allege that more than a
minute fraction of the detective force – itself only a small
part of the police – is ever guilty of these offences. As a
demonstration of this, there were the very successful prosecutions of the Richardson and Kray gangs in 1968 and
1969. Each of these involved over a hundred detectives,
and the rewards for betraying the police plans would have
been enormous. Yet dozens of important criminals were
arrested and the evidence against them marshalled, with
the effect that police morale was considerably raised, and
organised crime in London received a severe setback.

Part of the reason why corruption is rare – apart from the honesty of individual officers – is that their seniors always have this sort of consideration in their minds. They are alive to the possibilities, and look out for signs that they have been realised. The point of going into it all here is to illustrate the inward suspicion that is part of any honest police force.

The naïve observer, trying to deal rationally with unfamiliar ideas like bribery and the manufacture of evidence, tends to put them into separate receptacles in the mind. But there is no reason why they shouldn't happen together. One can imagine a scenario like this: a team of thieves plan to break into a safe deposit vault one week-end. The police have information and a squad is detailed to deal with the job. They keep observation on the men, see them, together and separately, reconnoitring the building. The men are clearly observed on several occasions.

Comes the day and a startling murder happens in another part of town. All available detectives (including the team working on this job) are employed over the week-end on house-to-house searches. The thieves strike that night, penetrate the wall of the vault with a thermic lance, dynamite the strong boxes, get what they came for and leave.

When they get home they take the greatest care to destroy all the evidence. In particular, the leader has his wife hoover his clothes to remove dust and splashes of metal. The police are called to the raped vault on Monday and at once go to see the men whom they have watched. There is no evidence of any sort, the men all have excellent alibis for the weekend which they decline to discuss, but for want of anything better, the police take their clothes for forensic examination. Tiny drops of metal are 'found' in the turn-ups of the leader's trousers. A spectrographic comparison with the rather unusual metal of the vault wall shows that they were identical. This will be a crucial piece of evidence at the trial.

The police go back and arrest the team. Before they are charged, the officer in charge of the detectives interviews the leader privately in the cells of the police station. This is a negotiation rather than an interrogation. He presents his difficulty. He doesn't know whether to charge them with unlawfully and maliciously causing an explosion of a nature likely to cause serious injury to property, for which the penalty is life imprisonment, or whether he'll have to settle for conspiracy – penalty two years or so. The leader sensitively appreciates his problem. He offers to plead to conspiracy – this will suppress the metal-splash evidence. But the detective is still doubtful. He and his men have worked hard ... The leader then suggests that, if an offer of £1,500 would clarify the detectives' minds, he for one would be glad to contribute.

Now when this case comes to court only a travesty of the real affair is presented to the jury. The accused and the police know the facts; counsel and the ushers can smell it, doubtless the Judge perceives more than he is told. Only the jury are at sea. This may seem far-fetched but something of the sort appears to have been attempted in recent years.

In November 1966, a Norman Smith and some friends were charged at the Old Bailey with receiving £18,000 worth of spirits. They alleged at the trial that the Inspector in charge of the case had been paid £150 not to press his opposition to bail in the lower court. The accused further complained that the police officers had then asked for £1,500 not to give false evidence – Smith said the Inspector showed him a notebook with evidence written out. The Common Serjeant, Judge Griffith-Jones, said in his summing-up to the jury:

'The advice I give you in the strongest possible terms, having regard to the possibility here of corruption and the police not having told the truth, is that you proceed to ignore and put out of your mind every fact given in evidence by the police which is in dispute by the defendants[1] ...'

The reader may feel that this is altogether too strong:

[1] *Private Eye*, 12 May 1967.

252

and he can only decide for himself whether such a thing is possible, and, if possible, likely. If it is, a pretty moral problem results. The criminal, who has been guilty of other crimes for years, and is guilty now, is convicted by false evidence. He gets two or three years: would society be better served if he went free? The policeman risks his career to plant the evidence, and gets as a reward, a moderate bribe. Who is *better* entitled to this money: the criminal who stole it, or the policeman who got him convicted?

Preventing Corruption

These crimes are as old as policing, and so are the countermeasures. The greatest of these is unceasing suspicion; nothing to a seasoned police officer is what it seems. Transactions that to the naïve bystander seem simple and straightforward can conceal a number of by-plots; the senior policeman must be alert to them all. This alertness is institutionalised under the name of *supervision,* and the Police Force is composed of two large groups: the people who get out on the street and do things and those who sit in offices scrutinising, correlating and comparing their reports.

In the Uniform Branch, 13,000-odd Police Constables and Sergeants are supervised by 3,500 more senior officers, a ratio of four to one: in the CID 2,300 2nd Class sergeants, Detective Constables and temporary Detective Constables are supervised by 700 higher ranks, a ratio of three to one. As another precaution, policemen, and particularly detectives, are seldom encouraged to go anywhere alone. This is partly for physical protection, but also to ensure that involvement and the profit of misdeeds would be spread as widely as possible. On the Flying Squad, a particularly sensitive place, there are eight operational teams of ten men, each headed by a detective inspector. The prudent DI makes every member tell the others what he is doing, so that, for instance, any bribe would have to be split ten ways, and so would be hardly worth taking.

Policemen are kept together; they are also kept in the character of police officers. I asked the Chief Inspector in charge of the C1 Drug Squad why he didn't employ young detectives in disguise, to penetrate the drug scene and uncover the pushers. His answer was an interesting commentary on police ethical thinking. He said: 'You would have to use young DC's of perhaps twenty-three or twenty-four, who have only been on the Department a couple of years. You've had no chance at all to assess their character, to make up your mind whether they're honest or not. If they're going to do the job you want, you're going to have to start dealing in drugs. That's the only way of getting near the top wholesalers. But think of the scandal if it came out! And then they could go bent on us – I hope most policemen would laugh at £500, but they might not.

'Anyway, they're in a great position to put on the screws – one of them could end up running the whole drug-scene with half a million in the bank – and all the time he's been sending us small fry. We might never suspect, and even if we did it would be harder to catch *him* than the bloke we were after first of all. Or it might go the other way: he might become a junkie. What do we say to his parents? What do we say to the Divisional Surgeon? What do we say to the Commissioner? I'm the officer in charge, I'm the one the finger's pointing at.'

Some Uniform Superintendents have employed young PCs in this way: perhaps they have more faith in human nature than the CID. But in general, it seems, the Metropolitan Police are unwilling to use people as *agents*. There are a number of good reasons: there is the impossibility of trusting, as a routine, a man in a position where convenience and profit both advise him to defect; there is the political explosion if he is discovered, and even if he stays loyal, there is strong feeling against the police being used in an *agent-provocateur* role.

It has happened, occasionally, on quite a large scale. The last occasion was perhaps with the formation of the Ghost

Squad, a small group of detectives instructed thus: 'You are to *infiltrate* into the underworld and establish and maintain contacts with anyone who can give information which will lead to the arrests of criminals. You must stay in the background but you must get the information and plenty of it. Once you have obtained it, you will pass it on to either the Flying Squad or one of the Divisional CID Offices. Remember that the whole success of this plan depends on strict secrecy.

'You will have complete freedom of movement. You will be released from your present duties and you will have your own office, with its own key. See that you leave nothing around. You will not be asked to sign off and on duty. You will not be asked any questions about the source of any information you may discover.[1]'

This group was broken up in 1958 for no very clearly-explained reasons. I was told by a senior officer that it was 'constitutionally objectionable to have people involved with criminals who don't come to court with them,' but this objection applies with equal strength to the present Criminal Intelligence organisation. Perhaps it was, as CID gossip suggests, because members of the Ghost Squad had become indistinguishable from the expert criminals whom they were chasing, were being caught by Flying Squad operations, and Scotland Yard repressed the Squad before it blew the police apart.

Finally, on the matter of corruption and the buying of information from police officers, the police must know very well it happens. There are seldom concrete signs, but one appeared in the *Evening Standard*[2], reporting a raid by 150 policemen on a club in Eltham. When the group assembled at the Yard beforehand, 'strict security precautions were taken. Senior police officers stood by telephones and not one of the officers used in the raid was allowed to leave the group after the briefing.'

[1] Gosling, John, *The Ghost Squad*, W. H. Allen, London, 1959.
[2] 6 January 1968.

I am even told that this leakage is accepted as inevitable. Senior officers realise they must have bridges with the underworld; that these bridges *can* carry information both ways, and that if there is enough money on the criminal side to buy warning, it will inevitably be bought. The police count on the trade balance to be in their favour, and in practice the flow may be self-regulating, because the officer who fails to get more information than he gives is not going to produce arrests of the quality and in the quantity he should. He will be removed.

So, a major index in the supervision of detectives is their arrest score. This defines the quality of the officer, but it also reveals a good deal about his ethical behaviour. If he is competent, but his arrest rate is low, then one may suspect that he is being bribed. If his arrest rate is abnormally high, and often of offenders of the same category – like the Aid to CID in the Mars-Jones inquiry who specialised in offensive-weapons cases – supervisors must wonder if he plants more evidence than God sends his way.

I have tried to discuss police wrong-doing at some length, not because it happens often, but because suspicion is always an unstated part of the furniture of the police world. Until I learnt to assess new situations in terms of these possibilities I wasn't seeing life in the same way as the policemen round me. But for all this, the tortious damage done by the Metropolitan Police to its fellow citizens as it goes about its work is remarkably small. The cost of compensation paid by the police in the financial year 1966–7 was £86,718. 3. 4d.[1] The force insures its own vehicle fleet, so most of this was paid on account of car accidents; and only £5,000 as compensation for false imprisonment, malicious prosecution, and assault. The total cost of civil damage done during the year was about four pounds per policeman – or two-pence halfpenny for each person living in the Metropolitan Police District.

[1] Financial Statement, Metropolitan Police Fund, 1966–7.

CHAPTER ELEVEN

Efficiency of the Police

One wants to ask about every organisation: 'How efficient is it?' and in most cases there is some sort of answer to give. With a business one looks at the balance sheet; profit is the major criterion. With an army one looks at the last battle; with a school perhaps at the university-scholarships list. There is often some simple, knife-edged test of success or failure. But nothing like this can be found for the police, because their job is completely artificial. They exist to absorb the tensions within society. Success in one state of public opinion may be failure in another; as an example of the way the police have to swing with the times, one might cite this not untypical prosecution of 1940:

Three men were arrested and charged under the Public Order Act of 1936 because: 'On a Sunday morning a steward at Muswell Hill Golf Club looked from his bedroom window and saw one of the accused approach the others and give them a Nazi salute. He was annoyed, as it "was not a thing one liked to see in this country", and he telephoned the police. Somewhat oddly, the police acted on this information and charged three offenders with *"insulting words and behaviour"*. In court, they explained it had been a joke; they were all loyal citizens of Great Britain. One of them, asked if he would say "Heil Hitler!", said: "Not on my life. I often say, when hitting a ball, I wish that were Hitler." The Magistrate, a colonel, dismissed the case, but said that it had been "rightly and properly brought[1]." '

[1] Turner, E. S., *The Phoney War on the Home Front*, Michael Joseph, London, 1961.

R

257

The Public Order Act has not changed, but the police have; a similar prosecution today would raise a storm of indignation. But, if the national temper warranted it, the police would doubtless change back.

So, in order to assess the efficiency of the police, one has to discover what people *really* want of them, and this is by no means easy. In theory the police exist to enforce all laws – laws which have been made by the people's representatives in Parliament. But in practice we vote, by our behaviour, on all the laws all the time, and the police are strongly influenced by this running plebiscite.

This is particularly apparent in traffic law enforcement, where the police are potentially confronted with mass lawbreaking. Here, a law that eighty-five per cent or more of people will voluntarily obey, once they understand it, is called 'enforceable', and one which fewer than that will obey is called 'unenforceable'. Thus, the thirty m.p.h. speed limit is unenforceable, but if a limit were set at thirty-eight m.p.h. it would be enforceable. The ban on parking between a zebra crossing and its studs is enforceable because people find it sensible, the ban on parking at yellow lines is less so. This situation is not confined to traffic. The old laws against street betting were, for example, quite unenforceable, and none were keener to have them repealed than the police.

There are many things the police could, or apparently should, do but do not, because the irritation generated, and the dislike and disrespect for law and order produced, outweigh the value of a mass of petty prosecutions. Jennifer Hart, writing in 1951,[1] said:

'Police do not try to enforce unpopular, or as they sometimes term them, unenforceable laws: e.g. certain parts of the gaming laws. Some of the most unpopular laws at present, such as fuel and price controls are, it should be observed, enforced not by the police, but by special enforcement officers of the Ministries concerned. In other words, there is some truth in saying that the police are popular because they are not too efficient.'

[1] Hart, J. M., *The British Police*, Allen & Unwin, 1951.

In the 1960s a new sort of unpopular law, against car parking, had a new sort of enforcement officer – the Traffic Warden, again relieving odium against the police.

Looked at rationally, this is inevitable. 20,000 policemen cannot *force* 8 million Londoners to do anything, and particularly since the low temperature of relationships between the State and the individual is one of England's most priceless possessions, it is important that they do not try. In the field of public order, the police can only guide and shepherd. The Metropolitan force can mobilise, at the very most, 10,000 men on the streets (there is no national guard to back them up).

This figure is not an accident; it has evolved over the years in an empirical way, and shows roughly how large an element of violent dissent British society will tolerate before we use conciliation. And this conciliation is a continuous process. For instance, at the autumn 'Demo' of 1968[1], the police adapted by yielding the street to the demonstrators, who could 'sit' as long as they liked. Before, this had been a reason for arrest. So the police, superficially, won the day; but a police win in London would be a 'no-fight' anywhere else.

This is obvious enough in public order, but it applies equally strongly to crime. It is quite impossible for the CID, with 3,000 members, to hold down 8 million potential criminals in any physical sense. The function of the CID is as a prosecuting agency. They do sometimes solve crimes *ab initio*, and occasionally from the unremarked clue – just like detectives in books. But fundamentally the State discourages crime by providing, as it were, a gun and crew with which the aggrieved citizen can avenge himself against the largest criminal. You are robbed, you go to the police. If the quarry is in sight, they aim the gun of law, the Judge pulls the trigger, and pow!

In the vast majority of cases, just like other policemen, detectives *react* rather than act. They prosecute most

[1] See above, p. 111.

crimes because non-policemen want them to, and provide them with the information and evidence which they need. It would perhaps surprise a layman to realise how seldom the CID can crack a case entirely through its own efforts. It would be even more surprising to realise how often prosecutions do not take place for want of help from interested citizens.

The Optimum Level of Enforcement

In theory the police job is to catch criminals, but on examination it is not even obvious that they should try to catch all of certain classes of offenders. A permanent police problem, in all societies, is presented by people who cater for ineradicable but disruptive public tastes, like prostitution, alcohol, drugs, gambling and pornography.

The police dilemma is this: if they take energetic measures, they can more or less easily repress the surface manifestations of these businesses and deny a bulk market to the organisers. But in doing so they do not eradicate the businesses, but compress and 'harden' them. The risks to be taken in supplying the forbidden delights become greater, and so they become more expensive. But there are always some people with enough money. The suppliers' organisation then becomes tough, secret and much harder to deal with, and is more likely to implicate powerful members of society. If, on the other hand, the police ignore the business, they lay themselves open to charges of laxity and even corruption.

One can distinguish two main kinds of damage done by these businesses: one, the 'hidden social damage', is due to the creation of hard, rich gangs, and the corruption of public figures.[1] The other, the 'overt social damage', is due

[1] As Hank Mossick shows in his book, *The Silent Syndicate*, Macmillan, New York, 1969, this apparently ineradicable American criminal organisation was directly created by legal repression during Prohibition.

directly to the proliferation of the undesirable service. Too much prostitution weakens marriage and the home: too many drugs means too many addicts and too many spoiled lives, etc.

By pruning the visible manifestations, the police can control the publicity these businesses enjoy, and so control the size of their markets. So we can draw two curves: (1) shows how the *hidden* social damage *increases* with police repression; (2) shows that the *overt* social damage *decreases* with repression.

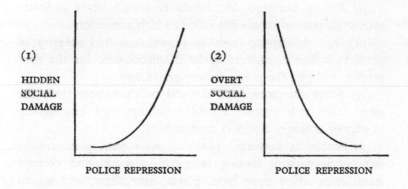

(1) HIDDEN SOCIAL DAMAGE

POLICE REPRESSION

(2) OVERT SOCIAL DAMAGE

POLICE REPRESSION

Added together, these curves suggest that the *least* total damage may be achieved at some level of repression between complete denial and complete permissiveness.

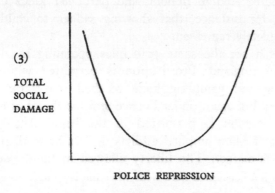

(3) TOTAL SOCIAL DAMAGE

POLICE REPRESSION

This effect can perhaps be seen in the way the police handle the pornographic book trade. Dirty bookshops operate publicly in London and all big cities, selling a product which most people would not openly have in their homes. They are obviously, to some extent, tolerated by the police, although all of them are continually committing offences against the law[1]. But the following advantageous effects result from moderate permissiveness:

(i) Although the prices charged are perhaps double the potential open-market price, it is not possible to make large sums from the trade.

(ii) Buying pornographic books is a sufficiently ordinary activity to put customers out of reach of blackmailers.

(iii) The deterrence (risk of prosecution and severity of penalty) is low enough to make it uneconomic for the proprietors to bribe the police in any grand way.

(iv) Since the bookshops depend on customers from the street, the trade cannot afford bombings and beatings-up as part of ordinary business competition.

(v) People in powerful positions who want pornography can get it without having recourse to secret and corrupt organisations that then have power over them, and so, to some extent, over the State.

(vi) Since the police do not make an all-out effort to eliminate the trade, they have powers in reserve to enforce minor points: window-displays must be decent, dirty books may not be sold to minors, and particular kinds of pornography, for instance, that showing sadism to children, can be completely repressed.

We can see the same principles operating in all similar fields in England. Prostitution is permitted within limits. Drinking and gambling have reached the status of legal activities, but again under licence and the threat of sanctions. Drug addiction is permitted in the belief that a modest number of State-supplied addicts do less harm than a vigorous black-market. The liberty allowed in these examples is

[1] We are not concerned here with what the law *ought* to be.

now a result of deliberate social policy expressed through
Acts of Parliament, but, none the less, they embody solutions
developed empirically by the police.

Punishment

The police take a simple-minded view of the end product
of the judicial process: the disposition of the court, the
punishment of the accused. Subtle distinctions between the
purposes of punishment mean little to them.

The policeman is set in motion by entries in a crime book.
To each entry there corresponds at least one criminal. The
object of the game is to detach him from the neutral mass
of civilians. Once a crime has occurred, a law-enforcing mechanism has failed. If the criminal is a first offender, the threat
failed to deter him; if he is an old offender, prison failed
either to deter or reform. The only purpose of punishment
then is to remove him physically from the field of play.
Those who are either deterred or reformed, or both, commit no crimes and so do not enter the policeman's calcula-
tions.

Most policemen would, I think, regard punishment for
most criminals like this, as simply a removal. They would
just like them away, out of it, preferably on some island,
'Where they can steal each other blind'. Most, too, would
probably agree that, after three convictions for serious, professional crime, a man should be removed for the rest of his
active life, to be released, say at fifty-five. They bear no
animosity against him: it just seems absurd that criminal
and detective should spend their working lives chasing or
being chased, with them catching him, letting him go, catching him, letting him go – a game that is ended by the retirement of both parties.

They realise that cooping criminals up in prison together
has its disadvantages. Her Majesty's attendance centres, detention centres, Borstals and prisons provide almost as efficient a system of criminal education as could be devised; a

sort of free university of crime. But this, too, is accepted as part of the game society wants the policeman to play.

They put up with this, but a common police complaint is of the leniency of punishment, a policy that seems to them to be designed to load them with work and failure. The over-all *deterrence* of the combined law-enforcement system, we might say, is the product of two factors: the chance of de-tection multiplied by the *severity* of sentence. Thus motor-ists are wary about parking on yellow lines because, although the penalty is low (a two pound fine), the *chance* of detection is high. Again, professional thieves are unwilling to repeat the Great Train Robbery because, although the chances of being caught are low, the penalty – thirty years – is high.

The police can only affect one half of this equation – the chance of detection – but they are judged by the success of the *whole* of it. For want of any better criterion, we say: 'Indictable crime went up five per cent last year – the police must be slipping', but we should take the scale of punishment into consideration as well. The relationship between crime and punishment is very complex indeed, and it takes a brave man to ascribe definite results to any penal system. As a demonstration of this we may look at the situation in London at the beginning of the nineteenth century.

The rise of large, disorganised, industrialised populations had completely wrecked the Tudor system of policing based on the parish constable. The chance of detection had fallen so low that adequate deterrence could only be maintained by a draconian code of punishments. This was the time when 400 or more offences were punished by hanging, and the success of the system has often been imaged by stories of pickpockets at work under the gallows where their colleagues kicked.

Although the introduction of the Metropolitan Police in 1829 is usually thought of as a watershed in law-enforcement methods, it in fact only completed a gradual series of im-provements which had begun in 1798 with the establish-ment of the Thames River Police. In 1805 the Bow Street

Magistrate had established the Horse Patrols to drive high-waymen from the outer roads. In 1821 the Unmounted Horse Patrol was set to patrolling the inner roads on foot, and in 1822 there was a special Foot Patrol at night. As a result, the detection rate improved enormously.

Hanging, a punishment that had been 'designed' to be occasional but salutary, then became routine and therefore terrible. Presented with streams of capital indictments for trivial offences, juries refused to convict. In practice, then, much of the criminal law was repealed, and those trades that had been to some extent protected by capital statutes found themselves naked in a hurricane of larceny.

The calico-printers brought the problem to a head. It was a capital offence to steal cloth from their establishments, but so much of their stocks was being stolen that they could not earn a living. They petitioned Parliament in 1811 to be given some workable protection in place of hanging. By 1819 there had been 12,000 similar petitions from trades left un-protected by the excessive severity of the laws.

The mass of offences punishable by death lingered on until 1839, ten years after the foundation of the Metropolitan Police, when, made unnecessary by more efficient detection, they were reduced to fifteen, and in 1861 to four (Murder, Treason, Piracy, and Arson in Royal Ships or Dockyards, which, except for murder, still stand).

A further defect of the draconian eighteenth-century system was its failure to provide for an escalating ladder of deterrents. It tried to divide society into two: the righteous and the wicked, but those who are as likely to be hanged for a sheep as for a lamb steal lambs too. We now have an elaborate ladder of punishments which has two functions: (i) to deter any crime, (ii) to deter people who have steeled themselves to one level of crime from stepping up to a more serious one.

The penal ladder is not only stepped, it is broad at the bottom and narrow at the top, like an orchard ladder: that is, many people may be prepared to risk light punishment to commit minor crime, but balk at the next rung. At each step up there should be fewer prepared to deviate that far and that expensively from the norm.

Since there are a fixed number of rungs – or crimes – the separation between each rung and the next – which is almost as important as the existence of the ladder itself – depends *only* on the height of the ladder, or the *maximum* punishment available. Thus the leniency of the courts, coupled with the abolition of capital punishment, affects the police in a very immediate and practical way. By lowering the height of the ladder it crams the same number of crimes into a smaller range of punishments. The effect of this is first seen at the top of the ladder, in the armed robbery figures.

It is the almost universal opinion of the police that murder and robbery with violence have increased since the end of hanging, and that the increase is due to the removal of this ultimate sanction. Detectives who know the robbing classes told me – as they told the Royal Commission of Capital Punishment – that criminals used to be afraid of being hanged and regulated their conduct accordingly; and this is confirmed by those criminals that I met who also move in the same circles.

Abolition is perhaps unconsciously resented because it spoils the unique position of the Police Force, and, in particular, that of the CID. They might be rough, uneducated, unpolished people, living obscure, dangerous and often squalid lives, but they were entrusted with this special task: to find sacrifices for execution. They were, in their way, under their rules and those of the law, something like the Aztec Priests of the Sun God, avenging angels in tweed suits. However fair the English system of trial – and abolitionists can point to some irreparable failures[1] – it was nevertheless true that, unless the CID chose us, we would not get hanged. Now that is taken

---

[1] In a recent (dates not stated) twelve-month period a total of 859 Free Pardons and remissions of sentence were granted on account of miscarriages of justice. A few of these were due to changes made in the law while sentences were being served. House of Lords Hansard, 29.1.70. One might imagine that a great many more went uncorrected.

away from them, their central mystery is empty, and they are civil servants like everyone else.

Luckily, even if a few murderers for gain are not deterred, law or society still seems to provide adequate sanctions to prevent a spate of killings. There has not been an enormous increase in killings in London since the abolition of capital punishment. What increase there is may partly be due to the new willingness of juries to convict on what would have been capital charges. On the other hand, the number of people prepared to *risk* killing by carrying out robberies armed with firearms has risen strikingly.

The graph on page 268 shows the numbers of lives taken by another's hand in some criminal act for each year since the War in London, per million inhabitants of the MPD. This includes: murder, manslaughter, infanticide, but excludes death by dangerous driving.

The armed-robbery curve shows the number of cases of robbery in which the attackers carried, or were thought to have carried, guns, per million inhabitants of the MPD.

The P.D. curve shows the *national* totals of those sentenced to Preventive Detention, or to Corrective Training.

For what it is worth, both curves show a marked fall after 1948 and the introduction of Preventive Detention. The robbery curve is something like an inverse to Preventive Detention, which frightened criminals by imposing long sentences *in addition* to the punishment for the crime on trial, without any possibility of remission. It was abandoned in 1966 because there was no more room in Her Majesty's prisons. The robbery curve shows its lowest point in the year after the Bentley and Craig case, when Bentley was executed for inciting Craig to shoot a policeman. Both curves show slight peaks after the introduction of diminished responsibility in 1957 – though this is perhaps accidental – and both have broadly speaking risen since then.

Clear-ups and Crime Rates

The success of the police in combating crime is measured

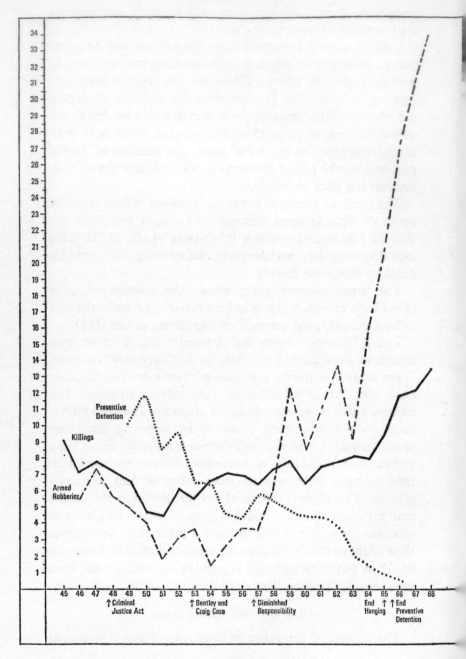

by the number of cases in which a criminal is detected and the crime 'cleared-up'. The moment of clear-up is 'at the time a person is arrested or summoned for committing the crime or when the offender asks for the crime to be taken into consideration by a court which has found him guilty of some other offence'. Also crimes are said to be cleared-up when the police know the offender, but he has died, left the jurisdiction, or has been charged or convicted of something so much more serious that the original crime becomes negligible.

The Metropolitan Police were asked to investigate some 270,000 indictable offences in 1967, of which they cleared-up twenty-four point three per cent. This average, overall figure is a good deal lower than it was, say after the last war, and gives rise to concern among policemen. But it also means that one only has to commit a crime four times to be arrested, which, when one considers the anonymity of people in London and the opportunities afforded for crime, is perhaps not bad.

This average, too, is a compound of widely varying rates for different crimes. Offences against the person which, in spite of public concern about violent crime, form only two point nine per cent of the total, are seventy-three per cent cleared up. This high rate is largely due to the fact that most attacks arise in a domestic or work situation, and the attacker is known to his victim; the police then just have to find him.

In general the clear-up rate for a particular crime strikingly reflects the size of the area of suspicion. That for ordinary larceny from the person – pickpocketing – was only thirteen per cent, because this crime can in practice only be detected if the perpetrator is caught in the act. Larcenies by servants, on the other hand, were ninety-nine per cent cleared up, because although, as we see below, many are not reported, those that are reported point instantly to a suspect – usually the sales assistant in charge of the deficient till. The clear-up rate for pedal-cycle larceny is low at eight point two per cent, because it is hardly worth anyone's time to make serious inquiries. Shoplifting, on the other hand, is ninety-one per cent cleared up because unless a store detective sees a shoplifter at work, there is no other evidence to prove that the offence happened. In this case the nine per cent failure rate represents people who managed to run away.

Some research has been done on a large collection of breaking offences by the Home Office Research and Planning Branch. In London these crimes form about fifteen per cent of the total and research finds that twenty-five per cent are solved straightforwardly – there is an obvious suspect, or they are taken into consideration by someone charged with another offence. Eight per cent are difficult to detect, in seven point five per cent there are some clues but no arrest, and in the remaining sixty per cent there are no leads at all. This result seems to confirm the true fact of the detectives' job: most of their work is as a prosecuting agency – citizens indicate offenders, or offenders ask for cases to be taken into consideration.

The police solve a third by their own efforts, but this is only eight per cent of all the crimes of this type reported to them, and perhaps only one point six per cent of the real total of crimes (see below). If this result is characteristic of the broad picture – and there is little reason to think that it is not – changes in the clear-up rate fade rather into obscurity, because the contribution made directly by the police to clear-up rates is so small that any *improvement* must be negligible in proportion to the total. An interesting pointer to the predominant role of the *citizen* in solving crime is given by these figures relating the sizes of police forces to their clear-up rates.

Number of men in force	Size of Community approx. (1,000s)	Average percentage of detection of known crime
Under 200	Under 120	60%
200—349	120—240	56%
350—499	240—300	51%
500—1000	300—600	48%
1000+	600+	38%
20,000 (Met)	8000	25%

The Association of Municipal Corporations[1] collected these figures over the years 1959–61, to resist the Home Office's Police Force amalgamation scheme by showing that similar forces were more efficient. But it is difficult to believe that the cause of these striking differences can lie solely within the police.

After all, training and methods are more or less uniform over England and Wales. It is more convincing perhaps to look for an explanation of the high clear-up rate of small forces in the greater cohesion of small communities, which encourages people to give information to the police, to act as witnesses, and the correspondingly greater visibility of criminals within them. One, but possibly less important, factor influencing police efficiency is perhaps to be found in the ease of sharing criminal information in a small force.

But surprisingly little is known about the effect produced by the police on the activities of criminals. The Home Office Police Research and Planning Branch has, in its short life since 1963, done some extremely interesting work. So far there is not perhaps enough material on which to base a firm opinion, but the indications are that the effect of the police is a good deal less direct than one would at first assume.

There are three relevant papers. The first examines the analogy between detectives catching criminals and animals catching their prey. As the prey-density goes up, or there are more criminals about, so the rate of 'kills' increases. But the kill-rate is not proportional to the prey-density, because the animal has to spend a certain amount of time eating. In the police situation this is equivalent to doing paper-work and taking prisoners to court. Unlike animals, who only kill to eat, the police are required to make as many 'kills' as possible, and are obliged to look at every animal track, or crime, that is found. If crime increases enough, then all the policemen will be fully occupied simply in going to visit scenes of crime, and one would expect the clear-up rate then to go *down* in spite of the abundance of criminals. Even if

[1] Cited by Whitaker, Ben, *The Police*, Eyre and Spottiswoode, 1964.

criminals queued up at police station doors, there is an upper limit to the number that can be arrested and charged, set by the detective-hours available to spend on preparation and the hearing of the cases.

An examination of police successes over the period of rising crime rates since the war shows that the largest number of criminals are caught when there are twelve point five to thirteen indictable crimes committed per policeman per year (or 125–130 per CID officer). After that the clear-up rate begins to fall. So it seems that the level of police success in the war against crime is, in the large scale, set as much by the amount of criminal activity as their own efforts.

The second paper describes an experiment to measure the effectiveness of the beat patrolman in reducing crime. The method of the experiment was to take, in each of four different cities, two similar areas, one for experiment and one for control. The control area was policed throughout as normal, while, on the experimental areas, patrol strength was varied from nothing at all, through one, two and three to four times as many officers as usual. To everyone's surprise, there was a slight increase of crime in the complete absence of policemen, but otherwise the variations had no effect at all.

It seemed that the cry, uttered by so many generations of senior officers, that more men on the beat would stop crime had no basis in fact at all. And this is perhaps confirmed by the attempt in London to staff a division at full strength for a year. No discernible effect was reported. But it was perhaps not so surprising. Any man who has walked a beat knows how little he can influence crime. See, for instance, the comment of the PC quoted on p. 61.

Interestingly, what seems to matter is not the *actual* number of policemen on patrol, but the impression which they make on the criminal. In London, the Special Patrol Group, a force of 130 uniform policemen with its own vehicles and communications, which descends on selected areas and patrols them intensively for a week or so, has a striking impact on crime. However, this may well be not because they are catching a large number of criminals, but because their vehicles are extremely conspicuous, and they themselves have a formidable reputation in the underworld. They are effective – for a while – because they frighten criminals off the streets. This effect was also found in two provincial forces where new and well-publicised methods of patrolling were introduced.

On a more theoretical level, a third paper examines the relationship between various social indicators, including police strengths and budgets, in various towns, and their crime rates. There is, indeed, something to be explained here: Liverpool shows nine point four crimes against property per year per thousand inhabitants; while Lincoln has only one point three six. Newcastle-upon-Tyne, with a fully staffed police force, has a crime rate of sixty per cent above the national average, while London, short of one policeman in three, has a rate almost identical to the average. It seems that police strength, or capital expenditure on police per head of policemen (that is, money spent on radios, cars, police stations), or the tactical deployment of the police, have no important effect on the crime rates. But population-density matters a lot, and so do wide extremes of distribution of wealth. This again suggests that the crime rate is an organic function of society, which the police can do little, directly, to modify.

The Dark Figure

So far we have been discussing the effect of police activity on the rate of *known* crime. But, in reality, we have no idea how successful the police are in detecting crime because we have no idea how many crimes are committed. True, the Home Office publishes totals of crime 'known to the police', and the police then achieve a score in clearing these up. But it appears that these known crimes are only a small proportion of the number of crimes committed.

s

Radzinowicz[1], writing in 1945, said:

'People may fail to notify the police of the offence committed for a variety of reasons. They may not believe in the efficacy of police investigations; they may consider the punishment which the law provides for the offence too hard or too lenient; they may fear the revenge of the offenders; they may not wish to lose time in making statements before the police and judicial authorities; they may consider the offence too insignificant to warrant modification. This list may be continued almost indefinitely.'

And another writer[2], in 1965:

'A large number of offences are never reported to the police. This may happen for a number of reasons:

1. All those involved may fail to realise that an offence has been committed. Children at play commit assaults and indecencies without being aware of their criminality;

2. All those involved may be willing participants. This is especially frequent in the case of abortions, homosexual offences, incest and carnal knowledge of girls under 16;

3. Even an unwilling victim may not wish to involve the offender in the consequences of prosecution. This happens not only with sexual offences such as indecent assault, but also in minor cases of pilfering, embezzlement, or fraud;

4. The victim may himself be antagonistic to the police. Many assaults in certain districts of the large cities are not reported because this would be regarded as handing the aggressor over to a common enemy;

5. The victim may regard the offence as too trivial to be worth the trouble of reporting. Many minor thefts are not reported for this reason;

6. The victim may be so pessimistic about the chances of bringing the offender to book that he does not bother to

[1] Radzinowicz, L., *English Criminal Statistics, a critical analysis*, in *Modern Approach to Criminal Law*, London, 1945.
[2] Walker, N., *Crime and Punishment in Great Britain*, Edinburgh, 1965.

report the offence. This is more likely with minor offences;

7. The victim may be too embarrassed to report the offence. Women – especially the very young – are often inhibited in this way from reporting indecent exposure. Men may keep silent about homosexual importuning in case they are suspected of attracting such advances. Parents of child victims of sexual offences may wish to spare the child the experience of interrogation and appearance in court;

8. The offence may be observed only by someone who disapproves of the law. Poaching is often unreported for this reason;

9. The victim or observer may be intimidated by the offender's threats of violence or by blackmail. Prostitutes' thefts from clients are seldom brought to the notice of the police;

10. The offence may be unknown to anyone but the offender, as must often happen in the case of speeding motorists.'

One might think that crimes of violence would be reported, but McClintock writes:

'It was naturally not possible to estimate, with any degree of accuracy, the size of the "dark figure" or undiscovered crimes of violence occurring in London each year. But as a result of discussions with the police, with probation officers, juvenile court officials, magistrates and other persons living or working in various areas in London it was found that most of the crimes of violence which are not reported to the police can be classified under one of five headings:

1. Offences resulting from quarrels between adults who were related or well known to each other and who lived in areas where a certain amount of violent behaviour is accepted as part of the pattern of ordinary social behaviour.

2. Offences between juveniles living in the same neighbourhood or attending the same school, where a certain amount of quite severe fighting is accepted as normal behaviour among the young.

3. Offences of violence between persons of the criminal

classes where there is an understandable lack of sympathy
or willingness to co-operate with the police and where there
is often fear of disclosure of their own illegal activities, such
as receiving, if the violence is reported to the police.

4. Offences against persons of apparent respectability
who fear the disclosure of some facts unfavourable to themselves such as homosexuality, or, if they are married, pro-
miscuous heterosexual relations.

5. Offences against persons who are inclined to feel the
police will be prejudiced against helping them, such as coloured people, Irish immigrants, vagrants and prostitutes[1].'

It was estimated that in many of the areas it would be
quite easy to find four or five times as many crimes of violence
that had *not* been reported to the police as had actually
been recorded by them.

If the dark figure for violence is surprising, that for theft
must be extraordinary. A study of crime in employment[2]
found that large numbers of detected offences were not
reported to the police and the offenders not charged.

	Large firms (%)	Smaller firms (%)
Stealing from firm	59	75
Stealing from fellow employee	66	33
Stealing from customer	29	100
Embezzlement	43	66

And these are only the offences detected within the firms.
Anyone who has worked in Britain knows about petty theft:
the 'fiddled' expenses, the tools and materials 'borrowed',
the couple of bags of cement that 'fell off the back of the
lorry'. If the departing work force of any factory were stopped
and searched at the gates, doubtless fifty per cent would
prove to have stolen something: spanners, drills, files, pencils,
a can of paint, myriad small things that are regarded almost
as the workers' perquisites; and which are certainly charged
for in the balance-sheets. And workers' thefts are not only
minor depredations. It is impossible to say how much of the

[1] McClintock, F. H. *et al.*, *Crimes of Violence*, London, 1963.
[2] Martin, J. P., *Offenders as Employees*, London, 1962.

goods is diverted by dishonest clerks and conniving delivery drivers.

There is enough to make it sometimes seem that there are two parallel economic systems at work in this country: one, overtly, operating through banks, the stock market, limited companies and so on – the mechanisms of capitalism; the other, a true co-operative working from the bottom which dissolves and erodes all the ideal channels of distribution, so that instead of goods and money flowing in well-defined, dredged streams, there are unsuspected soak-aways, secret canals, hidden connections. To adapt Clausewitz: Crime is commerce carried on by other means.

These hidden crimes are by no means trivial. Most joint stock banks show a loss of a million pounds or so in each year's balance-sheets, ascribed to 'bad mortgages' or some such: these often represent frauds which the managers are unwilling to prosecute for fear of demonstrating their carelessness in court. Many serious burglaries of jewels, cash and works of art, accumulated to avoid taxation, also go unreported. It is estimated that routine, unreported crime in England costs £150 million a year.

Radzinowicz sums up:

'But there is little reliable factual evidence on which to assess the total size of the dark figure. We have no more than a few fragmentary approximations and can only make a more or less inspired guess. My own would be that the crime fully brought into the open and punished represents no more than about fifteen per cent of the total. At every stage the total is increased: offences go unnoticed or unreported, offenders go undetected, unprosecuted or unconvicted. Who can say what our attitude towards the criminal – in emotional terms as well as in terms of practical policy – would be if the whole, or at least a large segment, of the 'dark figure' were brought to light and thus, to refer to England and Wales, another three or four million indictable offences were added to the recorded figures?'

In other words, the size of the puzzle which we set the police – that is, the crimes which we expect them to solve – has very little indeed to do with the actual amount of crime in the country, and a great deal to do with people's attitude towards crime and the police.

It is quite possible, for instance, that the 'crime wave' experienced in England since the war does not reflect any real increase in crime so much as an increased willingness in people to report crime. This might be because so many people have moved from the lower class – who see the police as an occupying army – to the middle class who see the police as providing a service which they pay for and deserve.

Moral Suasion

We are forced perhaps to some surprising conclusions: that the laws enforced by the police vary widely with public opinion, that the best social effects are sometimes gained by *permitting* a certain amount of crime, that the size, cost and organisation of police forces have no real effect on the general level of crime, and that the amount of crime reported to the police and prosecuted by them is an almost negligible fraction of the whole. What then are the police for? It is important to get the answer right, because the way we expect the police to behave turns on the result.

We are brought up to think of the police as white corpuscles in the blood stream of the body politic, whose function is to eat up *all* the germs, or criminals, and that this is the mechanism by which crime is prevented. If we take this view, that every criminal can and should be caught, then a low clear-up rate is a sign of failure, and it is worth straining every nerve to improve it. More seriously, in this view, the social damage done in short-cutting the law to increase arrests and convictions may be more than outweighed by the social benefits of neutralising criminals. We have recently seen two sad examples of the damage done by too much zeal; the Challenor affair will stand for the harm done in public order; the Sheffield business[1] for the harm done in crime.

Banton[2] writes:

'Though the police are concerned to a very important extent with law enforcement it is not a product, nor is it to be attributed to the police. Indeed the police are relatively unimportant in the enforcement of law. . . . control is maintained by the rewards and punishments which are built into every relationship and which are evident in the conferring and withholding of esteem, the sanctions of gossip, and the institutional, economic, and moral pressures that underlie behaviour patterns. Law and law-enforcement agencies, important though they are, appear puny compared with the extensiveness and intricacy of these other modes of regulating behaviour.'

In reality, those who get arrested, prosecuted and punished have been extremely unlucky. But what matters is not the physical effect on them, so much as the deterrence which their example exercises on the rest of us. The whole system of the police, courts and prisons works because the fate of the unfortunate few is designed to be extremely public, while the undetected majority remain in the shadows. The nicely-brought-up, law-abiding citizen has no means of judging the *real* risks of crime because only a fraction of the necessary information is available to him. He is deterred from committing serious crime because all he can see is a stream of criminals going through the courts. Judging on this evidence alone, as he must, the police are 100-per-cent successful in detecting criminals, and once a criminal is detected, he is very likely to be punished. Only the professional criminal – and the policeman – being in the shadows themselves, see the true risks.

So it appears that in crime, as well as in public order, the *existence* of the police is far more important than their efforts.

[1] Sheffield Police Appeal Inquiry.
[2] Banton, Michael, *The Policeman and the Community*, Tavistock, London, 1964.

If there were no law enforcement agency at all, few people would obey the laws. But if one exists, and is even only moderately efficient, then most people will not care to run the risk of getting into trouble. Given the fact of a police force, ready to prosecute if anyone asks them to, the level of criminality or good behaviour is then far more an organic characteristic of society. The mere existence of the police is their main contribution to whatever level of law-abidingness exists. The improvement that could be made by extra police effort is very small indeed.

It is important that the police should arrest the flamboyant criminals, the murderers and armed robbers, because these people create propaganda that will eventually nullify the deterrent. But apart from these cases, which are themselves important because they are themselves symbols, the major 'product' of the police is symbolic. In their own persons they embody respect for the laws. They persuade people to live honestly far more by their existence and example than because they physically remove wrong-doers from society. If *they* are dishonest or corrupt, then the citizen's strongest reason for honesty has gone. Civilised life would degenerate into a squalid scramble not to be found out. In effect, the police and the courts, with their odd clothes, archaic language and involved procedures, are an enormous theatrical production. As Plato thought of actors and the ancient Greek theatre, they portray vividly and passionately the downfall of evil and the eventual triumph of the gods, that man might become wiser. To say that the police job is fundamentally theatrical is not to denigrate it. If they were the ethical equivalent of corporation dustmen, who mechanically removed law-breaker from society like white blood-corpuscles gobbling up germs, it would not much matter how they behaved or what sort of people they were. But as things are it matters crucially. The policeman is the State made flesh. In his behaviour he demonstrates the true values of his society; his honesty, fairness and good sense are one supreme index of civilisation.

A New Procedure for Investigating Complaints?

It seems to the author that some of the problems of making justice visible in investigations of alleged police misbehaviour might be circumvented by a graduated scheme such as is sketched out below.

1. It should be permissible for any officer of Station Sergeant rank, or the equivalent in the CID, to try to settle a complaint informally.

2. If the complainant is not satisfied, he can opt to set the present system of investigation in motion.

3. At the end of this investigation, if the facts warrant it, there would normally be a private disciplinary hearing, with the complainant present while evidence is heard.

4. Or, either side could opt for a *public* hearing before a Police Disciplinary Review Board. 'Either side', because there might be times when the police would like to establish the justice of their cause without going to the lengths of a prosecution for wasting police time. The Review Board would operate in much the manner of a Tribunal; it would be necessary for legal aid to be available to complainants.

5. If there had been a *private* hearing (see 3), but the complainant was not satisfied with the result, he could refer the papers to the Review Board, now sitting as a sort of court of appeal.

6. The Review Board would in any case, as a routine part of its job, monitor the incidence and results of complaints against the police in its area.

This would deal, perhaps, fairly well with complaints that do not allege criminal offences against policemen. Most complaints would be settled in a few minutes, cheaply and humanely. Most of the rest would be settled quietly and not too expensively by a police disciplinary hearing, but because of the safety-valve of the Board, the public could feel that nothing was being hidden.

It is likely that few cases would get as far as the Board. It is true that the public hearing would impose a new strain on the few policemen likely to be subjected to it, but this is perhaps the price that has to be paid for good police-public relations.

Criminal accusations against policemen are another matter. These are investigated by the CID who report to the Chief Officer. If he is satisfied that no crime has been committed, he may deal with the matter as a disciplinary offence, or take no further action. If he is not so satisfied, he must refer the papers to the Director of Public Prosecutions, who may decide to prosecute or not.[1]

Only the last outcome, being self-publicising, is satisfactory from the point of view of the public interest. Too often complainants of criminality against policemen are fobbed off with form letters concealing one of these other steps. Since a complaint alleging crime must necessarily also allege a breach of police discipline, cases in which no prosecution is brought should be funnelled back into the complaints procedure suggested above.

The Board must consist of people whom the police respect. Suitable candidates might be: experienced solicitors and barristers, perhaps County Court Judges or retired High Court Judges. If the Inspectors of Constabulary were made members, in order to represent police interests, then they would bring with them their existing function of reviewing police complaints procedure, and the necessary staff in each of the nine English police districts.

Note: As this book was going to press, the Home Office announced the appointment of a working party to 'determine the best system of independent enquiries into serious allegations against police officers.'

[1] Police Act 1964, s. 49.

The Judges' Rules

1. When a police officer is trying to discover whether, or by whom, an offence has been committed he is entitled to question any person, whether suspected or not, from whom he thinks that useful information may be obtained. This is so whether or not the person in question has been taken into custody so long as he has not been charged with the offence or informed that he may be prosecuted for it.

2. As soon as a police officer has evidence which would afford reasonable grounds for suspecting that a person has committed an offence, he shall caution that person or cause him to be cautioned before putting to him any questions, or further questions, relating to that offence.

The caution shall be in the following terms: –

'You are not obliged to say anything unless you wish to do so but what you say may be put into writing and given in evidence.'

When after being cautioned a person is being questioned, or elects to make a statement, a record shall be kept of the time and place at which any such questioning or statement began and ended and of the persons present.

3. (a) When a person is charged with or informed that he may be prosecuted for an offence he shall be cautioned in the following terms: –

'Do you wish to say anything? You are not obliged to say anything unless you wish to do so but whatever you say will be taken down in writing and may be given in evidence.'

(b) It is only in exceptional cases that questions relating to the offence should be put to the accused person after he has been charged or informed that he may be prosecuted. Such questions may be put where they are necessary for the purpose of preventing or minimising harm or loss to some other person or to the public or for clearing up an ambiguity in a previous answer or statement.

Before any such questions are put the accused should be cautioned in these terms: –

'I wish to put some questions to you about the offence with which you have been charged (*or* about the offence for which you may be prosecuted). You are not obliged to answer any of these questions, but if you do the questions and answers will be taken down in writing and may be given in evidence.'

Any questions put and answers given relating to the offence must be contemporaneously recorded in full and the record signed by that person or if he refuses by the interrogating officer.

(c) When such a person is being questioned, or elects to make a statement, a record shall be kept of the time and place at which any questioning or statement began and ended and of the persons present.

4. All written statements made after caution shall be taken in the following manner: –

> (a) If a person says that he wants to make a statement he shall be told that it is intended to make a written record of what he says.
>
> He shall always be asked whether he wishes to write down himself what he wants to say; if he says that he cannot write or that he would like someone to write it for him, a police officer may offer to write the statement for him. If he accepts the offer the police officer shall, before starting, ask the person making the statement to sign, or make his mark to, the following: –

'I,   , wish to make a statement. I want someone to write down what I say. I have been told that I need not say anything unless I wish to do so and that whatever I say may be given in evidence.'

(b) Any person writing his own statement shall be allowed to do so without any prompting as distinct from indicating to him what matters are material.

(c) The person making the statement, if he is going to write it himself, shall be asked to write out and sign before writing what he wants to say, the following: –

'I make this statement of my own free will. I have been told that I need not say anything unless I wish to do so and that whatever I say may be given in evidence.'

(d) Whenever a police officer writes the statement, he shall take down the exact words spoken by the person making the statement, without putting in any questions other than such as may be needed to make the statement coherent, intelligible and relevant to the material matters: he shall not prompt him.

(c) When the writing of a statement by a police officer is finished the person making it shall be asked to read it and to make any corrections, alterations or additions he wishes. When he has finished reading it he shall be asked to write and sign or make his mark on the following Certificate at the end of the statement: –

'I have read the above statement and I have been told that I can correct, alter or add anything I wish. This statement is true. I have made it of my own free will.'

(f) If the person who has made the statement refuses to read it or to write the above-mentioned Certificate at the end of it or to sign it, the senior police officer present shall record on the statement itself and in the presence of the person making it, what has happened. If the person making the statement cannot read, or refuses to read it, the officer who has taken it down shall read it over to him and ask him whether he would like to correct, alter or add anything and to put his signature or make his mark at the end. The police officer shall then certify on the statement itself what he has done.

5. If at any time after a person has been charged with, or has been informed that he may be prosecuted for, an offence a police officer wishes to bring to the notice of that person any written statement made by another person who in respect of the same offence has also been charged or informed that he may be prosecuted, he shall hand to that person a true copy of such written statement, but nothing shall be said or done to invite any reply or comment. If that person says that he would like to make a statement in reply, or starts to say something, he shall at once be cautioned or further cautioned as prescribed by Rule 3(a).

6. Persons other than police officers charged with the duty of investigating offences or charging offenders shall, so far as may be practicable, comply with these Rules.

Vocabulary

A short vocabulary of Metropolitan Police slang. This is distinct from thieves' slang, although there are some thieves' words used by policemen, like 'slaughter', or, in inverted commas, 'old Bill.' There are some words used by both parties with different meanings: 'brief' means warrant or warrant-card to a policeman; a lawyer to a thief. Like any language, police slang is constantly changing. For example, every non-policeman knows that detectives call their working-area their 'manor' or 'patch'. The first I never heard used, the second only occasionally. What they actually said was 'ground'.

ACTIVE: an official term of praise for an enthusiastic detective.

ADVICE: a disciplinary tongue-lashing.

AGGRAVATION: harassment imposed either by the police or criminals on each other.

AID, AN: temporary Detective Constable. The rank used to be called 'Aid to CID'.

ALADDIN'S CAVE: the home or store of a successful thief.

AREA CAR: the black, obvious police cars that patrol each sub-division and respond to non-traffic 999 calls.

BEAT, A: the area patrolled by a uniformed policeman.

BENT, TO GO: to go back on a statement or a promise (of a witness).

BIRD: time in prison.

BLACK, THE: a blackmailer's information.

BLAG, TO: to rob.

BLAGGING, A: a robbery.

BLOCK, THE: an embargo on information, imposed from above.

287

BLOOD-PRINT: a print made by an attacker's finger, wet with his victim's blood. An excellent piece of evidence.

BLOW OUT, TO: for a case, theory, accusation, to fall down.

BLOW THROUGH, TO: to telephone information.

BODY, A: an arrested person.

BORROWED, TO GET: to be arrested.

BOTTLE: nerve, acumen.

BREAKER, A: a house or shop-breaker.

BRIEF, A: a warrant or warrant-card.

BUBBLE, TO: to put in for 'X': to disclose damaging evidence about 'X'.

BUSTLE PUNCHER, A: one who caresses ladies' bottoms in a dense crowd.

CATCHED, TO BE: caught.

CAST, TO BE: to be discharged from the Force.

CENTRAL: CI, the core of the CID.

CVI: Central Vehicle Index, kept in the Information Room, a record of all the cars lost or stolen in London, together with those of policemen and noted criminals.

CHUMMY: the neutral civilian and often witless actor in a criminal drama.

CIVVIE: the amorphous British public that is always getting lost and wanting to know the time.

CLAIM, TO: to arrest.

CLEAN PRINT: a specially treated finger-print form that takes a print without dirtying the fingers with ink.

CLEAR-UP: the basic counter in the CID game, the identification and capture—if possible—of the perpetrator of a known crime.

CLOCK, TO: to look at quickly and unobtrusively.

COAT, HAVE YOU GOT A?: intimation of arrest.

CO: Commissioner's Office, i.e. Scotland Yard.

CONS: previous convictions.

COP A DROP, TO: to accept a bribe.

COPPER, A: the word a policeman uses to describe himself.

COUGH, TO: to confess.

CRIME SQUAD: a Regional Crime Squad.

CID: Criminal Investigation Department.

CRO: Criminal Record Office. A 'CRO man' is one with a record.

DAB, TO BE ON: to be put on a disciplinary charge.

DEPARTMENT, THE CID.

DI: Detective Inspector.

DIP: a pick-pocket.

DIPPED, TO BE: to have one's pocket or handbag stolen from.

DONE FOR: convicted of e.g. 'Done for drunk', 'Done for speed'.

DOWN TO: thus: X is down to $Y = X$ is Y's responsibility.

DRAG, TO: to steal from cars.

DRINK, A: a bribe.

DRUM, A: a house or home.

ELIMINATION-PRINT: the print of someone who could legitimately be at the scene of a crime, like the owner of a broken-into house. His marks (qv) can be disregarded.

ENFORCEMENT CAR: an unmarked car run by Traffic Department to catch speed-limit exceeders; unlike the Q car, its crew is in uniform.

FACTORY, A: police station.

FEEL A COLLAR, TO: to arrest, with an implication of the rough and tumble of practical (qv) police work.

FENCE: one who physically receives stolen property (not often used).

FINGER, A: a disagreeable person.

FIVE DAY WONDER: graduate of the Special Course at the Police College.

FIX UP, TO: to concoct evidence against someone.

FLASH, TO: to expose oneself indecently. Thus a 'flasher'.

FLOUNDER, A: a taxi.

FORM: previous convictions.

FRAME: the general scene, the area of suspicion.

GO OUT WITH, TO: to share completely in someone's operations; the point being that real police work is done outside on the streets.

GOVERNOR: a superior in the Police, a term that expresses respect without servility. Also used face-to-face as 'sir'. Hence 'Government': one's superiors.

GRIEF: what a policeman's life is full of, for himself and other people.

GROUND: a policeman's area of operations. Usually a Division, and important because whose ground a job originates on determines who is responsible for dealing with it.

GUTTY: tedious, difficult to bear.

HANDED: a team of villains is said to work two—three—four —or mob-handed.

HAVE, TO: to accept or believe.

HAVE IT AWAY, TO: to escape, or to have sex.

HAVE OFF, TO: to arrest.

HAVE IT ON THE TOES, TO: run away.

HAVE OVER, TO: to trick or deceive.

HBI: House-breaking implements; possession of them is an offence.

HOUSE, TO: to find out where a suspect lives.

HUNGRY: a policeman who is impatient to catch criminals.

INFORMANT: a person who gives information about a job, either a member of the public who, say, dials 999 to report an accident, *or* a detective's informer. See Snout.

INFORMATIONS: the daily bulletin of London Criminal information published by CRO.

JOB, A: a piece of police work. To a traffic patrol, a street accident; to a Regional Crime Squad, the arrest of a team of bank robbers.

JOB: to do with the police, 'a job car'; 'a job dog'.

JOB, THE: the Police Force as an organisation, usually in its more oppressive aspects. Also, the title of the fortnightly newspaper of the Metropolitan Police.

KEEP, TO: one 'keeps a meet', or an observation.

KNOCK OFF, A: an arrest.

KNOCK OFF, TO: to arrest.

LARCENY-FINDER: larceny of something by finding it and making no effort to give it back to the owner.

LAW, THE: police.

LEGITIMATE ACCESS, ABBREV. LA: the exoneration applied to someone whose marks have been found at a scene of crime, but who could have been there anyway. He could still be proved guilty by other evidence.

MARK, A: a fingerprint found at a *scene of crime*, distinguished from a print (qv).

MARK, TO: to put a black thread across a door, or a leaf on a doorstep, so that intrusions may be detected.

MARK X'S CARDS, TO: to brief x discreetly.

MEET, A: rendezvous. Instead of making an appointment to see a practical (qv) police officer, one 'makes a meet', which is then 'kept'. The word has a particular importance to policemen because their most useful information comes from informal face-to-face chats rather than letters, telephone calls or formal interviews.

MET, THE: the Metropolitan Police—as opposed to other forces.

MIND, TO: to bribe on a regular basis.

MONKEY, A: an unpleasant person.

MUMPING: to accept cheap or free goods or services from tradesmen.

NAUGHTY: violent.

NICK, THE: police station.

NICK, TO: to arrest.

999: in the British telephone system, dialling this number

automatically connects a caller to emergency services: Hence: '999 call'.

NODDY: the lightweight silent motorcycle issued to beat men in the suburbs, so called because their riders cannot safely salute. When they were new, a legendary inspector aggrieved at this lack of respect growled: 'Well then, boy, when you see me, nod your head.'

NONDESCRIPT, A: a disguised police car or van for routine use, usually extremely conspicuous.

OBBO: an observation, which is 'kept' not 'made'.

OLD BILL: thieves' slang for police.

OVER THE SIDE, TO BE: to be about one's own affairs, usually sexual, during time on duty.

PANDA: the car used in Unit Beat policing, painted pale blue with a broad white stripe, controlled by its local police station.

PATCH, A: see Ground.

PETER, A: a safe or cell, something that locks.

PLACER, A: an underworld wholesaler in stolen goods, a broker—see Fence.

PLEAD, TO: to plead guilty.

PLOT UP, TO: to familiarise oneself with a criminal's habits and associates preparatory to arresting him.

POISON: an unflattering but accurate account of a convicted person's life and character given by the police in court before sentence is passed.

POLICE: one of the few words in the language that, like 'hounds', takes no definite article.

PONCE, A: a man who runs a prostitute. Also an all-purpose police insult.

PONCING, TO GO OUT: to search for ponces operating.

PORRIDGE: a prison sentence.

PRACTICAL: the highest police compliment; particularly of a senior officer who can still distinguish between the formal processes of law and the realities of police work.

PRINT, A: a finger-print made in ink on a record form—distinguish from Mark.

PROCESS: the method of initiating a prosecution by summons rather than arrest. Thus: 'to report for process'.

PULL, TO: to stop a vehicle.

PULL A STROKE, TO: to play a dirty trick.

PUNT AROUND, TO: to patrol.

PUT THE HANDS UP, TO: to confess.

PUT ONESELF ABOUT, TO: to swagger about, to impress.

'Q' CAR: disguised car with its crew in plain clothes; one patrols each division.

RESPECT, WITH THE GREATEST: ritual incantation used before disagreeing with a superior.

RIGHT: an emphatic.

RINGER, A: a car-thief who welds together parts of similar stolen cars to make it difficult to detect mongrels.

ROW IN—OR OUT, TO: to make an action implicating or exonerating a person from a crime in the eyes of a third party.

RUBBER HEEL: internal police investigation (in contrast to the noisy hard heel of the traditional police boot).

RUBBISH: most of a policeman's work; jobs that do not tax the abilities.

SCRATCH FOR WORK, TO: to make efforts to find arrests.

SCREW: Prison warder; (verb) to break into houses.

SECONDS, A TOUCH OF THE: used of a policeman who has been seen twice by someone he's following; also of, say, a witness who has had second thoughts about his evidence.

SETAC: specially equipped traffic accident car: an estate-wagon equipped with jacks, lights, road signs in order to deal with serious traffic accidents.

SHOP, TO: for a criminal to give information to the police about another criminal.

SHOUT, A: a call on the radio.

SHOW OUT, THE: the sign exchanged between a policeman

and informant meeting in a public place that it is safe to recognise each other (John Gosling in *Ghost Squad* uses it in this sense, but I have not heard it spoken).

SHOW OUT, TO: to give oneself away, or purposely to allow oneself to be recognised as a policeman.

SKIPPER: a sergeant; a 'second-hand skipper'; a second-class CID Sergeant.

SLAG: the aimless, feckless riff-raff of society; drunks, tramps, beatniks, hippies, etc.

SLAUGHTER, A: a concealed site where thieves divide the cargoes of stolen lorries.

SNOUT, A: a criminal informant, giving information in the hope of a reward or for revenge, or for favours expected.

SPECIAL PATROL GROUP: a unit of uniform policemen, about 130 strong, attached to no particular area. They are available for intensive patrolling, searches, guards, raids, etc.

SQUAD, THE: the Flying Squad.

STOP, A: the action of stopping and questioning a man or of a vehicle under s. 66 Metropolitan Police Act 1829.

SUS: suspicious behaviour within the meaning of the Vagrancy Act 1824. 'Done for sus': to be prosecuted for being a 'suspected person loitering' (Vagrancy Act s. 6 and 11).

SUSSES OUT, TO BE: to have one's disguise or hiding-place penetrated.

SUSSY: suspicious.

SWIFT: of a CID officer whose methods are scarcely legal.

TOM, A: a prostitute.

TURN: a police shift.
Early turn from 6 am to 2 pm.
Late turn from 2 pm to 10 pm.
Night turn from 10 pm to 6 am.

UNIFORM: the uniformed branch of police, who do not always wear uniform, as opposed to CID, who normally wear plain clothes.

UNIFORM CARRIER: a policeman content to walk his beat and bother no one.

VERBALS: a self-incriminating verbal statement made to the police after the arrest of a man, and given in evidence by them. Verbals are often said to be manufactured by the police. Hence to 'put the verbals on so and so', or 'to verbal up'.

VILLAIN: a respectable criminal, a worthy opponent. A 'right' villain implies viciousness; a 'good' villain is one who plays the police-criminal game as the police understand it.

WELL, THIS IS IT: the conclusion to almost any police conversation. It implies a resigned acceptance of the idiocies of the world.

WORK: a policeman's arrests and reports for prosecutions.

WPC: Women Police Constable.